WATER AND STATE IN EUROPE AND ASIA

Water and State in Europe and Asia

Edited by

PETER BORSCHBERG
MARTIN KRIEGER

MANOHAR
2008

First published 2008

ISBN 81-7304-776-6

Published by
Ajay Kumar Jain for
Manohar Publishers & Distributors
4753/23 Ansari Road, Daryaganj
New Delhi 110 002

Typeset by
FineCurve Computers
1, Prahalaad Nagar
Meerut City 250 002

Printed at
Lordson Publishers Pvt. Ltd.
Delhi 110 007

Contents

Preface

Water is indispensable for all life on earth. This insight is the first and a very basic step towards an exploration of water and water resources on the two continents of Europe and Asia through time. The availability of fresh water for irrigation and its storage in times of low rainfall enabled the production of agricultural surpluses that could be redistributed through trade to other regions. Irrigation technology and the transfer of irrigation know-how facilitated the production surpluses to meet the increasing demands of a growing population. Water—whether lakes, rivers or even the sea—has been used since time immemorial to transport agricultural surpluses to distant regions, meeting the market demand, forging patterns of exchange and establishing networks of trade. Where water is readily available, markets and trade, political power and the competition to control this resource is never far away. Water, it seems, emerges as a crucial factor in the consolidation of political authority and the exercise of state power, and in many instances a cornerstone in modern state formation. Taken in this sense, water is more than just as a sustainer of life, it also serves to unite or divide people across time and space.

Since ancient times, the control of freshwater resources and also the sea contributed to the rise of communal structures and states. Many states consolidated central authority by creaming off agricultural surpluses from irrigated lands. Rulers collected surpluses as taxes from farmers or landholders. Such agricultural goods could be easily converted into cash which the central authority could use to sustain its administrative structures and coercive authority. The more effective the irrigational systems, the higher state revenues tended to be. Such irrigation-based communities are characteristic for Asia and can be found, for example, in the Harappan and Ganges civilizations, the riverine states of south India as well as Angkor, Pagan or China. Even in Europe irrigation constituted an essential aspect of state formation, especially in some parts of the Mediterranean. The knowledge of constructing dams, canals, artificial lakes and water-lifting devices was an indispensable asset of society. States not only relied on their own traditions, but also sought to adapt foreign know-how. Technologies of water management often emerged as instruments of cultural exchange between Europe and Asia or also between Europe and the New World.

For much of the twentieth century, research on such community-based irrigation was dominated by Karl August Wittfogel's discourse on 'Hydraulic Despotism'. In sum, Wittfogel contended, that Asian centralistic and 'despotic' states derived their major power from control of water resources. It cannot be denied that his thesis provided a valuable platform for further analysis and research at the time of its primordial formulation. This model is now seriously disputed, and it seems imperative that current research move away from the debate over the merit and viability of Wittfogel's thesis.

So much for the irrigational states. Sea-borne empires could flourish as a result of their commercial success and naval strength. For such maritime polities, indispensable facets of statehood included military power at sea, successful control of marketplaces and domination of maritime trading routes. In this context, know-how encompassed shipbuilding technologies, knowledge of navigation as well as military techniques and innovations. The control of waterways and channels could be paramount, such as in the case of the Danish Sound or the Malacca Straits. Historians are particularly interested in investigating the extent to which maritime power contributed to state income or centralization of state authority. Examples of maritime empires or states can be found in Asia as well as in Europe. For Asia, Srivijaya or pre-colonial Malacca come to mind, and for Europe, the Hanseatic League or the Dutch Republic.

This volume is a collection of papers presented at the international colloquium on 'Water and State in Europe and Asia' held in June 2004 at the University of Greifswald and is generously supported by the Fritz Thyssen Foundation. The meeting brought together by inviting established and also younger experts from Asia and Europe to explore the interdependence of water and state formation on both continents from a comparative point of view. Participants explored regional developments and common patterns of irrigational states and seaborne empires, together with the transfer of technology and know-how between the different regions under review. The colloquium deliberately pursued an ambitious programme. The initial picture was that of different sets of research periods and locations, but upon closer examination these melted into a mosaic of shared patterns of state formation and consolidation.

The colloquium did not intend from the onset to revisit Wittfogel's thesis on 'Hydraulic Despotism', but it soon became clear to all participants that his analysis could not be ignored. The discussions following the individual presentations brought together different strands and parameters of analysis. Participants thrashed out a number of core insights that are mirrored both in the shape and sequence of the final papers. The present collection offers a representative cross-section on the wider theme of 'water and state formation', even if some specific aspects may very well be absent. Unfortunately, it was not possible to include papers on the role of water and state formation in East Asia, specifically China, Korea or Japan. Despite this shortcoming, the editors deem the present volume useful and interesting, and hope that it may serve as a primordial and authoritative step toward a more comprehensive exploration of this crucial theme.

The volume is divided into two basic parts. The first explores the situation in Asia, and the second focuses on Europe. Each of these two basic parts is further subdivided into articles on sea-borne powers as well as on fresh water or irrigational states.

Hermann Kulke begins the section on the maritime powers of Asia with his paper on trade and politics around the Bay of Bengal. His study covers the period from the tenth to the thirteenth century, but pays special attention to the eleventh century CE. Kulke provides a valuable survey on the dynamics of culture, trade and politics of the Srivijayan confederation with its neighbours in south India, Java, Sumatra, the Malay Peninsula, Angkor and Imperial China.

The decline of Srivijaya is followed by the the rise of the Malacca Sultanate. In the second chapter, Peter Borschberg explores the historiographical frameworks that have shackled studies in the past, critically comments on some interesting primary sources and identifies problem areas for special consideration. His principal aim is to trace continuities and discontinuities in Malacca in the period between the Malay Sultanate of the late fifteenth century and the city's transfer to Portuguese colonial rule in the early sixteenth century.

Ranabir Chakravarti explores the hydraulic resources of north and central India, beginning with the Harappan period and spanning into the Middle Ages. He argues that, as a result of climatic changes and especially drought conditions, north India saw a transformation of water resource management. Chakravarti focuses particularly on the arid regions of north-west India—Gujarat and Rajasthan—where artificial lakes, tanks and reservoirs were constructed to feed an expanding network of irrigation lines. Conservation of water resources also became a concern in India, with Maharashtra and Karnataka meriting special attention.

Chakravarti's contribution on northern, largely arid parts of India is supplemented by a range of very different insights from S. Jeyaseela Stephen's exposé on the hydraulics of south India. Gleaning evidence from inscriptions and other key sources, Stephen contends that village assemblies took a special interest in the construction and maintenance of canals, dams, reservoirs, tanks, irrigation facilities and embankments. These hydraulic facilities placed emphasis on the reorganization of food production and the transformation of unproductive land for agricultural use.

With an eye cast on India under colonial rule, Martin Krieger explores the continuities and discontinuities in the planning and construction of dam projects in India by distinguishing two distinct phases. The first phase, in the eighteenth century, saw the transfer of Spanish dam engineering know-how to India under British rule. The second phase, spanning the twentieth century, saw dam planning and construction under colonial rule shifting away from strictly irrigational purposes. In post-colonial India, emphasis was placed on a combination of hydroelectric power generation and agricultural irrigation.

Moving across the Bay of Bengal, Maitrii Aung-Thwin contends with shifting historiographical tenets that underpin the study of hydraulics in Asia, and focuses specifically on the relation of water and state in Burma. Inspired by Victor Lieberman's analysis, Aung-Thwin raises questions on how the study of hydraulic networks and technology can expand the scope of enquiry beyond the now familiar debate on centre-periphery relations to unveil fresh insights into South-East Asia's conceptual world.

The second part of the present volume is dedicated to the hydraulics of Europe. Focusing attention first on the maritime powers of Europe, Horst Wernicke examines the Hanseatic League as a maritime force during the late Middle Ages. He distinguishes two phases in the history of the League: its beginnings as a confederation of merchants, later to transform itself into an association of cities or towns concentrated around north Germany and the Baltic. Although the League came to command a powerful fleet, this was not deployed for expansionist purposes, but strictly to defend trade routes or ensure the security of member towns. The loose nature of the League, moreover, rendered the financing of war, and the raising of troops or equipment a cumbersome undertaking.

At the onset of the early modern period, the Hanseatic League lost its leading position as a mercantile power in northern Europe and made way for the emerging territorial kingdoms of Denmark and Sweden. Jens E. Olesen investigates this process of transformation and shows how Denmark eventually supplanted the Hanseatic League by transforming itself into a centralized power featuring modern state institutions and a navy. Despite this, the ruler of the Danish Sound found himself vulnerable to emerging rivals, especially Sweden.

Shifting from the Baltic to the Atlantic seaboard, Karel Davids surveys naval power of the Dutch Republic from the end of the sixteenth to the end of the eighteenth century. He is particularly interested in examining the question: how is it that a loose confederation of sovereign provinces like the Dutch Republic could emerge as one of the greatest maritime powers of early modern Europe? Davids investigates a spectrum of problems ranging from funding and revenue raising for the fleet to the chronic shortage of manpower, to political decision-making, and the proverbial feet-dragging of entrenched mercantile interests.

Moving the focal point of attention across the Channel to the British Isles, Allan I. Macinnes examines the circumvention of state power by the Scottish merchants between 1660 and 1707. He especially investigates Scotland's traditional trading networks in North America and the Caribbean and elucidates competing mercantile interests that opposed, but also contributed to, the creation of the British Empire around 1700.

Salvatore Ciriacono's paper focuses on hydraulic states in Europe and the exchange of know-how and technology between Europe, Asia and the Americas. He investigates the issue from a global, comparative perspective and sketches how technological innovations found their way from the Iberian Peninsula, Italy or even the Netherlands to other parts of the early modern world.

The final paper by Andreas Klinger entitled 'Particularism, Canals and Watercourses in the Old Reich' investigates the case study of commerce and canal building through a dense patchwork of princely territories in early modern Germany. In his meticulous reconstruction, Klinger familiarizes his readers with the concerns, circumstances and shifting economic policies of the Duchy of Saxe-Gotha from its foundation in the seventeenth century through to the early 1800s. It transpires how political particularism and commercial competition from Saxe-Gotha's neighbours came in the way of repeated plans to link the Duchy, its agricultural production and its flourishing bulk trade into a commercial network that spanned navigable rivers and even canals to marketplaces in northern Europe.

In reworking the present collection of papers for press, the editors undertook all reasonable efforts to harmonize use of language as well as the orthography, abbreviation and transliteration of foreign names, titles and concepts. Still, it was deemed both fair and feasible to respect as far as possible the contributing authors' preferences and individual styles.

A broad spectrum of institutions and individuals contributed to the successful organization of the 2004 colloquium and the preparation of the present volume. The editors wish to extend their sincere gratitude first and foremost to the Fritz Thyssen Foundation for generously supporting the 2004 colloquium as well as the publication of the present volume. The Ernst-Moritz-Arndt-University of Greifswald merits special mention here for kindly placing its facilities at the disposal of the colloquium participants. In addition, Peter Borschberg expresses his special acknowledgement to the Netherlands Institute for Advanced Studies (NIAS) in Wassenaar for its generous institutional support. Finally, special thanks are to be expressed to all the 2004 colloquium participants, as well as to those who tirelessly assisted in organizing and managing the 2004 colloquium and to Mr Ramesh Jain of Manohar Publishers for his close cooperation in editing and producing this volume.

July 2007

PETER BORSCHBERG
MARTIN KRIEGER

Contributors

MAITRII AUNG-THWIN is an Assistant Professor in the Department of History at the National University of Singapore. He has published several pieces on colonial Burma.

PETER BORSCHBERG is Associate Professor in the Department of History at the National University of Singapore. In 2005 he was also a resident fellow at the Netherlands Institute for Advanced Studies (NIAS) in Wassenaar. He has published on trade, diplomacy and colonial politics in early modern South-East Asia.

RANABIR CHAKRAVARTI is Professor of history of ancient India at the Jawaharlal Nehru University, New Delhi. His major research interest is the economic history of ancient India.

SALVATORE CIRIACONO is a Lecturer of history at the Università degli Studi di Padova, Italy. He has specialized in the history of technology, particularly in irrigational systems in Europe and the New World.

KAREL DAVIDS is Professor of history at the Vrije Universiteit Amsterdam. He has extensively studied the maritime power of the Dutch Republic and has specialized in global history.

ANDREAS KLINGER is an Assistant Lecturer of early modern European history at the Friedrich-Schiller-University, Jena. He has published studies on German territorial states, and his doctoral thesis was on the principality of Gotha.

MARTIN KRIEGER is a Lecturer of early modern history at the Ernst-Moritz-Arndt-University, Greifswald. His major areas of interest are economic, cultural and environmental history. He has published on a range of subjects, including the history of Asia and Germany.

HERMANN KULKE is Emeritus Professor of history of Asia at the Christian-Albrechts-University of Kiel, Germany. His interests focus on the east coast of India (especially Orissa), the Bay of Bengal and the Indianization of South-East Asia. He has authored and edited several books on Indian history.

ALLAN I. MACINNES is Professor of early modern history at the University of Aberdeen, Scotland. His research interests are British state formation and Scottish history.

S. JEYASEELA STEPHEN is Professor at the Vishwa Bharati University, Shantiniketan, West Bengal. He has authored several books on trade and social structures of eastern India during the medieval and modern periods.

HORST WERNICKE is Professor of medieval and Hanseatic history at the Ernst-Moritz-Arndt-University, Greifswald. He holds the only Chair in Germany dedicated to Hanseatic history. He has published extensively on the history of the Hanseatic League and the Baltic.

PART I

ASIA: MARITIME POWERS

CHAPTER 1

Trade and Politics in Eleventh-Century Bay of Bengal

HERMANN KULKE

In the year 1025, the south Indian King Rajendra Chola was eulogized in one of his inscriptions for 'having despatched many ships in the midst of the rolling sea and having caught Saṅgrāma-vijayottuṅga-varman, the king of Katarām [Srivijaya], together with the elephants of his glorious army, (and) the large heap of treasures, which (that king) had rightfully accumulated'.[1] The inscription also lists thirteen port cities on the Malay Peninsula, Sumatra and the Nicobar Islands which were raided by Rajendra Chola's navy.

The Chola king's mighty overseas expedition against Srivijaya was a unique event in India's history and its otherwise peaceful relations with the kingdoms of South-East Asia. These had come under India's strong cultural influence since almost a millennium. The justification for this naval expedition remains a moot point as the sources are silent about its exact origins. In his monumental work on the Cholas, Nilakanta Sastri concluded 'we have to assume either some attempt on the part of Srivijaya to throw obstacles in the way of the Chola trade with the East, or more probably, a simple desire on the part of Rajendra to extend his *digvijaya* to the countries across the sea'.[2] The American historian G.W. Spencer interpreted the naval expedition of the Cholas as the apex in their politics of plunder and expansionism pursued for decades during their wars in south India and Sri Lanka.[3] All these explanations probably contain a grain of truth. But there are reasons to assume that south India's war against Srivijaya has to be placed within the wider context of contemporary political and economic developments around the Indian Ocean.

The late tenth century witnessed the synchronous rise of three new and powerful dynasties: the Fatimids in Egypt (CE 967) the Song in China (CE 960), and the Cholas (CE 985), which began to interfere in the Indian Ocean trading system. The decline of the Abbasids of Baghdad and the corresponding rise of the Fatimids in Egypt as the dominant power of the Islamic world not only led to the shift of Muslim trading activities from the Persian Gulf to the Red Sea, but also considerably increased the importance of the Malabar coast in the hinterland of the Cholas. Whereas trade between the Persian Gulf and India followed mainly the coast-line to the great harbours of Gujarat, ships from the Red Sea and Aden easily crossed the Arabian Sea directly to the Malabar coast of south India, especially during the monsoons. In the Far East, the Song dynasty began to promote and control maritime trade far more successfully than any previous Chinese dynasty. India and South-East Asia, too, emerged at this time as active participants in the international power struggle and in maritime trade between the Near East and China. The Cholas' attack on Srivijaya has to be seen in this larger context of the rise of new powers, the shift of trade routes and, as a consequence of these dramatic changes, a struggle for market share.

The rise of the Cholas from CE 985 to 1025 took place with breathtaking swiftness. From their dynastic core region around the Kaveri delta, King Rajaraja subdued all kingdoms in south India along the coast, penetrated Central India and conquered the offshore islands of Sri Lanka and the Maldives. In the 1120s, his son Rajendra undertook two unique expeditions to Bengal and South-East Asia, as a culmination of this Chola expansionism. The Cholas appear to have followed a systematic plan, even though it may have evolved only gradually. After the conquest of the whole of south India and its flourishing ports on the Coromandel and Malabar coasts, they occupied Sri Lanka and the Maldives as important maritime trading centres in the Indian Ocean. Furthermore, they subdued all possible Indian opponents on the east coast up to Bengal (e.g., the Somavamsa of Orissa) and finally attacked Srivijaya, which dominated South-East Asia's trade routes through the Malacca and Sunda Straits.

During the closing centuries of the first millennium CE, India and South-East Asia witnessed similar processes of state formation that elsewhere is known under the rubric 'early to imperial kingdom'.[4] The outcome saw an increased capacity of the state to extract socially produced surplus and to mobilize men and means. At this juncture the rise of the Rashtrakutas in Central India in 752 and of the Angkor state in 802 are to be mentioned. Almost simultaneously with the expansion of the Cholas under Rajaraja and Rajendra, the kingdom of Angkor for the first time pushed its frontiers far beyond its dynastic homelands and subjugated parts of Laos, central Thailand and the northern region of the Malay Peninsula. It rose to become the dominant power around the Gulf of Siam and mainland South-East Asia. It was, therefore, bound to come into conflict with Dai-Viet and Champa that were competing for control of the vital maritime trade routes along the eastern coast of mainland South-East Asia.[5] Significantly, Angkor penetrated directly into Srivijaya's sphere of interest on the northern Malay Peninsula. For centuries, Srivijaya had controlled the southern part of the Malay Peninsula up to Ligor and Chaya and even the Isthmus of Kra for some time.

Since the mid-eleventh century another 'imperial kingdom' and important competitor emerged in the north-eastern Bay of Bengal. The kingdom of Pagan united central and coastal Burma with parts of the north-western coast of the Malay Peninsula. Perhaps for the first time in the history of South-East Asia, Pagan was able to link maritime trade in the northern Bay of Bengal directly with China via the overland route to Yunnan. During this period Burma's relations with countries on the western side of the Bay of Bengal and with Sri Lanka appear to have been very strong. This is corroborated by the influence of Orissan architecture in early Pagan.

The Malay region comprising present-day Malaysia and Indonesia was divided between Srivijaya in the west and the kingdom of Mataram on Java. In the early tenth century, Mataram shifted its capital from the vicinity of Yogyakarta in south-central Java to

Surabaya in north-east Java. What caused the abandonment of one of Asia's most impressive sacred spaces around Borobudur and Prambanam remains shrouded in uncertainty. However, there are good reasons to assume that this shift aimed at controlling the fertile rice growing plains to the south-west of Surabaya and gaining more direct access to, and perhaps even control over, the spice trade with the Molukkas that skirted the northern coast of Java. The western region of Island South-East Asia and its important trade routes came under the control of Srivijaya since the late seventh century. Sometimes dubbed a thalassocracy or 'Ocean State', Srivijaya was a confederation of harbours and their respective hinterlands and not a centrally administered agrarian state.[6] Its riches were almost legendary. In 956, just as the aforementioned great powers rose around the Indian Ocean, the Arab geographer Ma'sudi reported that even the fastest ship would not be able to visit in two years all the islands of this kingdom whose Maharaja extracted greater profit from his own country than any other ruler of the world.[7]

Relations between the South-East Asian states and their great neighbours, India and China, were close but dissimilar. For South-East Asia, India was the holy land of Buddhism and Hinduism and an important trading centre. But politically and economically, China was the 'Middle Kingdom'. All kingdoms of South-East Asia, particularly the petty states oppressed by their neighbours, dispatched tributary missions to the imperial court of China.[8] For South-East Asian historiography as well as for the historiography of the Indian Ocean trading network it is of paramount importance that Chinese officials had meticulously reported about these missions, their gifts, requests, etc. China's own interest in the 'southern barbarians' of *K'un-lun*, the countries of South-East Asia, increased considerably during the T'ang dynasty (618-907).[9] Their rule coincided with the apex of transoceanic trade between the Arab and Near Eastern merchants and China.

The reunification of China under the Song dynasty and the ascent of the Fatimids and the Cholas in the second half of the tenth century heralded a new era in the maritime history of Asia. Shortly after his ascending the throne, the first Song emperor issued orders to regulate maritime trade and revenues. Nearly two decades later, a 'Bureau of Licenced Trade' was established for acquiring foreign goods that were subsequently resold by a government-held monopoly. In 987, the Chinese imperial government issued an instruction that engendered enduring struggle and change around the Bay of Bengal. In the same year, China dispatched four official missions with gifts that sought to induce 'foreign traders of the South Sea and those who went to foreign lands beyond the sea' to call at Chinese ports more frequently. They were also promised special facilities and import licences.[10]

Srivijaya was the first to respond to the Chinese offer and dispatched a tribute mission the following year. While in China, members of the mission were informed that Srivijaya had been attacked by the east Javanese kingdom of Mataram. On their return, they received news in Champa that Mataram was still at war with Srivijaya. The mission was left with no other option but to return to China, and the imperial government placed Srivijaya under its protection. A Javanese embassy to China confirmed in 992 that the war had not been concluded.[11] The reasons underlying this armed confrontation are uncertain. It may be assumed, however, that it was closely related to the fierce competition between the two polities, not least because Srivijaya and Mataram were closely involved in the spice trade with China.

During the years of heightened tension, a number of peculiar 'rituo-political' donations were made by South-East Asian rulers to China and India. The annals of the Song dynasty report that in 1003 the king of Srivijaya 'sent two envoys to bring tribute'. They informed that in their country a Buddhist temple had been erected to pray for the long life of the emperor and that they wanted a name and bells for it by which the emperor would show that he appreciated their good intentions. An edict was issued by which the temple received the name of *Ch'êng-t'ien-wan-shou* (ten thousand years of receiving [blessings] from heaven [i.e. China]) and bells were cast to be given to it.[12] The following year Srivijaya dispatched more envoys to China who were followed by four more embassies by 1018. Evidently, Srivijaya was eager to win China's favour.

At the time when Srivijaya's king had a temple constructed for the welfare of the Chinese emperor, Srivijaya also established diplomatic relations with the Chola state. In 1005, Rajaraja donated the revenue of an entire village for the maintenance of a Buddhist shrine which the King of Srivijaya had constructed in Nagapattinam, the major port of the Chola state. The foundation stone of this shrine may have been laid already in 1003, i.e. when Srivijaya's king informed the Chinese emperor about the construction of a Buddhist shrine for his welfare. It is tempting to assume a direct connection between these two quite unusual and more or less synchronous deeds of the Srivijaya king whose name, Chulamanivarmadeva, is clearly mentioned in both Chinese and Indian sources. Srivijaya obviously sought to establish friendly relations with the two great powers of East and South Asia in order to enhance its privileged position in the maritime trade in eastern Asia. Previously China may have been more important for Srivijaya than south India. But after the conquest of south India's ports, the Maldives and Sri Lanka, the Cholas controlled the central section of the Indian Ocean trade routes in a similar manner as Srivijaya dominated the south-east. During this period of incipient trade rivalry in the Bay of Bengal, both states, Srivijaya and the Chola state, still sought to maintain friendly relations. After ascending the Chola throne in 1014, Rajendra continued this policy. In 1015 he commissioned an inscription confirming his father's donation to Srivijaya's temple at Nagapattinam. In that year and again in 1018, he received precious gifts from Srivijaya for a Hindu temple and its Brahmins at the Chola port.[13]

During that period, Angkor, mainland South-East Asia's major power, established rituo-political relations with the Cholas. In 1012, King Suryavarman under whom Angkor became the dominating power around the Gulf of Siam, chose a very unusual gift for the Chola king. For the protection of his own royalty (*ātmalakṣmī*) he presented to Rajaraja a war chariot with which he had defeated his enemies. Again, no reasons are given for this princely gift from the King of Angkor to his Chola counterpart. It is likely that Angkor had entered troubled waters with its penetration into Srivijaya's sphere of influence on the Malay Peninsula. The Isthmus of Kra offered an alternative to the long and often dangerous maritime trade route to the Gulf of Siam via the Straits of Malacca and Singapore, particularly for those merchants who shunned the rather restrictive staple rights of Srivijaya. It is likely that in the early eleventh century Angkor tried to revive the overland route across the Isthmus of Kra which would have diverted a portion of the maritime trade between the Bay of Bengal and China directly through the Gulf of Siam, which at that time was under Angkor's control.

In general, none of the sources make any mention of a direct conflict between Srivijaya and Angkor in the eleventh century. In the eighth century, however, several inscriptions found in Champa report on how frightful 'men living on food more horrible than cadavers, came in ships' from Java and other islands and desecrated temples and idols.[14] In the mid-eleventh-century Sadasiva, Suryavarman's *purohit* and brother-in-law, mentioned in his famous Sdok Kak Thom inscription that his forefather Sivakaivalya had consecrated Angkor's 'state cult' in 802, the Devaraja cult, in order 'to prevent his land of Kambuja from ever being [again] dependent (*āyatta*) on Java'.[15] This reference in an inscription dating from 1052 demonstrates how in eleventh-century Angkor, Java was still perceived as a threat, and this reference would have also encompassed Srivijaya. The desire to forestall fresh dependency on Java may have prompted the ruler of Angkor to present his own war chariot to the south Indian king. Obviously, the Cholas had emerged as rivals to Srivijaya and consequently potential allies of Angkor.[16]

It is not surprising that during this period of hectic diplomatic wrangling among the states around the Bay of Bengal, the Cholas dispatched their first embassy to the imperial Chinese court. It remained in Srivijaya for several months and reached China in 1015. As this took place ten years before the Chola navy swiftly attacked Srivijayan ports, it may be assumed that the south Indian envoys amassed intelligence with an eye on a future conflict with Srivijaya. The mission to China was a great success. The Cholas were recognized as a 'Tributary State of the First Class', the highest possible distinction for a non-Chinese state by the imperial court. The Cholas thus acquired the same status as the Fatimids, Srivijaya and Java. Together with China, these states represented the major powers of the region.[17]

As mentioned earlier, Rajendra Chola initially sustained his father's policy of friendly relations with Srivijaya. But there are reasons to assume that during his period competition among the major powers around the Bay of Bengal increased considerably. In 1016, the Javanese kingdom of Mataram was attacked and its capital sacked with the obvious approval, or even the active support, of Srivijaya. For more than a decade, Mataram ceased to be Srivijaya's rival in the spice trade. Aware of its newfound position as the foremost maritime power in South-East Asia, Srivijaya dispatched envoys to China in 1016, 1017 and 1018.

The Cholas did not remain mere spectators to Srivijaya's rise to unrivalled regional domination in South-East Asia. They began to eliminate possible rivals on the islands of South Asia. In 1017, the last vestiges of the ancient kingdom of Sri Lanka were destroyed. Polunnaruva, with its easy access to the east coast and its ports, became the new Chola capital of Sri Lanka. In the following year, Kerala and its important Malabar ports were eventually subjugated, and the 'many ancient islands', being the Maldives, faced fresh attacks. In 1020, the Cholas sent more ambassadors to the imperial court.[18] In 1022-3, the Cholas marched through Kalinga up to the Ganges and in the process eliminated all potential rivals along the eastern seaboard.

It appears as if the Chola state sought to copy the Srivijayan model, i.e. to gain undisputed control over ports and maritime networks that penetrated its sphere of influence. It is not clear as to why these two major maritime powers of South and South-East Asia discontinued their successful rituo-political diplomatic relations or why the Cholas attacked Srivijaya in 1025. Competition evidently reached a level where conventional means of conflict resolution were no longer applicable. In 1023, the Chinese emperor urged Arab envoys to shift their trade from the overland Central Asian Silk Road to the 'Silk Road of the Sea'.[19] In this scenario, the significance of sea-borne trade may have induced the influential south Indian merchant guilds of the *Ayyavole* and *Manigraman* to assume a more active role in this expanded maritime power game. They may have tried to influence the Chola court in a way similar to the pressure exerted by the (British) Rangoon Chamber of Commerce on the British government in 1885, on the eve of Upper Burma's annexation. This is only conjecture as the available sources are totally silent on this issue.

The Chola raids on fourteen flourishing port cities of the Malay Peninsula and Sumatra sent shock waves throughout the courts of South-East Asia; none of them were able to muster envoys to China for three years. In 1028, the Song emperor lamented that 'in recent years foreign shipping rarely came to Canton'. He issued instructions to the Fiscal Superintendent of Canton to entice merchants to return. Weeks later a mission from Srivijaya arrived and was received with great honour. O.W. Wolters observed in this context that 'Srivijaya was still in business'.[20] Although hampered by internal struggles between several port cities (possibly a result of the Chola raid), Srivijaya reestablished its dominant position in the western Malay world and the adjacent Straits. It revived its traditional diplomacy in order to enhance its position in the imperial Chinese court. In 1079, it donated 600,000 gold pieces for the repair and maintenance of a Taoist shrine in Canton.[21] According to a Chinese report of the twelfth century, Srivijaya 'is the most important port-of-call on the sea-routes of the foreigners, from the country of Sho-po (Java) on the east and from the countries of the Ta-shi (Arabs) and Ku-lin (Quilon) on the West; they all pass through it on their way to China'.

The Cholas were rather reluctant to convert their military successes into an enduring political domination. They could have done so, for example, by establishing a fortified settlement of Tamil merchants along the Straits of Malacca. In fact, such a settlement of the *Manigraman* merchant guild already existed at Takuapa on the Isthmus of Kra during the reign of Pallavas in the late eighth century.[22] After attacking Srivijaya, the Cholas confined themselves to dispatching yet another mission to China in 1033. At the close of the eleventh century, notably under the reign of Kulottunga I (1070-1118), they stepped up their activities around the Bay of Bengal.[23] In 1068, they sent a naval expedition on behalf of a contender to the throne of Kadaram, Srivijaya's second capital on the Malay Peninsula. At the Chinese court, however, their support to a Srivijayan prince did not enhance their reputation as they were perceived as a tributary or 'vassal' state of Srivijaya. This is the viewpoint that transpires from the Chinese annals. This skewed perception may have been deliberately painted by Srivijaya's envoys at the Chinese court. The 'misunderstanding' was corrected only in 1077 following the dispatch of a Chola mission to China under Kulottunga which comprised 72 persons most of whom were traders. China accorded them two exceptionally high privileges of protocol. Srivijaya was compelled to dispatch two additional missions in 1079 and 1088 to receive the same honour.[24] The involvement of the Cholas, and specifically of Kulottunga, in Srivijayan affairs remains a controversial issue. A Chinese transliteration found in the Canton inscription of 1029 mentions Kulottunga as the ruler of Srivijaya, and the same name is also used to refer to the Chola king who sent a mission in 1077.[25] From this and other scattered evidence it may be inferred that the Cholas supported a particular faction either at the Srivijayan court or at a particular port-city within the Srivijayan confederation. This was a period of intensive factionalism within Srivijaya. A few decades later, Palembang lost its dominant position in Srivijaya to Jambi. According to a 1088 inscription of the *Ayyavole* guild found near Barus on Sumatra, Indian merchants continued to trade with Srivijaya.[26]

Kulottunga also maintained friendly relations with the two great kingdoms or mainland South-East Asia. In 1114, soon after ascending the throne, Suryavarman II, the famous builder of Angkor Wat, sent a mission to the Chola court and a gift of precious stone for Kulottunga. In an inscription at Pagan, Burma's King Kyanzittha (1077-1112) claims to have converted the 'Choli prince' to the teachings of Buddha through a personal letter written on gold leaves in which he extolled the greatness of the Buddhist *triratnas*.[27] All these rituo-political missions and donations were probably connected with the promotion of trade, because Kulottunga was the only Chola king whose name was associated with a harbour. The renaming of

Visakhapattanam as Kulottungacholapattanam indicates Kulottunga's interest in trade with countries around the Bay of Bengal, i.e. with Burma and even with Cambodia beyond the Isthmus of Kra.[28]

The decline of the Cholas from the late twelfth century onward did not in any way precipitate a decline in south Indian trade in the Bay of Bengal and with China. The twelfth and thirteenth centuries saw heightened activity by the two south Indian guilds, the *Ayyavole* and *Manigraman* merchants, mainly in south India and also in Sri Lanka.[29] In Burma, too, south Indian merchant guilds congregated during this period. An inscription from the thirteenth century found at the sole Hindu temple in Pagan reports a donation by a member of the south Indian *nānādesi* merchants.[30] The decline of the Chola state in the mid-thirteenth century gave an opportunity to other kingdoms around the Bay of Bengal to participate more actively in the Indian Ocean trade. This can be inferred from the famous Motupalli inscription of King Ganapati of the Kakatiya dynasty (northern Andhra Pradesh) who promised in 1244 'safety to traders by sea starting for and arriving from all continents, islands, foreign countries and cities'.[31] Recent excavations at Manikapatnam, an ancient maritime harbour at the Chilka Lake in Orissa, corroborate the growth of Chinese trade during this period.[32]

Evidence dating from the thirteenth century is particularly impressive for the presence of a large south Indian merchant community in China, and for Chinese traders in south India. Recent discoveries at Quanzhou (which under the Southern Song dynasty surpassed Canton as China's main port and place of foreign merchants) have brought to light a well preserved lower portion of a Hindu temple along with nearly 200 sculptures, all in purely late but localized Chola style.[33] This temple and the large number of Hindu sculptures are the earliest known pieces of evidence supporting the existence of a large south Indian colony in China. A bilingual Tamil-Chinese inscription of 1281 reveals the dedication of a Saiva statue in another Hindu temple in Quanzhou. Its author was probably the son of the last Chola King Rajaraja III who may have sought assistance from the Chinese emperor two years after losing his dynastic fortunes.[34] Two months before this dedication, a

Mongol envoy, Yang Ting-pi, had been dispatched to India—most likely to south India—'underscoring the reciprocal nature of this relationship'.[35]

The evidence supporting the presence of a Chinese merchant community in south India during this period is equally impressive. Until 1867, ruins of a three-storeyed Chinese pagoda were seen in Nagapattinam which was constructed in 1267 according to Chinese sources. Apparently China followed the example of Srivijaya and its Buddhist monastery at Nagapattinam. A total of 1,838 Chinese coins have been unearthed in the neighbourhood of Nagapattinam, most probably belonging to a coin-hoard. They are dated from the second to the thirteenth century. The latest of them belong to the 1265-75 period which corresponds to the date of the construction of the Chinese pagoda. The findings of Chinese ceramics in south India as well as this body of evidence—the largest number of which belongs to the thirteenth and fourteenth century[36]—clearly indicate that these centuries saw intense and direct trade relations between south India and China.[37]

The establishment of the Delhi Sultanate in 1206, its temporary expansion to central and south India in the early fourteenth century, the subsequent establishment of the Deccan and Madurai Sultanates, as well as the spread of Islam throughout India's ports and along the maritime trading routes in South-East Asia also underscored India's importance in the Indian Ocean trading system. Through its Indian and foreign Muslim trading community India's ports became more directly linked with the 'international' maritime Muslim trade. South Indian Muslim merchants like the Telugu Klings and Tamil Chulias were particularly active in the Malay world.[38] The conquest of Bengal by Muslim armies gave a considerable boost to the maritime activities of Bengal. It drew the harbours of Bengal into the orbit of the Delhi Sultanate as well as transoceanic trade of Muslim merchants. This maritime network connected the Near East and south India with South-East Asia and China. Envoys regularly sent by Bengal to China during the early fifteenth century furnish ample proof of the heightened trading activities between Bengal and China.[39]

In the early fifteenth century, two events proved paramount for the Indian Ocean trading system before the arrival of Europeans: the foundation of Malacca and the maritime expeditions of the Ming dynasty under Zheng He. Six expeditions between 1405 and 1433 firmly established China's contemporary hegemony over the 'Southern Sea', i.e. South-East Asia, and gradually extended China's dominant maritime position to Sri Lanka, south India, the Persian Gulf, the Red Sea and East Africa.[40] Whilst Malacca rose to become a major commercial centre initially under the direct influence of Zheng He's expedition,[41] the Ming called off their maritime expeditions as suddenly as they had begun. Both the foundation of Malacca and Zheng He's expeditions marked the climax of tightly knit all-Asian processes that have been exemplified here through the eleventh-century struggles for political and economic dominance in the Bay of Bengal. The outcome of these processes and the forces driving them was the rise of an intricate network of political, economic and cultural relations spanning the whole of the Indian Ocean. At the very base of this Asian maritime network were interlocked regional networks, each with its own distinct history in the Near East, South, South-East and East Asia. The presence of this web of distinct yet inter-linked networks facilitated the swift and successful entry of the early European powers and merchants into the Indian Ocean trading system.

NOTES

1. Archaeological Survey of India, ed., *South Indian Inscriptions*, Madras/New Delhi, 1890-1990, vol. 2, p. 109.
2. K.A.N. Sastri, *The Cōḷas*, Madras, 1955, p. 220.
3. G.W. Spencer, 'The Politics of Plunder. The Chōḷas in Eleventh-Century Ceylon', *Journal of Asian Studies*, vol. 35, 1976, pp. 405-20. G.W. Spencer, *The Politics of Expansion: The Chola Conquest of Sri Lanka and Srivijaya*, Madras, 1983.
4. H. Kulke, 'The Early and the Imperial Kingdom: A Processural Model of Integrative State Formation in Early Medieval India', in *The State in India 1000-1700*, ed. H. Kulke, New Delhi, 1995, pp. 233-77. Kulke, 'The Early and the Imperial Kingdom in South-East Asian History', in

Southeast Asia in the 9th to 14th Centuries, eds. D.G. Marr and A.C. Milner, Singapore, 1986, pp. 1-22.

5. K.R. Hall, 'Eleventh-Century Commercial Developments in Angkor and Champa', *Journal of Southeast Asian Studies*, vol. 10, 1979, pp. 420-34.
6. Kulke, '"Kadātuan Śrīvijaya"—Empire or Kraton of Srivijaya. A Reassessment of the Epigraphical Evidence', *Bulletin de l'École Française d' Extrême Orient*, vol. 80, 1993, pp. 159-80.
7. G.R. Tibbetts, *A Study of the Arabic Texts Containing Material on South-East Asia*, Leiden, 1979, p. 38.
8. The report on an early mission from Holatan on Java in CE 430 is very informative for this type of East Asian diplomacy.

   'My country once had a large population and was prosperous [and] never bullied by other countries. But now the situation is different and we have become weak. My neighbours vie with each other in attacking me. I beg Your Majesty to extend Your protection from far. I also hope that there will be no trading restrictions which will affect the coming and going [of our merchants]. If you pity me I hope that you will send missions ordering these countries not to maltreat us so that Your Majesty's reputation as the protector of the weak will be known everywhere. I hope that you will instruct the Canton officials to send back my ship and not permit them to rob and hurt [my traders]. I wish hereafter to send missions every year.'

   Liu Sung Shu, 5, 33b, quoted by O.W. Wolters, *Early Commerce: A Study of the Origins of Śrīvijaya*, Ithaca, 1967, p. 151.
9. Wang Gungwu, 'The Nanhai Trade: A Study of the Early History of Chinese Trade in the South China Sea', *Journal of the Malay Branch of the Royal Asiatic Society*, vol. 31, no. 2, 1958, pp. 1-135. See also P. Wheatley, 'Geographical Notes on Some Commodities Involved in Sung Maritime Trade', *Journal of the Malay Branch of the Royal Asiatic Society*, vol. 32, no. 2, 1959, p. 21. Jung-Pang Lo, 'Maritime Commerce and its Relation to the Sung Navy', *Journal of the Economic and Social History of the Orient*, vol. 12, 1969, pp. 57-101.
10. See Wheatley, 'Geographical Notes', pp. 24 ff.
11. G. Coedès, *The Indianized States of Southeast Asia*, Honolulu, 1968, p. 132.
12. W.P. Groeneveldt, *Historical Notes on Indonesia and Malaya Compiled from Chinese Sources*, Jakarta, 1960, p. 65.
13. For the policy of the Cholas during the eleventh century see Sastri, *The Cōḷas*, p. 220. Spencer, *The Politics of Expansion*. K.R. Hall, *Trade and Statecraft in the Age of the Cōḷas*, New Delhi, 1980.

14. G. Coedès, *The Indianized States*, p. 91.
15. Kulke, 'The Devarāja Cult', in *Kings and Cults: State Formation and Legitimation in India and Southeast Asia*, ed. H. Kulke, New Delhi, 1993, p. 344.
16. K.R. Hall, 'Khmer Commercial Development and Foreign Contacts under Suryavarman I', *Journal of the Economic and Social History of the Orient*, vol. 18, 1975, pp. 318-36.
17. Ibid.
18. N. Karashima, 'Relations between South India and China in Chola Times', in *Professor K.A. Nilakanta Sastri Felicitation Volume*, Madras, 1971, pp. 69 et seq.
19. K.N. Chaudhuri, *Trade and Civilization in the Indian Ocean. An Economic History from the Rise of Islam to 1750*, Cambridge, 1985, p. 56.
20. Wolters, *Early Commerce*, p. 251.
21. Tan Yoek Soeng, 'The Sri Vijayan Inscription of Canton (AD 1079)', *Journal of Southeast Asian History*, vol. 5, 1964, pp. 17-26.
22. K.A.N. Sastri, 'Takuapa and its Tamil Inscription', *Journal of the Malay Branch of the Royal Asiatic Society*, vol. 22, 1949, pp. 25-30.
23. See particularly K.R. Hall, 'International Trade and Foreign Diplomacy in Early Medieval South India', *Journal of the Economic and Social History of the Orient*, vol. 21, 1978, pp. 75-98. Sastri, *The Cōḷas*, pp. 316 ff.
24. O.W. Wolters, *The Fall of Śrīvijaya in Malay History*, London, 1970, p. 93.
25. For details see Tan Yoek Seong, 'Inscription of Canton'. I am grateful to Tansen Sen who sent me a copy of his unpublished paper, *Relations between China and the Cōḷa Kingdom of South India: AD 850-1279*. See also his recent publication *Buddhism, Diplomacy and Trade: The Realignment of Sino-Indian Relations. 600-1400*, London, 2003.
26. Sastri, 'A Tamil Merchant Guild in Sumatra', *Tijdschrift voor Indische Taal-, Land- en Volkenkunde*, vol. 72, 1932, pp. 314-27.
27. J. Stargardt, 'Burma's Economic and Diplomatic Relations with India and China from Early Medieval Sources', *Journal of the Economic and Social History of the Orient*, vol. 14, 1971, pp. 38-62.
28. R. Chakravarti, 'Kulottunga and the Port of Visakhapattanam', *Indian History Congress Proceedings*, vol. 42, 1981, pp. 142-5.
29. M. Abraham, *Two Medieval Merchant Guilds of South India*, New Delhi, 1988, pp. 127-81. B. Stein, 'Coromandel Trade in Medieval India', in *Merchants and Scholars: Essays in the History of Exploration and Trade*, ed. J. Parker, Minneapolis, 1965, pp. 47-62.

30. *Epigraphia Indica,* VII, pp. 197-8.
31. Ibid., p. 196.
32. D. Pradhan, P. Mohanty and J. Misra, 'Manikapatana: An Ancient and Medieval Port on the Coast of Orissa', in *Archaeology of Orissa,* ed. K.K. Basa and P. Mohanty, Delhi, 2000, pp. 473-94.
33. J. Guy, 'The Lost Temples of Nagapattinam and Quanzhou: A Study of Sino-Indian Relations', *Silk Road Art & Archaeology,* vol. 3, 1993-4, pp. 291-310.
34. T.N. Subrahmaniam, 'A Tamil Colony in Medieval China', *South Indian Studies,* 1978 (quoted by J. Guy, 'Lost Temples', p. 298). J. Wisseman Christie, 'The Medieval Tamil-language Inscriptions in Southeast Asia and China', *Journal of Southeast Asian Studies,* vol. 29, 1998, pp. 239-68.
35. Guy, 'Lost Temples', p. 300.
36. The same picture emerges from the few findings of Chinese ceramics which have become known from Manikapatnam. For south India see, Y. Subbarayalu, 'Chinese Ceramics of Tamil Nadu and Kerala Coasts', paper presented at the international seminar on Techno-Archaeological Perspectives of Seafaring in the Indian Ocean (with Focus on 4th century BC - 15th century AD), New Delhi, 1994.
37. H. Ray, 'Trade between South India and China 1368-1644', in *Commerce and Culture in the Bay of Bengal 1500-1800,* ed. Om Prakash and D. Lombard, New Delhi, 1999, pp. 37-46.
38. S. Arasaratnam, 'The Chulia Muslim Merchants in Southeast Asia 1650-1800', paper presented at the 10th Conference of the International Association of Historians of Asia, Singapore, 1986.
39. T. Yamamoto, 'International Relations between China and the Countries Along the Ganges in the Early Ming Period', *Indian Historical Review,* vol. 4, 1977-8, pp. 13-19. H. Ray, *Trade and Diplomacy in India-China Relations. A Study of Bengal during the Fifteenth Century,* New Delhi, 1993.
40. R. Ptak, *China and the Asian Seas. Trade, Travel and Visions of the Other (1400-1700),* Aldershot, 1998.
41. W. Gungwu, 'The Opening of Relations between China and Malacca, 1403-5', in *Malayan and Indonesian Studies: Essays Presented to Sir Richard Winstedt,* ed. J. Bastin and R. Rollvink, Oxford, 1964, pp. 87-104.

CHAPTER 2

Malacca as a 'Sea-Borne Empire'—Continuities and Discontinuities from Sultanate to Portuguese Colony (Fifteenth and Sixteenth Century)

PETER BORSCHBERG

INTRODUCTION

The history of pre-colonial Malacca under the sultans has been the subject of much interest and research in recent years.[1] This may be partly due to the widespread commemorative activities organized and hosted on mainland China, Taiwan, as well as the firmly established overseas Chinese communities in South-East Asia. In accounts of the voyages of Admiral Zheng He, the name Malacca is mentioned on several occasions, and most importantly, it was through the great 'Three-Jewelled Eunuch' acting on behalf of the 'Son of Heaven', that the 'chief' of Malacca was formally raised to the status of 'king'.[2] This elevation and investiture met with dissatisfaction from the King of Siam, Malacca's great neighbour to the north and traditional rival on land and at sea.[3]

Malacca's more distant past has sparked renewed interest as revealed by the eager fund-raising activities of numerous 'Admiral Zheng He Societies' which have mushroomed across East and South-East Asia.[4] Since the return of Macao to China in 1999 and the resolution of the 'East Timor Question', Portuguese scholars have developed a keen interest in the region and its place in Portugal's colonial past. The 'Lisbon School' has seen the production and publication of several arguably seminal studies, chiefly under the auspices of Luís Filipe Thomaz, which include not only his own contributions, but also other noteworthy studies by Jorge Alves (Aceh and Malacca), Paulo Pinto (Malacca and Johor), Manuel Lobato (Malacca and the Moluccas) and Maria Anna Marques Guedes (Pegu and Ava).[5] These works have contributed meaningfully toward diversifying the approaches to Malacca's historical past: as a repository of culture in the Malay world, as a trading entrepôt that connected the Bay of Bengal and the South China Sea, or as a birthplace of a hybrid *mestiço* culture that benefited later European colonial powers. The Dutch and the British later established and consolidated their own presence in and around the Peninsula and the Straits.

The results of research fall into three broad categories.

First, the accounts that base their insights predominantly on European colonial sources without adopting a critical mindset are almost inevitably characterized by the fallacies of imperial rhetoric and inflated claims. Admittedly, this genre generally comprises older contributions on the subject, written at the height of British imperialism on the Peninsula. Imperial history, not surprisingly, produced a seriously skewed vision due to its almost exclusive recourse to English language sources, documentation, narratives and cultural outlook. These histories would have probably long faded into a more distant horizon, had they not been regularly pulled out of the closet of discarded ideas and put on public display in museums or exhibits around the South-East Asian region. Their predictable line of argument is that Malacca was a great and mighty port polity that controlled vast regions around it. The port and city represented the central node of trade in South-East Asia, if not the world! This famed port polity was wrested by the Portuguese who managed to hold on to it until the Dutch, at the beginning of the seventeenth century, made their forays into the region. This made it most difficult for the *Estado da Índia* that was drained of financial resources and resolve through a highly parasitic personal union with Spain. The

1580-1641 period is considered as the 'dark ages' of Portugal's imperial history. Malacca was taken over by the Dutch, but fell victim to a myriad of policies that centralized commercial activities in and around Batavia. With the benefit of hindsight, the outcome was almost inevitable: Malacca was reduced to a commercial backwater, a sad spectre of its former glorious self. This was the state of the city and port when the British formally assumed control in 1795. But it was too late to revitalize Malacca, for Penang was already established and Singapore was on its way to prominence as Raffles' 'naturally conditioned' node of trade and commerce. Malacca was forever left behind in the shadow of its own fabulous past. This is the storyline known to most persons weaned on school history textbooks up to the late 1990s.

A second group of texts emanates from the consciously non-Eurocentric interpretations of the post-colonial period. Indigenous texts like the *Sejarah Melayu* (Malay Annals) have acquired greater importance as independent testimonies of historical events in their own right.[6] The question though remains which parts can be trusted, and how one is to read this and related texts that impart chiefly prescriptive moralizing narratives with little concern for historical veracity.[7]

Mirroring political developments of the 1950s and 1960s, post-colonial works seek to place Asian history on an autonomous footing, and rightly so. Decoupling events and developments on the Peninsula from imperial histories, especially British imperial history, was and still remains an important and necessary task. With particular focus on Malacca, Van Leur and Meilink-Roelofsz deserve many accolades for steering research in the right direction.[8] Credit goes to Van Leur for acknowledging that the role of European trade in Asia for much of the early modern period was not as 'substantial' or even 'overwhelmingly dominant' as many of the imperial and company histories, written for the European home market, would like their readers to believe. Meilink-Roelofsz should be commended, amongst other achievements, for meticulously reconstructing the main networks of trade with their many side branches, mainly by recourse to early colonial documents. However, her reliance on the

Suma Oriental has been criticized. Meilink-Roelofsz has nevertheless instilled modern researchers with a newfound faith in the historic value of colonial texts and documents. They contain, as is now widely accepted, at least nuggets of useful information. Some of these were gleaned from either written indigenous sources, or collective memory that are now lost. Van Leur, Meilink-Roelofsz and others who followed similar strands of thinking were willing to adduce a broad array of sources, but it is unfortunate that many younger scholars, especially in Asia, are unwilling—or perhaps unqualified—to follow in their footsteps. The propensity today in Singapore as also in Malaysia, is to defer to British Colonial Office documentation or the English East India Company records. This has resulted in overemphasis and overreliance on nineteenth- and twentieth-century history. At the same time, there is a vacuum *vis-à-vis* the early modern period that remains inaccessible largely as a result of linguistic inability. Chinese sources could offer a vast repository of knowledge,[9] but these too remain largely untapped, because young researchers trained to read simplified characters struggle with Chinese classical script.

The third category of publications is contextual analysis, not unlike what the 'Cambridge School' is to early modern European history. This approach seeks to place sources and nuggets of information within the context in which they were written or conceived, and the (supposed) purpose they were to serve. Information is often gleaned from reading against the grain, and can also be independently verified or juxtaposed by critically comparing statements with other independent testimonies, often of Asian origin. This process of independent re-verification of facts or events could be a very tricky and challenging task. The problem is not so much the comparison of, say, Dutch and Portuguese testimonies. The real challenges arise in comparing testimonies from different Asian civilizations and their specific 'cultural baggage'. The conclusions drawn regarding Malacca using this approach provide somewhat different perspectives on the famous emporium. These occasionally stand in direct conflict with views expounded in works of the 'imperial' and 'post-colonial' genre.

II

PROBLEMS WITH SOURCES AND INTERPRETATIONS

After this survey, it is important to explore some of the key sources that reveal something about the continuities and discontinuities in Malacca's *Thalassocracy*, a term employed on several occasions by the geographer and historian Paul Wheatley in the 1960s. One may follow the footsteps of Wheatley and Meilink-Roelofsz (who worked extensively on that critical transition from sultanate to Portuguese colony) and even refer to the *Suma Oriental*. But work conducted and published during recent decades has posed a series of questions about the integrity of Pires and the transmitted text. One needs to be both aware and critical of the exact terminology he employs.[10] Equally, one is painfully aware of how different the terminology can be between the Paris manuscript (probably late sixteenth century) published and translated by Armando Cortesão in 1944 and the significantly shorter Lisbon manuscript edited and published for the first time as a self-standing text by Rui Manuel Loureiro in 1996.[11] The linguistic style and terminology of the latter manuscript are probably more honest and authentic, and one cannot help but shudder at Cortesão's own frank admission in his foreword to the *Suma Oriental* that he sometimes had to 'best guess' what Pires was trying to say.[12]

Other early Portuguese texts fare a little better; Duarte Barbosa represents another point in case. However, one has a hard time appraising what parts were frivolously added by Giovanni Battista Ramusio in his collection *Delle Navigazioni e Viaggi* to 'exoticise' the story for European readers, or alternatively, reconstructing the parts that were censored by the Portuguese authorities from the original manuscript(s) because the text revealed commercially 'sensitive' and therefore 'classified' information.[13] A third classic Portuguese text, the *Declaraçam de Malacca* by Erédia, also has serious problems. First, it dates from a much later period, i.e. the early seventeenth century. A comparison of this text with Erédia's earlier exposé, the *Informação da Aurea Chersoneso* (*c.* 1597), reveals considerable inconsistency in the way terminology is employed and also in some of the basic insights expounded, for example, what Erédia says about the home of the

Malays. In the *Declaraçam de Malacca* he claims this to be Pahang, but in his earlier text, the home of the Malays is placed unconventionally in Patani.[14] Did Erédia change his mind? Or, was there no consensus on this very issue? Other authors claim that the Malays are from Malacca, or Sumatra, or Lingga, etc. Who really knows? Although the view may very well be sustained that Erédia's treatise ultimately represents an 'honest' effort, there are several as yet inadequately researched points of friction (terminological and otherwise) between the draft dating from around 1597 and the final text version of 1613.[15]

Among historians of early modern Malacca and the Straits, there appears to be an acknowledged consensus, tacit or otherwise, that past accounts have relied perhaps too heavily on Pires and the handy English language translation produced by Cortesão. It is perhaps against the backdrop of this discomfort and acknowledged over-reliance that one should specially appreciate the partial translation of Gaspar Correia's *Lendas da Índia* by Manuel Pintado and published by Malaysia's National Archives in the early 1990s.[16] Correia is certainly not the most reliable author nor is he always critical of the material he has incorporated into what can be safely deemed a truly monumental work. The author's own peccadillos are compounded by Pintado's occasionally sloppy translation that adds glaring errors (he mistranslates *cravos* as 'cinnamon' instead of 'cloves') to his evidently inadequate understanding of the early modern spice trade (he renders the Portuguese term *drogas* as 'medicine' or 'medicinal substances' which in this form, is strictly speaking, incorrect).[17] In defence of Pintado's translation efforts, there is no doubt that this volume represents a first important step in weaning the modern historian away from an over-reliance on Pires to meaningfully broaden the range of early Portuguese colonial sources that are readily accessible.

Malay language texts, as far as they even exist, present the modern historian with a very different set of challenges. First, there are very few sources that date, or claim to date, from the period around the fall of the Malacca Sultanate. Most of them do not come anywhere close to their 'original text', and so what is extant represents later codified version(s) of oral tradition and/or public memory. The meaning and intention of the text is by no means consistent, and one may talk here of such texts as the *Sejarah Melayu* or 'Malay Annals'. This text as it stands today clearly dates from the period after the fall of the Malacca Sultanate to the Portuguese (1511) and the core objective of this work is to rally the Malays behind the Johor sultan by stressing lineage, providing 'prophetic' statements and testaments, as well as employing moral suasion, the language of obedience, or in stressing the benefits of mutual obligation.[18] In any case, there is little, if anything, in the *Sejarah Melayu* that may serve the underlying theme of the present paper on water-borne states.

This leaves one with the two legal digests of Malacca, the *Undang-undang Melaka* (or Laws of Malacca) and the *Undang-undang Laut* (or [Malacca] Maritime Code).[19] Both purport, and are widely accepted, to trace their origins to the period of the Malacca Sultanate (1450-1511). Like any other legal text, these digests represent diverse strands of thinking at different periods of time, both pre-colonial and colonial Malacca as well as their acclaimed successor states. The Malay Concordance Project at the Australian National University traces the origin of both texts to the fifteenth century, but advises caution. On the surface, this caution is justified for the text of the *Undang-undang Laut*, where certain clauses incorporated into the main body of the text bear specific dates from the seventeenth century. The *Undang-undang Melaka* is far less transparent. The editor, Liaw Yock Fang, simply observes that the digest is pieced together from different texts and most likely across the reign of several Malacca rulers.[20] The question that inevitably arises is exactly which laws belong to which period?

Liaw Yock Fang traces the origins of the *Undang-undang Melaka* to the rule of Muzzaffar Shah (1445-58), i.e. a period that can be safely deemed the 'golden age' of the Malacca Sultanate.[21] By this time the erstwhile 'pirates lair' of Parameswara[22] (to borrow the terminology from Wheatley) had grown from a fishing village under the influence of Pasai on Sumatra and nominal suzerainty of the King of Siam[23] to a separate kingdom in its own right.[24] Admiral Zheng He's famous visit, at a time when the ruler of Malacca was elevated from chief to the status of king or *raja* was almost half a century in the past. Malacca was at that point the large emporium that the Portuguese and other early European visitors, including Ludovico de Varthema and Giovanni da Empoli, described with passion and admiration in their famous writings.[25] Figures cited by Wheatley reveal a population of around 6,000 inhabitants in the year 1424, a figure that had supposedly been inflated by 'later arrivals [of *orang laut*], scavenging along the coast and lured by the promise of early gains. [They] had taken up their preferred site, close against the water's edge.'[26] Agriculture was not the preferred activity of the immigrants, and as a result, food supplies remained in short supply.[27] Sago, vegetables and fruit were the staple food in Malacca at that time. Under Sultan Muzzaffar, Malacca is thought to have expanded from a city state to an 'imperial' power. The peoples of the Western Peninsula as well as Pahang, Siak on Sumatra and the Riau archipelago are thought to have been absorbed into an expanding polity centred in Malacca.

III

THE *UNDANG-UNDANG MELAKA*

Against this historic backdrop one needs to place and understand the *Undang-undang Melaka.* Like all other digests, this text also contains provisions reflecting a process of gradual evolution. It encapsulates a tested hybrid of Islamic and indigenous (Malay) laws. Reflecting Arabic preoccupation with family and progeny, it is no surprise that clauses pertaining to what could be generously deemed 'family law' generally conform to Islamic principles, but it is chiefly in the sphere of criminal law that one recognizes the remnants of pre-Islamic Malay or indigenous society rising to the surface.[28] The scarcity of labour and food is frequently addressed.[29] There are many provisions on slaves and debt bondage, on feeding slaves and obtaining recompense for the cost of food, or on starving persons entering into debt bondage in exchange for food.

A clause in the *Undang-undang Melaka* that reflects a traditional Malay mindset *vis-à-vis* land and space appears at the beginning of

Fasal 20. Introduced here is the concept of *tanah mati*, which is literally translated as 'dead land'.[30]

There are two kinds of land, first the 'living land' (*tanah hidup*) and second the 'dead land' (*tanah mati*). With regard to 'dead land', nobody has property rights to it, [when] there is no sign of its being under cultivation by someone, [then] certainly nobody can lay claim to that land. If someone cultivates it ... no one can proceed against him. That is understood by 'dead land'.[31]

The concept of *tanah mati* is an interesting one as it reveals several important facets of Malay thinking about space and land: first, the criterion for ownership is regular cultivation. Land, on its own, uncultivated, is evidently worthless. Uncultivated land—primeval jungle or abandoned fields or orchards—is not specifically assigned to anyone in the *Undang-undang Melaka*, not even to the *penghulu* (village chief) or the sultan. Perhaps, the question whether land fell under the auspices of the village chief or ruler never arose and it may have just been taken for granted. Of course, the word *mati* (dead) is not to be understood in a 'biological' sense. The land is not 'dead', and the 'jungle' (*hutan*) is full of plants, insects, animals and also tribes of *orang asli* or native hunter-gatherers which are found across much of South-East Asia. These shy people who did not necessarily speak a language that was readily understood by urban dwellers gathered forest produce like lignaloes (*gaharu*, eaglewood, agarwood, *kalambac*), beehives, monkey stones and porcupine bezoars (*guliga landak, pedras de porco d'espinha*), tree resins (dammar, benzoin, camphor), lakawood and bird's nest, that were all treasured especially by the Chinese merchants.[32] Roaming through the thicket in search of forest produce was not a sufficient legal basis to claim ownership. The land had to be cultivated, tilled and planted. One is reminded here especially of a *padi* field, or a fruit orchard. The land was 'dead', meaning uninhabited and uncultivated by sedentary Malays. Malay dictionaries by William Marsden (1812) and Cornelis Elout (1825) date of course from the later centuries,[33] but they may in some way encapsulate the more complex and far less specific meaning of the word *tanah* from earlier times. During the time of Marsden and Elout the word also carried a more abstract meaning of 'zone', 'sphere', 'region' or 'space'. *Tanah mati*, more than just meaning 'dead soil' or 'dead land', could broadly be interpreted as 'dead space', or even liberally as 'empty space'.

For a polity that was, in the testimony of most early authors, including Chinese observers, not particularly interested in agriculture,[34] the provisions reproduced in the *Undang-undang Melaka* for fruit orchards and roaming domesticated animals are rather impressive. Luís Filipe Thomaz described a Malacca surrounded by marshland or swamp, that may have been suited for *padi* and even fruit orchards, but not vegetables. Are these provisions an echo of Malacca's colonial period under the Portuguese or Dutch? Do they perhaps echo pre-Islamic, pre-imperial attitudes common to any *kampong*, reflecting chiefly the concern of a *penghulu* or village chief? What about the reference to roaming (domesticated) pigs? Are these echoes of Malacca's pre-Islamic past, or simply an expression of colonial realities?

For a great and mighty waterfront polity that acted as an emporium for commerce from across Asia, played host to so many foreign merchants, and by the mid-fifteenth century had reportedly embarked on an awesome trail of territorial expansion, one is disappointed to find that so few provisions deal with the very issues of (water-borne) trade, commerce or the presence and treatment of foreigners.[35] It is indeed difficult to accept that considerably more attention is paid to roaming domesticated pigs and buffaloes (where there was supposedly little or almost no farming going on), to illicit sexual encounters or fugitive slaves, than to hard monetary issues related to maritime trade and commercial interaction, that vital source of Malacca's almost legendary wealth!

There remain many questions, few of which can be easily answered. The most important ones are: Why are the provisions so parochial? Why is the digest so introverted? If the *Undang-undang Melaka* is as old in its origins as one generally opines, can this digest be taken as the expression of the self-confident, expanding empire in the Malay world rivalled only by Srivijaya and Majapahit? Does this digest (in its reconstituted form at least) represent the sad remains of Malacca as a trading port under colonial rule with the occasional echo of a more distant, but glorious past?

What about the sea? The problem with this digest is that it hardly addresses the sea.[36] What few provisions exist pertain to naval craft of various sizes adrift in open waters, either by negligence of their owner or by malice of other persons. In the event that the craft should bear a cargo, the laws state what measures need be taken. Like the *orang asli* who roamed the hinterlands of the Peninsula for forest produce, the *orang laut*, or sea gypsies, lived along the waterfront or on boats on the open sea and formed an integral and important component of Malaccan society, probably since the earliest times of Parameswara or even before.[37] The *orang laut*, moreover, were instrumental in ensuring that the Malacca Sultanate enforced its 'control' or 'monopoly' over the Straits.[38] The rights of this people are codified in these laws, which, at least in the author's opinion, is the most important concession to maritime trade in the whole document as it has been handed down in modern times. One surmises that traditional thinking held that ships are like wild beasts in the forest. The sea is not unlike *tanah mati*, here to be translated as 'dead' or more accurately 'uncultivated' space, and the analogy of a junk passing over the open waters of the Singapore and Malacca Straits and a wild beast stalking through the thick jungles of the peninsular highlands are not as far apart as one may initially believe. They both belong to whoever can overwhelm and catch them. What about a fully laden, unmanned junk hopelessly adrift during or after a storm? A provision for this had to be made, depending on how far away from the shore that particular junk was when it was picked up by the *orang laut*. Half the value of the cargo was the absolute minimum to be ceded to the 'rescuers', and additional penalties had to be paid to the port master at Malacca supposedly as a punishment for genuine negligence, but one suspects also for the effort of having to intercede and negotiate with the *orang laut* to restore the vessel and the other half of the salvaged cargo. Both parties seemed to have been satisfied with this arrangement, and the problem was evidently significant and sufficiently widespread to have been provided for in law.

This leads to the important issue of foreign residents in pre-colonial Malacca. Much has been written about the cosmopolitan nature of the city when the Portuguese first assumed control of the port and city. In this context, a passage from Tomé Pires has been quoted *ad nauseam*, according to which no less than eighty-four languages were used at any time in the streets and the markets of Malacca.[39] Even if one assumes that legislation tends, by its very nature and intention, to lag behind times, one is nevertheless stumped by the provisions of the *Undang-undang Melaka* regulating the presence of foreign traders or visitors. They are not exactly as hospitable and generous as one might duly expect from a cosmopolitan city where scores of languages were used on any given day, and a port polity that played host to an estimated 4,000 to 5,000 foreign merchants.[40] According to the *Undang-undang Melaka*, 'If a Sea-Captain overstays due to business dealings, [and misses the monsoon and cannot proceed to another port], the fine inflicted is the same as above [i.e. five *emas*] because the Sea-Captain is held negligent toward the junk or small vessel.'[41] What the word 'overstay' actually implies is not explained in any detail. One can surmise from the narrow meaning of the text that traders were permitted to stay for one single trading season, and were then expected to leave. They had to ensure payment of all their port dues before they set sail for home, otherwise, on return to Malacca, they would be charged double the fees.

Were these provisions comparatively generous? Did Malacca become such a great port to do business because restrictions were few? Was the regulation of commercial affairs largely in the hands and at the discretion of certain Malaccan officials, such as the *shahbandar* or the *bendahara*?[42] Could the attraction of Malacca have been that it was comparatively 'free', free from constraints, from the myriad of maritime legislation and fee structures that characterized other port cities in Asia, especially, say, Spanish Manila, or perhaps such rival ports as Pasai and Pedir?

Why is there a lack of provisions for maritime trade? Why are these codified laws not hospitable to foreign merchants? As one trawls the *Sejarah Melayu* and other early testimonies for clues—including Pires for that matter—as well as some of the better secondary works on the subject of Malacca's earliest founding, it is hard not to stumble time and again over that image so brilliantly expressed by Wheatley: Malacca has its origins as a 'pirate's lair'. This view is evident in the Pires' work as well. Is this the main clue to unlocking these problems and questions? Could it be that Malacca was not a sophisticated, regulated marketplace one knows from the Mediterranean or the Near East? It was not suffocated by a myriad of laws and regulations that officials and sometimes even merchants wanted in place to protect their interests. More befitting to its environment along the shores of the Malay Peninsula and in South-East Asia, Malacca was largely an 'unregulated'—or at least minimally regulated—marketplace. A place where the *orang laut* could come and 'dispose of' their 'acquired' ware from ships taken at sea, or from vessels wrecked on the rocks, shoals and sandbanks of the ever treacherous Singapore and Malacca Straits.[43] Did Malacca's original attraction lie in the fact that it was an 'unregulated' (or minimally regulated) marketplace, where pirates could unload their wares and bargain-hunting businessmen pick up goods on the cheap? Perhaps, merchants were also occasionally compelled to call at the port and trade there. Are these conditions truly the ones that enabled Malacca to rise rapidly from little more than a seafront *kampong* of *orang laut* and Malays and 'compete' effectively with the nearby and far more established port polities such as Pasai or even Singapura?[44]

Then there are provisions pertaining to the presence of foreign merchants, especially those who overstay. Evidently, it was common to remain in Malacca only for as long as was absolutely necessary, i.e. until one's barter trade had been conducted and the winds of the monsoon had changed. Again, does this express the provisions of a colonial port settlement or a (supposedly) cosmopolitan sultanate?

If one compares these images with information gleaned from early Portuguese colonial documents and chronicles, one fares scarcely any better. Certainly, the claim of Gaspar Correia proudly expounded in his *Lendas da Índia,* that Malacca was a great trading city since the eighth century, cannot be sustained by any stretch of the imagination. Nor should one give much credence to the testimonies of many European scholars from the age of Renaissance and Humanism, especially those who were trapped and shackled by the tenuous and mostly unverifiable names derived from Ptolemaic geography. Erédia's widely acclaimed *Declaraçam de Malaca* and perhaps his earlier *Informação da Aurea Chersoneso* should be added to this category. Rather, one should be drawn to the more sobering scholarly enquiries of Rouffaer, Obdeijn and later Wheatley,[45] none of whom believe that Malacca was much more than a fishing village—nay a little more than a wretched 'pirate's lair'—before the eve of the fifteenth century. Malacca early on was a marketplace for all sorts of merchandise, including ill-gotten ones, and it was only after the marriage of Iskandar Shah with a Pasai princess,[46] and later the arrival of Chinese merchants following Zheng He's expeditions that the port polity assumed regional prominence.

In closing this section, two testimonies will be discussed that shed some light on the state of commercial affairs in Malacca around the time of its political transition from a sultanate to a Portuguese colony. The first derives from a maritime digest that supposedly traces its origin to the times of the sultanate (specifically the reign of Sultan Mahmud), and was subsequently appended (one suspects considerably) during Portuguese and Dutch occupation.[47] The provisions made in this digest concentrate mainly on the authority of captains and officers on ships and junks, the obligations and duties of the crew, and the punishments for such crimes as adultery, fornication and theft. There is little that this digest could genuinely contribute to the purposes of this exposé, except—and this is important—for a very interesting statement made in the preamble about the historical origins of the text. Here it is claimed that the merchants of Malacca were clamouring for a legal code to regulate more stringently their business affairs, and the present compilation was intended to serve precisely this objective.[48] This is most fascinating. One, this may be taken as an indication that first the maritime code did not historically belong together with the digest *Undang-undang Melaka*.[49] It transpires further that for much of the period of the sultanate, there was evidently no codified legislation to govern the affairs of maritime trade. There were probably unwritten, customary laws (*adat*), or there may have been varying degrees of 'self-regulation' through the various *shahbandars* as has been stipulated earlier.[50] This was the situation during the reign of Mahmud (1488-1511), i.e. during the period immediately preceding the Portuguese takeover.

The second testimony derives from Tomé Pires. He writes in his *Suma Oriental*:

> It is an old custom in Malacca that as soon as the merchants arrive they unload their cargo and pay their dues or presents,[51] as will be said. Ten or twenty merchants gathered together with the owner of the said merchandise and bid for it, and by the said merchants the price was fixed and divided amongst all in proportion. And because time was short and the merchandise considerable, the merchants were cleared, and then those of Malacca took the merchandise to their ships and sold them at their pleasure; from which the traders received their settlement and gains, and the local merchants made their profits. And through this custom the land lived in an orderly way, and they carried on their business.[52]

This excerpt contains two nuggets of useful information: first, it explains the mechanisms by which trade was conducted, and that 'gifts' or 'fees' for the sultan and his officers were an integral part of the commercial transaction. Measures were in place to contain bribery and corruption, but there are many lingering doubts about their efficacy.[53] The other point is far more intriguing. The final sentence needs to be mentioned again: '[T]hrough this custom the land lived in an orderly way'. Custom? What does that mean? Are these customs formally prescribed and codified in law? Or, are they just 'widely accepted' or 'widely practised' (*adat*) that were, ultimately, very flexible and subject to continuous reformulation and reinterpretation?

IV

THE ADVENT OF PORTUGUESE MALACCA

At this juncture it is appropriate to turn to a second question-complex raised by the present exposé: What, if anything, changed when the Portuguese seized control of Malacca? What are the aspects and dimensions of self-perception that altered insofar as these can even be reconstructed?

The task of answering these questions has been considerably simplified by the array of studies that have been published over the past one and a half decades, mainly in Portugal, and to a lesser extent in Asia.[54] Interpretations based chiefly on imperial Portuguese histories, that emphasize efforts to gain military hegemony over the Muslim world, conquest, colonial acquisition and economic remoulding, have made way for more sobering accounts that highlight societal accommodation, mercantile insertion, as well as extensive co-operation with native elites. Again, the works of Luís Filipe Thomaz, Alves, Pinto and Guedes merit special mention in the context of early colonial South-East Asia, and António Saldanha for issues pertaining to early Portuguese expansion into Asia generally.[55]

Malacca was seized in a military operation headed by Affonso de Albuquerque in 1511 that lasted for about three weeks.[56] The developments leading up to the conflict with the sultan's troops as well as the fall of the city are described at considerable length in most of the early Portuguese chronicles, including Correia, Castanheda and in the letters of Affonso de Albuquerque and Empoli.[57] According to Pires, after the sultan had fled, Albuquerque 'took possession of the city. The city and the sea were cleared up and authorities were appointed.'[58] This observation omits important information provided by Empoli who underscores that 'almost every day they [the enemy troops] attacked us, now from one side, and now from another, now by sea and now by land.'[59] These attacks, also mentioned by Correia, occurred mainly at night.[60] Food supply was very limited with more Portuguese soldiers and merchants dying of famine and fever than in combat with the sultan's men.[61] Empoli testifies:

> We had nothing to eat save rice, so that all our people began to fall sick,[62] wherefore in one month about seven hundred of our men died and as many [Gujaratis].[63] . . . [T]he dead lay in the captain's quarters for two or three days, for no one to bury them could be found.[64]

Similar testimonies of the tragedy are found in Correia's *Lendas da Índia* where it is also explained that the fugitive Sultan Mahmud and his men effectively strangled food supplies to the city (probably with the active assistance of the *orang laut*):

> Many in Melaka were dying of hunger, for the sultan sent men to block the routes to Melaka, and no food could get through. People ate only rice and oil. The biscuits available were putrid. If anyone had to take a laxative he had only fish soup (to strengthen oneself with), for a chicken, if it was available, cost thirty cruzados and an egg two cruzados, and there was no other food.[65]

It is in the light of these conditions that one should try to understand the formal diplomatic initiative reported amongst other Portuguese chroniclers by Correia, whereby Albuquerque immediately set out to 'normalize' relations with the neighbouring and regional princes.[66] Resuscitating trade and commercial interaction was certainly a priority, but the special treaties with Siam, Pegu and Java are probably linked to scarcity of food in the immediate aftermath of the Portuguese takeover.[67]

Malacca was supposedly one of the prized possessions of the *Estado da Índia,* an emporium unlike any other in Asia and probably the world.[68] Correspondingly, early Portuguese colonial sources show a propensity to dwell on the grandeur and glory of Malacca, but also provide figures that are scarcely credible. Rui de Araújo estimated the number of households in Malacca at 10,000, a number that was probably as high as the largest European settlements of the sixteenth century. Correia gave an estimate of well over 200,000 (making Malacca the largest city in 'All of the Indies', i.e. East and South-East Asia).[69] Pires claimed that Malacca could muster 100,000 men-at-arms, implying a population of over 200,000![70] Castanheda, by contrast, gave a more modest estimate of 120,000. At any one point in time, there were reportedly 'thousands' of craft and ships of various sizes plying the waters of Malacca harbour and the river. According to Empoli, the harbour was large enough for 2,000 vessels and could accommodate smaller craft in the river.[71] These figures are about as inflated as the vast armies in the books of Chronicles and Kings of the Old Testament. It would be extremely naïve to accept them uncritically and at face value, as some authors have done in more recent decades, but what they do express are the views of foreign observers who were evidently 'impressed'. Still, Malacca appears to have diminished in size and population. The Flemish diamond merchant Jaques de Coutre who visited Malacca in 1603 reported that it was possible to identify stakes or poles belonging to former houses. Orchards that once surrounded residential areas extended some two or three miles from the Portuguese city centre. This area where evidently a larger and more expansive city once stood was increasingly overgrown with tropical thicket. De Coutre estimated that about 600 craft of various sizes annually called at the port.[72]

Francesco Carletti, the intrepid merchant from Tuscany whose travels on the eve of the seventeenth century brought him to the port of Malacca and indeed, around the world, explained that the houses of this city of spice and commerce were constructed of wood and located under shady trees.[73] This description does not differ significantly from Chinese accounts written one and a half centuries earlier.[74] Carletti also observed that the sailors of vessels at anchor spent the night on board, rather than on shore. This is similar to the statement made by Varthema during the period of the sultanate. According to Carletti's fellow Italian, the dangers to the merchants at Malacca were truly considerable, and Varthema probably did not exaggerate when he claimed that during the sultan's rule in Malacca, scores of merchants were killed in cold blood 'like dogs'.[75] It can be presumed that with so many ships arriving and departing, and with the *orang laut,* the Bajau, Aru and Batak scouring the waters outside the port, the merchants had to be on the alert.[76] In any case, the Portuguese authorities—just like their Malay counterparts around Sumatra and the Peninsula—reportedly sealed off the waterfront each night by trawling a series of logs linked by chains across the mouth of the port.[77] This was to stop 'merchants' from setting sail under the cloak of darkness without paying their dues, and also to prevent ships from vanishing into the night without a trace. The logs and chain may very well also have served the purpose of forestalling an attack on the city from the sea by the *orang laut* and other tribes that regularly engaged in plunder and slave raiding. With regard to the latter, Pires' testimony speaks for itself:

> The Kingdom of Aru is a large kingdom . . . and it is not rich through merchandise and trade, for it has none. This king has many people, many lancharas. He is the greatest king in all Sumatra, and the most powerful in plundering raids. . . . His mandarins and people go robbing at sea, and they share with him because some part of the armada is paid by them. Since Malacca began, he has always been at war with Malacca and has taken many of its people. He pounces on a village, and takes everything, even the fishermen, and the Malays always keep a great watch out for the Arus. . . .[78]

Given the limited space and the considerable traffic in the port, ships sometimes had to anchor at a distance away from the shore, with the result that they were out of reach of cannon fire from the Portuguese fortress. It was thus imperative to permanently deploy an armed vessel which was stationed around Pulau Jawa and often cruised the waters outside the harbour.[79]

V

BUSINESS AND MERCHANTS IN PORTUGUESE MALACCA: CHANGE AND CONTINUITY UNDER LUSITANIAN RULE

The following discussion focuses on the conduct of business in the city. Correia emphasized that the merchants of Malacca were not ruined by the military defeat of the sultan and the supplanting of political authority by the Portuguese. In his words:

> He [Albuquerque] was aware that they [the Portuguese] had taken only one-third of the wealth of the town, much of which was buried in underground vaults with strong walls. He was also glad that the traders and people of the town did not feel that they were ruined, for they had returned to the town and rendered him much honour and generosity.[80]

How business was managed and conducted in early Lusitanian Malacca has been described at some length by Pires which has been the base of several exposés on Malacca's model in secondary literature over the past five decades.[81] Consensus has it that the institutions and regulations of Malacca favoured a quick processing of the cargo, disposal, and turnaround time. It may be assumed that he has provided in this instance generally reliable information. Pires and other sources dating from the period of Portuguese presence reveal two interesting facets: first, the Portuguese sought to quickly normalize relations after the takeover, and made minimal changes to the way business was conducted in Malacca. The second facet concerns co-operation with the established business élite of Malacca. This mutually beneficial co-operation is mixed in Correia's *Lendas da Índia*. The 'early spirit of co-operation' was best exemplified in the persons of Utimutiraja (Timutaraja) and later by Nina Chatu.[82] According to Correia, 'the Governor [Albuquerque] entrusted a great deal of the administration of Malacca to Utimutiraja, a rich and powerful Muslim merchant who acted as though he was a King.'[83] Correia further states that this wealthy Javanese merchant was 'treacherous' and an 'opportunist', hatched plans 'to become sultan . . . by any means possible' and also played a game of dual loyalty with the Portuguese and the fugitive Sultan Mahmud of Malacca.[84] Utimutiraja's actions and the treacherous plot to kill all the Portuguese and restore Malacca to the erstwhile sultan,[85] certainly brought the Muslim faction disgrace[86] and benefited Nina Chatu who was appointed (albeit briefly) *bendahara* under the new Lusitanian masters. The latter was also the leader of the influential Kling merchants.[87] For evidently religious reasons, the Hindu Klings were favoured by the Portuguese over the Muslim Gujaratis who had been the most powerful foreign contingent of traders under the sultan.[88] This appointment led to a constellation of power that tightly knit the office of *bendahara* with the interests and concerns of the kling merchant community.[89] According to Luís Filipe Thomaz,

> Nina Chatu evidently envisioned a trade mechanism in the area which at times was not understood by the Portuguese. . . . His collaboration in the expansion of the Portuguese trade in the South Seas was not merely technical or verbal but was also financial. Truly, the first ships that sailed with Portuguese goods from Malacca after its conquest were trading in the ports of the region. On board ship the first trading agents of the Crown of Portugal ensured that the proceeds were shared equally between the Crown and the faithful Bendahara of Malacca.[90]

Cracks in this early but relatively close cooperation became more visible in the later decades, notably under the influence of the Counter-Reformation in the second half of the sixteenth century. As the resolutions of the Council of Trent were gradually imposed by the Portuguese authorities in Asia, the interests of the Kling merchants became severed from the office of the *bendahara*. The disassociation of interests was openly manifest by 1570 when a Christian from the Moluccas was appointed to the position of *bendahara*.[91]

During the final years of the sultanate, merchants paid as a rule of thumb imposts of 6 per cent on the value of their cargoes if they arrived from ports to the west of Malacca, i.e. from the Gulf, India as well as ports around the Bay of Bengal,[92] 3 per cent from around the Straits and the Malay Peninsula, and no tax from the eastern ports. In the latter case, however, it was customary to bring gifts for the sultan and his officials in the absence of formal taxes. Merchants who settled with their families in Malacca also paid a royal fee between 3 and 6 per cent. This information is derived from the *Suma Oriental* for whatever it is worth.[93] Under the early Lusitanian colonial administration, Asian merchants were charged a preferential rate of 6 per cent compared to 10 per cent from the Portuguese traders.[94] By the close of the sixteenth century the fee structure had changed considerably to the advantage of the Lusitanian parties. The Portuguese paid 6 per cent duty, while the Javanese and other foreigners paid 14 per cent.[95] Other sources of colonial revenue included profits reaped from the crown monopoly voyages known as *viagens*. These appear to be a Portuguese creation, though it is also true that during the period of the sultanate, the Malacca monarch was a large owner and operator of vessels.[96]

As can be seen from this discussion, offices, institutions, as well as rules and regulations pertaining to commerce and trade underwent only a gradual transformation during the initial period of Portuguese colonial administration.[97] The reasons for this are sufficiently clear: the new Lusitanian masters were keen to send the message to the regional trading communities that Malacca was open for business as usual, and the Portuguese set out almost immediately (compelled in part by necessity and famine) to mend fences with the powerful neighbouring princes, rajas and merchants.[98] This was the situation during the years immediately following the fall of the Malacca Sultanate.[99] Whether the merchants responded in a way that satisfied the Portuguese authorities is another question altogether, but Lusitanian chroniclers routinely echo enthusiasm in this regard.[100] Hostility toward the Muslim traders and the concept of *daulat* (with all the prestige and aura attached to it in the Malay world) are conventionally cited to explain the apparent decline in business in the Malacca port after 1511. After that year, the port was increasingly competing against several, rapidly (re-)emerging centres of trade on Sumatra and the Peninsula.

By contrast major shifts took place in the way Malacca (at least from an official point of view) understood its strategic location, its hinterland and its relation to the sea. The shifts were abrupt, sudden, and significant for understanding how Malacca functioned during the period of Portuguese colonial administration. In the early documents the name 'Malacca' was used loosely to refer to a broad range of geographic features. In a narrow sense, it can be understood as the city of Malacca. It referred also to the environs of the city, to the lands up and down the western coast of the Peninsula, even to the entire Malay Peninsula and the lands around the Malacca Strait. According to Correia, Portuguese citizens owned (sometimes large) 'farms' outside the city which probably changed or at least mitigated the ever-precarious supply situation.[101] Echoing other reports, including Chinese ones, Varthema denied that the land around Malacca was fertile. He even denied that there was much wood available. A few decades later, Varthema was decried as a liar by the famed medic Garcia da Orta. Probably both were right, but at different points in time. Commercial intelligence reports reveal a keen Portuguese interest in supplies of (highly profitable) jungle produce, as well as the provenance of metals such as tin and gold. Because of strained relations with the neighbouring princes, especially in the later decades with the Sultanates of Johor and Patani, the Portuguese evinced a keen interest in overland trading routes and tried to exercise control over them. The works of Erédia are enlightening in this regard, and the arrival of the Dutch in the

Malacca and Singapore Straits only served to significantly sharpen this interest of the *Estado da Índia,* mainly a matter of political and economic survival.[102]

The sea was perceived by the new Portuguese masters in a different light from their predecessors. They shared with the sultanate the view that the sea was the commercial lifeline of the city; they shared the view that waters of the sea did not divide or separate, but connected the port to the outside world. It was widely believed that the sultan relied on the *orang laut* (his navy since the founding of the entrepôt or even before)[103] to enforce his 'monopoly' of trade in the early phase of Malacca's founding, but not necessarily in later times.[104] The concessions to the *orang laut* in the *Undang-undang Melaka* have been highlighted earlier. The *orang laut* continued to prey on merchant ships plying the waters of the Straits, operating in accordance with the same principles and rules as they did before 1511. They were not loyal to the Portuguese colonial administration, but to 'the Sultan of Malacca' and his 'legitimate heir', the Sultan of Johor.[105] This changed the dynamics of seaborne trade on a number of fronts. First, the *orang laut* played a role in sabotaging the *Estado da Índia* by attacking and seizing Portuguese vessels, to the extent that providing security for inbound shipping to Malacca became a serious as well as a costly affair. Of course, the *orang laut* were not alone, as the other tribes around the Straits were very much active. The Portuguese could hardly raise the funds, let alone operate a navy sufficiently large to effectively patrol waters around the Straits of Malacca, Singapore, Sabam (Kundur) and to the east as far as Tioman and Pulau Condor (southern Vietnam). Second, as during the period of the sultanate, the *orang laut* played their role in re-routing (native Asian) trade to alternative ports, thus 'taking potential business away' from Portuguese Malacca. This ties-in with the widely accepted view that after the Portuguese takeover, Malacca declined in significance as a regional and transregional port.

The Portuguese could not exercise effective control over much land beyond the city and its immediate surroundings, and for a short period of time also over the Straits of Malacca where a toll of 7 per cent was charged on the value of the cargo.[106] The optimism expressed in earlier testimonies such as those of Pires or even Empoli about Portugal's acquisition of an 'empire'—a vast territorially-based empire—proved to be little more than an illusion. Portuguese Malacca came to be viewed as something of a confined space, and 'insular thinking' could be used to describe the growing exasperation after the arrival of the Dutch in the waters of the Malacca and Singapore Straits (1603). Malacca was seen increasingly as a city under siege, precariously dependent on the regular delivery of food supplies from as far away as Java, Pegu and Siam. It was tenuously linked by an unpredictable, financial cord with Goa. Its shipping routes to the Moluccas and Bandas, Timor, Macao and Firado were vulnerable to attack and disruption. Funds to beef up security were neither generously dispensed nor readily forthcoming, and that explains why officials in their reports to Goa and Lisbon routinely dramatized and exaggerated the nature of problems, challenges and threats, painting a truly frightening and alarming picture. But can these documents be accepted at face value? The challenge of 'reading against the grain' of imperial rhetoric, inflated claims, accusations of corruption or even pervasive bureaucratic frustration is truly a daunting one.

VI

CONCLUSION

Extant source material of both European and especially Asian origin, needs to be critically scrutinized. Accounts have their inherent limitations and also cultural biases or baggage. In some cases exaggerations form a part of the acceptable and even expected rhetoric. In this context the exhortation of Gaspar Correia reverberates strongly: 'If we do not give the king the dividends due to his expenses, he stands to lose greatly.'[107] The immense costs to the Crown of early colonial expansion in Africa, Asia and also the Americas had to be explained and justified, failing which leading representatives of the Crown entrusted with responsibility and enjoying the confidence of the monarch would fall from grace and favour.

Despite the inherent and acknowledged shortcomings of the extant source materials, what can be observed about the continuities and discontinuities in Malacca as a trading centre during the period of transition from a sultanate to a Portuguese colony?

First, Asian as well as European sources reveal that in the years immediately preceding the Lusitanian takeover of Malacca, the sultanate faced a number of difficulties. The polity had rapidly grown during the early fifteenth century, possibly as an 'unregulated' or a minimally regulated marketplace. In this context, the deep dissatisfaction of the merchants was particularly striking, who evidently clamoured for a more efficient and effective management of the trading environment. When the Portuguese took over Malacca, they emphasized cooperation with the native elites in the region around the Straits and also with the merchant community in Malacca. This mercantile and societal accommodation facilitated a certain continuity from sultanate to colony. But questions remain as to how important Malacca really was as a marketplace in relation to its regional competitors (especially in northern Sumatra) and how fragmented, diverse and opportunistic Malacca's merchant community behaved.

Malacca's self-perception as a mercantile centre during the period of the sultanate is reconstructed with difficulty. This is because extant Malay sources accentuate different facets and purposes of society than those of European origin. In the past, scholars relied heavily on the *Suma Oriental* of Tomé Pires and accepted at face value his descriptions of the arrangements prior to the Portuguese takeover in 1511. Pires, as a source, has serious difficulties which have till now not been adequately addressed by modern scholarship. There are text versions of his celebrated work that show substantial differences in outlook and use of terminology. Often it is not what Pires said, but what he did not, or simply suppressed, that evokes much interest. More research needs to be conducted that is based on other period sources.

The self-perception of the polity that emerges from sources such as the *Undang-undang Melaka* is one where Malacca stands within a complex web of personal allegiances and commercial relationships as a nodal centre which draws at the peripheries. The term *mandala* system has been used to describe such varying and ever shifting degrees of patron–client relationships. Certainly, the Portuguese including Pires were mistaken (or perhaps deliberately skewed information in order to please their masters in India or Europe) that Malacca comprised a European sort of territorial empire. Still, both the sultanate and the colony evidently shared something of an insular mindset where the sea connected the port to the outside world, and the thick jungle of the hinterland divided or acted as an almost impenetrable barrier. Malacca was thus an 'island' of a special sort, a status which it incidentally maintained till its formal transfer to permanent British administration and sovereignty with the ratification of the Anglo-Dutch Treaty in March 1824.

NOTES

1. Peter Borschberg is an Associate Professor in the History Department at the National University of Singapore and at the time of completing this paper was a resident fellow at the Netherlands Institute for Advanced Studies (NIAS) in Wassenaar. He expresses his gratitude to the following libraries for granting access to their collection of rare prints and charts: Amsterdam University Library; Bayerische Staatsbibliothek, Munich; Leiden University Library; The National Library of Australia, Canberra; as well as the Central Library, National University of Singapore. Special thanks are extended to Prof. Roderich Ptak (LMU, Munich), Prof. Anthony Milner (ANU, Canberra), Dr. Geoff Wade (ARI, Singapore) and Jerry Lee (Singapore) for their critical comments on earlier drafts of this paper.
2. According to the Ming Annals and Teixeira, this occurred in the year 1403. See M. Teixeira, *The Portuguese Missions in Malacca and Singapore*, vol. 1, Lisbon, 1961, p. 15.
3. See also R. Ptak, 'Reconsidering Melaka and Central Guangdong', in *Iberians in the Singapore-Melaka Area and Adjacent Regions*, ed. P. Borschberg, Wiesbaden/Lisbon, 2004, p. 7. O.W. Wolters, *Early Indonesian Commerce: A Study of the Origins of Srivijaya,* Ithaca, 1967, p. 224. See also fn. 64.
4. For a recent critical evaluation of the Ming voyages of 'exploration', see G. Wade, 'The Zheng He Voyages: A Reassessment', *Journal of the*

Malayan Branch of the Royal Asiatic Society (hereafter *JMBRAS* vol. 77, no. 1, 2005, pp. 37-58.

5. See especially L.F.R. Thomaz, *De Ceuta a Timor*, Lisbon, 1994. L.F.R. Thomaz, 'The Malay Sultanate of Melaka', in *Southeast Asia in the Early Modern Era: Trade, Power and Belief*, ed. A. Reid, Ithaca, 1993, pp. 69-90. J.M. dos Santos Alves, *O domínio do norte de Samatra: A história dos sultanatos de Samudera-Pacém e de Achém, e das suas relações com os Portugueses (1500-1580)*, Lisbon, 1999. P.J. de Sousa Pinto, *Portugueses e Malaios. Malaca e os Sultanatos de Johor e Achém, 1575-1619*, Lisbon, 1997. P.J. de Sousa Pinto, 'Melaka, Johor and Aceh: A Bird's-Eye View Over a Portuguese Malay Triangular Balance', in *Nouvelles Orientations de la Recherche sur l'histoire de l'Asie Portugaise, Actes du Colloque, Paris, 3-4 Juin, 1994*, Paris, 1997. M. Lobato, *Política e comércio dos Portugueses na Insulíndia. Malaca e as Molucas de 1575 a 1605*, Lisbon, 1999. M.A. Marques Guedes, *Interferência e integração dos Portugueses na Birmânia, ca. 1580-1630*, Lisbon, 1994.
6. Several editions of this important historic text are extant. I have relied here on the translation of John Leyden, a contemporary and friend of T. Stamford Raffles. See *John Leyden's Malay Annals*. Introduction by V.M. Hooker and M. Barry Hooker, rpt., Kuala Lumpur, 2001.
7. C.H. Wake, 'Melaka in the Fifteenth Century. Malay Historical Traditions and the Politics of Islamiziation', in *Melaka. The Transformation of a Malay Capital, c. 1400-1980*, vol. 1, ed. K. Singh Sandhu and P. Wheatley, Kuala Lumpur, 1983, pp. 129-30.
8. M.-A.P. Meilink-Roelofsz, *Asian Trade and European Influence in the Indonesian Archipelago between 1500 and about 1630*, The Hague, 1962. J.C. van Leur, *Indonesian Trade and Society: Essays in Asian Social and Economic History*, tr. J.S. Holmes and A. van Marle, The Hague, 1955. See the original Dutch work *Eenige beschouwingen betreffende den ouden Aziatischen handel*, Middelburg, 1934.
9. See, for example, the survey by G. Wade, 'The Portuguese as Represented in Some Chinese Sources of the Ming Dynasty', in *Ming Qing Yanjiu*, ed. P. Santangelo, Naples Rome, 2000, pp. 89-148.
10. A. Milner, 'Who Created Malaysia's Plural Society?', *JMBRAS*, vol. 76, no. 2, 2004, pp. 1-24.
11. R.M. Loureiro, *O Manuscrito de Lisboa da 'Suma Oriental' de Tomé Pires Contribuição para uma Edição Crítica*, Macao, 1996. See also the more recent exposé: 'O Sudeste Asiático na Suma Oriental de Tomé Pires', *Revista de Cultura*, vol. 4, 2003, pp. 107-23.

12. T. Pires, *The Suma Oriental of Tome Pires. An Account of the East from the Red Sea to Japan: Written in Malacca and India in 1512-1515*, 2 vols., ed. A. Cortesão, New Delhi, 1990 (facsimile reproduction of the edition originally printed in London, 1944). For Cortesão's ominous statement, see ibid., vol. 1, p. xvi.

    'The present copy of Pires' *Suma* is not the original he himself wrote, and the copyist has left only too many instances of his own carelessness. Pires' style is far from clear, and this, added to the transcriber's mistakes and the most anarchic punctuation, or absolute lack of it, makes the interpretation of the text often extremely difficult; sometimes the translation has to be very free, perhaps even more of a guess than anything else.'

    Cortesão also describes the original Portuguese text of the Paris manuscript (ibid.) as 'very difficult and etymologically very interesting'.
13. For the latest Portuguese language edition see *O Libro de Duarte Barbosa*, introduction and notes by N. Águas, Lisbon, no date. The relevant passages on Melaka cover ibid., pp. 164-8.
14. M.G. de Erédia, *Informação da Aurea Chersoneso, ou Peninsula, e das Ilhas Auriferas, Carbunculas e Aromaticas*, Lisbon, 1807, p. 76.
15. The 1613 manuscript now in possession of the Royal Library in Brussels was published as M.G. de Erédia, *Malaca, L'Inde Méridionale et le Cathay (Declaraçam de Malaca)*, ed. and tr. M.L. Janssen, Brussels, 1882. The earlier draft of this work appeared together as Erédia, *Informacão da Aurea Chersoneso* (as in n. 14), pp. 95 ff.
16. *Portuguese Documents on Malacca,* vol. 1, 1509-11, collected, tr. and annotated by M.J. Pintado, Kuala Lumpur, 1993. See especially pp. 210 ff.
17. For these specific examples, see ibid., para 90, p. 233 and para 294, p. 277.
18. Hj.M. Khalid-Taib, 'Sastera Sejarah in the Malay World. A Structural and Contextual Study of Folkloristic Elements in a Transitional Genre', unpublished doctoral dissertation, Indiana University, 1981, p. 126. 'It has now been generally agreed among the Malay Studies scholars that the *Sejarah Melayu's* prototype was a kinglist. This kinglist was a very sketchy compilation which emphasized the genealogical relationships of the Malacca royal dynasty.' See also Ch.B. Walls, 'The Legacy of the Fathers. Testamentary Admonitions and the Thematic Structure of the Sejarah Melayu', unpublished doctoral dissertation, Yale University,

1974, pp. 15, 17-18, 22, 27, 40-7, 91, 95, 117-20. Thomaz, 'The Malay Sultanate of Melaka', p. 80.

19. *Undang-undang Melaka. A Critical Edition,* ed. Liaw Y.F., Proefschrift Leiden/The Hague, 1976. R. Winstedt and P.E. de Josselin de Jong, 'The Maritime Laws of Malacca. Edited, with an Outline Translation', *JMBRAS*, vol. 29, no. 3, 1956. On the question as to whether the *Undang-undang Melaka* and the *Undang-undang Laut* represent actual legal codes or digests (compilations), see Liaw Y.F., 'The Undang-undang Melaka', in *Melaka,* vol. 1, ed. Singh and Wheatley, pp. 170, 181, 183.

20. Influence is also traced to Indian laws, see C.H. Alexandrowicz, *An Introduction to the History of the Law of Nations in the East Indies,* Oxford, 1967, p. 63, n. 12.

21. *Undang-undang Melaka,* p. 38. Liaw, 'The Undang-undang Melaka', in *Melaka,* vol. 1, ed. Singh and Wheatley, pp. 182, 185.

22. Parameswara and his band thieves and hoodlums are described as having been previously very active around Singapura (where he murdered his host) and then Muar. See [J. de Barros?] *Held-dadige Scheeps-togt van Alfonso de Albuquerque na de Roode-Zee In het Jaar 1506, en ervolgens gedaan: behelsende de geleegendheyd, opkomst en voortgang van de Koningrijken Ormuz, Goa, Malacca, etc.*, Leiden, 1706, pp. 202-3, where the name of the assassinated king of Singapura is given as 'Sangesinga', and who is also identified as the son-in-law of the Siamese monarch. The latter was to avenge his murder and dispatched a large army with elephants and a fleet, inflicting punishment on Parameswara and his 2,000 *celates*. See also Pires, *Suma Oriental,* vol. 2, p. 232: '[Parameswara] remained there [Muar] for six years, and there he planted things to live on; and they [i.e. Parameswara and his men] used to fish and sometimes robbed and plundered sampans. . . .' See also ibid., p. 233. Similar sources were evidently used in Teixeira, *Portuguese Missions,* vol. 1, p. 17; Wolters, *Early Indonesian Commerce,* pp. 222-3.

23. See also the Chinese testimonies of Fei-Hsin (1436) and Ma-Huan (1451) reproduced in translation by Wheatley in his *Golden Khersonese,* pp. 321-5, where it is reported that Malacca (evidently even after the chief was elevated to the position of king by the Chinese emperor) paid an annual tribute to Siam of '40 taels' in gold (ibid., pp. 321, 324). On the origin of this tribute, see also *Held-dadige Scheeps-togt,* p. 206. Also J. Hageman, 'Geschiedenis der Verovering van Malakka en der Oorlogen Tusschen de Portugezen en Maleijers', *Verhandelingen*

van het Bataviaasch Genootschap van Kunsten en Wetenschappen, dl. 24, Batavia, 1852, p. 11.

24. On the origins of Malacca, see also Thomaz, 'The Malay Sultanate of Melaka', pp. 75-7.
25. See *The Itinerary of Ludovico de Varthema of Bologna from 1502 to 1508*, tr. J. Winter Jones and ed. N.M. Penzer, London, 1928 (original in Italian, 1510). G. da Empoli, *Lettera*, ed. A. Bausani, Rome/Djakarta, 1970. M. Spallanzani, *Giovanni da Empoli. Un mercante fiorentino nell'Asia portoghese*, Florence, 1999.
26. Wheatley, *Impressions of the Malay Peninsula*, pp. 132-3. Also *Held-dadige Scheeps-togt*, p. 203, '. . . [S]y (i.e. the *orang laut* or celates) haar woonplaats aan de kant van een Rivier maakten, dat Malacca tegenwordig gelegen is'.
27. *Held-dadige Scheeps-togt*, p. 204, where for Malacca a form of *convivencia* is described between the *orang laut* (celates) and the Malays.
28. Liaw, *Undang-undang Melaka*, p. 38. 'The Undang-undang Melaka', in *Melaka*, vol. 1, ed. Singh and Wheatley, pp. 182-3.
29. L.F.R. Thomaz, *Nina Chatu and the Portuguese Trade in Malacca*, tr. M.J. Pintado, Melaka, 1991, p. 31, '. . . the town being surrounded by swampy land and covered with thick jungle, and therefore unsuitable for growing any edible greens'.
30. In its present-day use, the term is applied to land that has been 'abandoned' (and thus forfeited?) by its legal (former) owners.
31. Liaw, *Undang-undang Melaka*, p. 110.
32. See also J. Everaert, 'Erédia: Humaniste ou Aventurier?', in M.G. de Erédia, *Suma de Árvores e Plantas da Índia Intra Ganges*, ed. G. Everaert, J.E. Mendes Ferrão and M. Cândida Liberato, Lisbon, 2001, p. 55. Anonymous, 'Riquesas que produs o Estado da Índia', in *Documentação Ultramarina Portuguesa*, vol. 2, p. 116. Heredia, *Malaca, l'Inde Méridionale et le Cathay*, fol. 39 verso. Erédia, *Informação da Aurea Chersoneso*, pp. 80, 82-4, 89. L.F.R. Thomaz, *Early Portuguese Malacca*, Macao, no date, p. 54. See also L. Andaya, 'A History of Trade in the Sea of Melayu', *Itinerario*, vol. 24, no. 1, 2000, pp. 87-110, esp. pp. 89 ff.
33. W. Marsden, *Dictionary of the Malayan Language, in two Parts, Malayan and English and English and Malayan*, London, 1812. C.P.J. Elout, *Nederduitsch en Maleisch Woordenboek, gevolgd van een Fransch en Maleisch Woordenboek. . . . Naar het Engelsch en Maleisch Woordenboek van den Hr. W. Marsden*, 2 vols., Haarlem, 1826. For the relevant entry on *tanah*, see ibid., vol. 1, p. 115, 'Tanah djin dan dewah' which Elout translates into French as 'la région

des demons et des ésprits célèstes' (i.e. the region [sphere, space] of demons and celestial spirits).

34. See also Thomaz, 'The Malay Sultanate of Melaka', p. 72.
35. See also 'The Undang-undang Melaka', in *Melaka*, vol. 1, eds. Singh and Wheatley, pp. 191-2.
36. Note the following observation in *Held-dadige Scheeps-togt*, p. 204, '. . . sy alle maar een volk uytmaakten, ende sig met haar gewoonelijken arbeyd onder malkander erneerden, namentlijk de Cellates ter See en de Maleyers met de vrugten van't Land.' According to this, the sedentary Malays were essentially little interested in the 'sea'.
37. This finds firm endorsement in Pires, *Suma Oriental*, pp. 233 et seq.
38. On this point see M. Dunn, *Kampf um Malakka: Eine wirtschafts geschichtliche Studie über den portugiesischen und niederländischen Kolonialismus in Südostasien*, Wiesbaden, 1984, pp. 56, 88. But Meilink-Roelofsz denies, for example, that any force was applied to re-route shipping to call at Malacca's port, see Meilink-Roelofsz, *Asian Trade*, p. 33.
39. Pires, *Suma Oriental*, p. 269.
40. L.F.R. Thomaz, 'La présence iranienne autour de l'océan Indien au XVIe siècle', *Archipel*, vol. 68, 2004, p. 130. Thomaz, *Early Portuguese Malacca*, p. 24. Thomaz, 'The Malay Sultanate of Melaka', p. 80.
41. *Undang-undang Melaka*, pp. 117, 119.
42. See also D. Heng, 'Reconstructing Banzu, a Fourteenth Century Port Settlement in Singapore', *JMBRAS*, vol. 75, no. 1, p. 73.
43. See also Wolters, *Early Indonesian Commerce*, p. 223.
44. According to the *Held-dadige Scheeps-togt*, p. 207, weather rather than man-made advantage is to be seen as leading to the demise of Singapore, 'De voornaamste oorsaak van dit bedert van den ouden staat van Cingapura door den nieuwen van Malacca waren de gestadige stormen en onweders, die sig voor de eerste van de twee Steeden openbaarden.' See also, ibid., p. 209, Singapore was apparently not as well situated to effectively exploit the shifting monsoon winds:

    'En die tijd hadde mede die geene van nooden, die door de Oost-Zee voeren. Want sy moesten so lang tot Cingapura toeven, tot dat de geene, die uyt het Westen quamen, met hare goederen aldaar waren, om met malkander te handelen. En also alle die geene, die buyten om het Eyland voeren, wijl de Reys sekerder hoewel langer, was, so waren sy versekert, als binnen door gaande, te overwinteren'.
45. G.P. Rouffaer, 'Was Malaka Emporium vóór 1400?', *Bijdragen tot de*

Taal-, Land- en Volkenkunde van Nederlandsch-Indië, vol. 77, 1921, esp. pp. 383 ff. V. Obdeijn, 'De oude zeehandelsweg door de Straat van Malaka in verband met de geomorfologie der Selat-Eilanden', *Koninklijk Nederlandsch Aardrijks kundig Genoot schap*, 2de Serie, vol. 59, 1942, pp. 751 ff. P. Wheatley, *The Golden Khersonese. Studies in the Historical Geography of the Malay Peninsula before A.D. 1500*, Kuala Lumpur, 1961, esp. pp. 306-25. P. Wheatley, *Impressions of the Malay Peninsula in Ancient Times*, pp. 119-76.

46. M. Yusoff Hashim, *The Malay Sultanate of Malacca. A Study of Various Aspects of Malacca in the 15th and 16th Centuries in Malaysian History*, Kuala Lumpur, 1992, p. 185.
47. See also Ram Prakash Anand, 'Maritime Practice in Southeast Asia until 1600 A.D. and the Modern Law of the Sea', *The International and Comparative Law Quarterly*, vol. 30, no. 2, 1981, p. 445.
48. Winstedt and de Jong, *The Maritime Laws of Malacca*, p. 51,

    §1: These are the laws given by Sultan Mahmud Shah, . . . know these laws, in order that all matters be peacefully settled.

    §2: The sea-captains desiring a code of maritime law, the Dato Bendahara, Paduka Seri Maharaja Mangkubumi put their request to Sultan Muhammad [sic] Shah. The Sultan consented. This code, which was composed in the days when Malacca was still powerful, under the rule of Mahmud Shah, is now set down in writing.
49. 'The Undang-undang Melaka', in *Melaka*, vol. 1, ed. Singh and Wheatley, p. 183.
50. Ibid., p. 186.
51. Pires, *Suma Oriental*, p. 273, 'A present is paid to the king, and the Bemdara [i.e. Bendahara] and the Tumunguo [i.e. Temenggong] and the Xabandar [i.e. the Shahbandar] of the nation in question, and these presents will amount to one or two percent.'
52. Ibid., pp. 273-4.
53. Ibid., p. 273.
54. See n. 5 for a select list of recently published sources. See also Sar Desai, 'The Portuguese Administration in Malacca', pp. 501-12. Thomaz, 'The Malay Sultanate of Melaka'.
55. A.V. de Saldanha, *Iustum Imperium. Dos tratados como fundamento do império dos Portugueses no Oriente*, Macao, 1997.
56. Thomaz, *Nina Chatu and the Portuguese Trade in Malacca*, p. 26.
57. Giovanni da Empoli reported from his second voyage to the Malay

Peninsula on 14 July 1517 that he personally met Tomé Pires. See M. Spallanzani, *Giovanni da Empoli. Un mercante fiorentino nell'Asia portoghese*, Florence, 1999, p. 237.

58. Pires, *Suma Oriental*, p. 280.
59. Empoli, *Lettera*, pp. 138 ff. See also D. Ferguson, *Letters from Portuguese Captives in Canton: Written in 1534 and 1536*, Bombay, 1902, p. 3.
60. Pintado, *Documents*, para 201, p. 259.
61. See also Hageman, 'Geschiedenis der Verovering', p. 28.
62. Pintado, *Documents*, para 201, p. 259, traced widespread illness to hunger and the heavy rains.
63. See also *Held-dadige Scheeps-togt*, pp. 261 ff.
64. Empoli, *Lettera*, p. 139.
65. Pintado, *Documents*, charter 29, para 198, p. 257.
66. Ibid., pp. 211, 259, 'Since the main objective [of the Portuguese] was trade, which could not be carried out in conditions of war, the Governor sought to make Malacca safe, and this could only be done under conditions of love and peace.'
67. Pintado, *Documents*, para 283, p. 275, Albuquerque 'decided to establish peace treaties with the neighbouring kingdoms'. Also ibid., para 284, 'Albuquerque greatly desired to establish peace with all the neighbouring countries which desired it.' Further ibid., para 291, p. 277, 'A messenger from Java came with a request for a peace treaty . . . [Albuquerque willingly ratified the treaty] as Java was a very productive country and connections with it would be advantageous to Malacca, for it would be assured of [food] supplies from it.' *Held-dadige Scheeps-togt*; pp. 253-4, 280-1.
68. Pintado, *Documents*, para 96, p. 233: 'Malacca is the most populous town in the Indies . . .'. Also para 185, p. 255, 'This is the principal town in these parts, rich in trade . . .'. Ibid., para 304, p. 281, [Melaka] 'the greatest trading centre in the world'. Similar statements can be gleaned from other early Portuguese sources, including Pires and Barbosa.
69. Pintado, *Documents*, para 216, p. 261. See also Hageman, 'Geschiedenis der Verovering', p. 4.
70. Pires, *Suma Oriental*, p. 279. Thomaz, 'The Malay Sultanate of Melaka', p. 71.
71. L.A. Noonan, 'The Travels of John of Empoli. A Study of a Florentine

Trader in the Service of Portugal, 1503-1517', unpublished doctoral dissertation, University of Western Australia, 1970, p. 111.

72. J. de Coutre, *Aziatische Omzwervingen. Het levensverhaal van Jaques de Coutre, een Brugs diamanten handelaar, 1591-1626*, tr. J. Verbeckmoes and E. Stols, Berchem, 1988, pp. 108-9 (original in Spanish).
73. Thomaz, *Early Portuguese Malacca*, pp. 51 ff. See also Hageman, 'Geschiedenis der Verovering', pp. 4, 9.
74. On this point see Ptak, 'Reconsidering Melaka and Central Guangdong', p. 3.
75. Varthema, *Itinerary*, p. 84.
76. Pires, *Suma Oriental*, pp. 145-7. Concerning the Bajau in Malacca, see Thomaz, *Early Portuguese Malacca*, p. 3.
77. On this practice in the Malay world, see D. Heng, 'Reconstructing Banzu', pp. 71, 84-5. Note should be made of his claim, ibid., p. 84. 'Malacca, for example, was not recorded for having a [chain] boom'.
78. Pires, *Suma Oriental*, pp. 146-7.
79. Thomaz, *Early Portuguese Malacca*, p. 53.
80. Pintado, *Documents*, para 187, p. 255.
81. See, for example, shorter contributions by Thomaz, *Nina Chatu and the Portuguese Trade in Malacca; Early Portuguese Malacca;* 'The Malay Sultanate of Melaka', pp. 69-90. R.W. McRoberts, 'The Examination of the Fall of Malacca in 1511', *JMBRAS*, vol. 57, no. 1, 1984, pp. 26-39. D.R. Sar Desai, 'The Portuguese Administration in Malacca, 1511-1641', *Journal of South-East Asian History*, vol. 10. no. 3, 1969, pp. 501-12. In fact, Pires is extolled as the single most important source on Malacca during the period of transition, see classicly C.G.F. Simkin, *The Traditional Trade of Asia*, London 1968, p. 163. R.M. Loureiro, 'Sixteenth Century Iberian Accounts of Indonesia. A Preliminary Survey', in *Indonesia-Portugal: Five Hundred Years of Historical Relationship*, ed. I.C. de Sousa and R.Z. Leirissa, Lagos, p. 23.
82. See *Held-dadige Scheeps-togt*, p. 239. It is revealed here that Utimutiraja was at the time 80 years old, was a very powerful merchant, he lived in Upe and exercised command over a massive entourage and (ibid., p. 241) wielded almost complete power in Upe. Reportedly the Malacca sultan wielded no authority there: '[Utimutiraja] . . . had een volkoomen magt in sijn woon-plaats op alle die geene, die daar in leeftend, schoon het hare slaven niet waren, sonder dat de koning daar yewats te seggen had.' He evidently also had problems with the ruling sultan (ibid.): 'Dese [Utimutiraja] also hy den koning niet al te wel genegen was. . . .'

this may explain why he initially cooperated with the Portuguese. Concerning Nina Chatu, see ibid., pp. 264, 282. Nina Chatu was not popular, he 'poisoned' several prominent businessmen in town and was deposed in 1513. He was succeeded in office by the 'King of Kampar' who had recently taken up residence in the city of Malacca (ibid., p. 455). See also Hageman, 'Geschiedenis der Verovering', pp. 5, 15, 19, 22, 32 ff.

83. Pintado, *Documents*, para 246, p. 267. Also see *Held-dadige Scheepst-togt*, pp. 239 ff.

84. Pintado, *Documents,* esp. paras 221-3, 226, p. 263, paras 248 ff., pp. 267 ff. According to *Held-dadige Scheeps-togt*, p. 272, Utimutiraja also kept tally of all the Portuguese who were killed (in battle or ambushed) as well as those who succumbed to sickness and disease.

85. Pintado, *Documents*, para 273, p. 273. *Held-dadige Scheeps-togt*, pp. 273 ff. on the arrest and execution of Utimutiraja. See also Teixeira, *Portuguese Missions*, vol. 1, p. 48.

86. Pires glosses over this entire episode. He merely records that the Javanese merchant 'Timutaraja' was executed (p. 255), a claim repeated later in the text where it is simply stated that he (p. 281) was 'beheaded because they (the Timutiraja, his son, son-in-law and another relative) were found engaged in Malayan intrigues and trying to darken the cloves', i.e., engaged in high treason and fraudulent business practices in high value commodities like cloves.

87. Concerning Nina Chatu, see Pires, *Suma Oriental*, pp. 258 (esp. n. 1), 281, 283, 287-9. L.F.R. Thomaz, 'Nina Chatu e o comércio português em Malaca', in *De Ceuta a Timor*, pp. 487-512. See also: *Nina Chatu and the Portuguese Trade in Malacca*, Appendix 1, 'The Grant Made to Nina Chatu' (1514), ibid., pp. 44-9. Thomaz, *Early Portuguese Malacca*, pp. 112-15.

88. *Held-dadige Scheeps-togt*, p. 233.

89. P. Pinto, 'Purse and Sword—D. Henrique—*bendahara* and Portuguese Melaka in the Late 16th Century', *Santa Barbara Portuguese Studies*, vol. 2, 1995, pp. 75-93.

90. See also Thomaz, *Nina Chatu*, pp. 28-9.

91. Thomaz, *Early Portuguese Malacca*, pp. 121-2.

92. Pires, *Suma Oriental*, p. 273. Thomaz, 'The Malay Sultanate of Melaka', p. 74. Sar Desai, 'The Portuguese Administration in Malacca', p. 505.

93. Ibid., pp. 273-4. This information is used by most authors writing on early Portuguese Malacca.

94. Thomaz, 'Os Portugueses nos mares da Insulíndia no século XVI', in *De Ceuta a Timor,* pp. 574, 577. Thomaz, 'The Malay Sultanate of Melaka', p. 78.
95. *Regimentos das Fortalezas da Índia,* ed. P.S.S. Pissurlencar, Goa, 1951, pp. 256-7, Alvará of the viceroy Marias de Albuquerque (1595). Also quoted in Thomaz, *Early Portuguese Malacca*, p. 120.
96. The mechanisms of the viagens are described in considerable detail by M. Lobato, *Política e Comércio dos Portugueses na Insulíndia,* Macao, 1999, pp. 241-90.
97. In fact, there appear to have been few genuine cash transactions, as explained by Correia in Pintado, *Documents*, para 232, p. 265, 'In Malacca there had been no coins of gold or silver, because all commerce had been done by barter. Retail trade in the markets and shops had been done with the use of tin coins called calayns.' Thomaz in *Nina Chatu*, p. 31,

    'It was equally necessary to have a good knowledge of trading techniques, and for all the products traded in, for the bulk of the trade carried out in Malacca was not made in cash, but by a system of taking the goods out of pawn, that is, by barter system.'

    Despite the minting of gold and silver coins soon after the Portuguese takeover, barter continued to enjoy importance. The indication of this is given by Correia, Pintado, *Documents*, para 299, p. 279, 'The Governor [Albuquerque] sent a junk to Pasai to load it with pepper for Malacca, so that the Chinese and the Liu-Kius [i.e. Ryukyans, now Japan] who arrived there would not find nothing to take back with them.'
98. See also *Held-dadige Scheeps-togt*, p. 251.
99. This interpretation does not necessarily square with the testimonies of early Portuguese chroniclers such as Pires and Barbosa.
100. While some authors contend that Malacca was 'restored to its former greatness', Meilink-Roelofsz and Dunn argue that Malacca lost out to the emerging competition. See M. Dunn, *Kampf um Malakka,* pp. 88, 92. Meilink-Roelofsz, *Asian Trade*, p. 136.
101. Reports as late as the eighteenth century, when Malacca was under Dutch control, hold out the prospect of an impending famine in the city.
102. See P. Borschberg, 'Remapping the Straits of Singapore. New Insights from Old Sources', in *Iberians in the Singapore-Melaka*, esp. pp. 120 ff.

103. Wolters, *Early Indonesian Commerce,* p. 224, citing Pires as his source.

104. See also *Held-dadige Scheeps-togt*, pp. 205-6, it states that the activities of the *orang laut* in forcing ships to call at Malacca led to the demise of Singapura as a viable commercial port.

105. Pires, *Suma Oriental*, p. 264, states that they had made (or moved) their base to the island of Bintan. The loyalty of the *orang laut* was later transferred to Johor, see P. Floris, *His Voyage to the East Indies in the Globe, 1611-1615*, ed. W.H. Moreland, London, 1934, p. 102. J. de Coutre, *Andanzas asiáticas*, vol. 16, ed. E. Stols, B. Teensma and J. Werbeckmoes, Madrid, 1991, p. 398.

106. See R. Fitch, *Aanmerklyke Reys van Ralph Fitch, Koopman te Londen, Gedaan Anno 1583 tot 1591 Na Ormus, Goa, Cambaya, Cacola, Chonderi, Pegu, Jamahay in Siam, en weer na Pegu: van daar na Malacca, Ceylon, Cochin en de geheele Kust van Oost-Indien*, Leiden, 1706, p. 36, 'Den 8 Februarij quam ik tot Malacca, daar de Portugeesen aan de Zeekant een Fort hebben, maar het land effen buyten de Vesting, behoord de Maleytsche. . .'. Also Dunn, *Kampf um Malakka*, p. 88.

107. Pintado, *Documents*, para 96, p. 233.

PART II

ASIA: HYDRAULIC STATES

CHAPTER 3

Interacting with Hydraulic Resources—Early Indian Experience

RANABIR CHAKRAVARTI

INTRODUCTION

The sustained urge for interdisciplinary studies in recent decades has fruitfully led to major cooperations between the earth sciences and human sciences. One of the most significant fruits of this cooperative endeavour has been a growing concern for environmental issues and their crucial impact on human societies, both on immediate as well as long-term considerations. It has been recognized that mere maximization of available natural resources, including water resources, for the material and political 'progress' and 'advancement' of human beings may not ultimately lead to lasting good of this planet or its inhabitants—the floral, faunal, aquatic and human species alike. Understanding nature and the gifts of nature in pre-modern, 'traditional' societies, often located in non-European cultures of the 'Third World', therefore demands a close scrutiny. This leads to a probing into the early phase of Indian history, up to *c*. CE 1300. The Indian subcontinent is known for its almost perennial dependence on agriculture as the mainstay of its people from at least the fifth millennium BCE to the present times. Agriculture has not merely been rooted to the life and livelihood of the majority of Indian people over millennia, but it is also an inseparable and indispensable factor in the formation of Indian society, its religio-cultural life and political formation. If, in writing the political history of early India, scholars have stressed empires and other powerful entities; such formations largely stem from sedentary agriculture generating considerable surplus with which state functionaries and the army—the latter as the most visible form of the coercive authority of state power—could be maintained. The subcontinent is even today heavily dependent on the rains, which in turn are tied to the 'monsoon regimes'. A good monsoon leads to a rich harvest whereas a bad one proves perilous to the Indian peasantry, the people at large and the state. In the various approaches to understanding the environment in India, the significance of the monsoons and its effects on the very lifeline of India have taken a backseat to the issues of forestry, deforestation, floral and faunal wealth. These are of primary concern to environmentalists and historians of the environment.

In the light of these antecedent statements, this paper presents an overview of the early Indian experience of interacting and utilizing hydraulic endowments, especially the extent to which the state in early India sought to manage and nurture sources as well as the supply of water. This survey, however, confines its analysis to north India and the Deccan. A separate contribution in this volume examines the situation in the south.[1] North India is noted as much for the vast tracts of riverine plains as for the rainfall during the monsoons (June to September). There are great rivers like the Indus and its eastern tributaries, the Ganga, the Yamuna and the Brahmaputra, which are of glacial origin from the Himalayas and therefore perennial in character. These rivers carry, at the height of the monsoons, enormous volumes of silt. This is the most significant feature of the alluvial soil of the north Indian plains which is naturally conducive to crop production. Scholarly probings into the history of flood control in India reveal that it was only under British rule in India that efforts were made to construct perennial irrigation channels in major river systems of north India. The general pattern of using hydraulic resources in pre-modern India was to ensure seasonal irrigation by storing water during the monsoons. This was seen as a major break from the indigenous, traditional system of water management in India after the late eighteenth and early nineteenth century.

II

FROM HARAPPAN CIVILIZATION TO THE VEDIC PERIOD

That the north-western part of the subcontinent had a good harvest of crops as early as the third millennium BCE is amply borne out by the Harappan civilization (*c.* 2600-1750 BCE), known for its diverse types of cereals, cotton as well as granaries. The vast extent of the Harappan civilization (half a million sq. m.) and its surprising uniformity in material culture indicate the prevalence of an administrative system of a very impressive kind—occasionally labelled 'empire'—though the actual nature of the organization is not known. One of the most significant aspects of the urban layout and city planning in the Harappan civilization was the elaborate drainage system in the cities. The celebrated Great Bath at Mohenjo-Daro provides testimony to the skill of the Harappans in providing water storage facilities for urban dwellers. Excavations at Dholavira in Kutch, one of the largest urban centres of the Harappan civilization, show that it was laid out on a sloping terrain between two stormwater channels. The gradient between the higher east and the lower west of Dholavira is 13 m. which is ideally suited for reservoirs. A series of reservoirs surrounds almost the entire city. It is not exactly known if the authorities of the Harappan civilization took measures to provide hydraulic facilities to agriculturists in villages. Combined efforts by hydrologists and archaeologists, however, reveal that there was an indigenous method possibly dating to the pre-Harappan times, known as the *gabarband*, or a dam built of stone rubbles. *Gabarbands* usually consisted of a series of platforms, about 60-120 cm. in height and rising in receding steps, gradually narrowing at the top. These were effective in controlling flood water and retaining alluvium coming down from the hills.[2]

The earliest literary images in India of the monsoons, the rivers and their role in the development of human settlements, can be traced back to the voluminous Vedic literature (*c.* 1500-600 BCE). The most celebrated instance of this is Rgvedic hymn X.75 in praise of rivers (*nadistuti*). The *Rgveda* appears to have been more familiar with the Indus and its eastern and western tributaries than the eastern rivers like the Ganga and the Yamuna. The congenial role of the rivers and the valleys in the emergence of human settlements is recognized under the name of 'Suvastu' (present-day Swat), literally meaning that it was 'good for habitation'. Of the various Rgvedic divinities, Indra (the king of gods) looms large, who was also the wielder of the thunderbolt. Varuna was simultaneously the presiding deity over the cosmic order (*Rta*), justice and clouds. Parjanya was the god presiding over rainfall. It is little wonder that the later Vedic literature (*c.* 1000-500 BCE) shows more mature understanding of the changing seasons and suitable crops than the *Rgveda*. One comes across references to channels (*kulyah*) and digging for water (*khanitrima apah*). But there is otherwise little evidence of any political initiative, or interest, to provide facilities of water storage for drinking and irrigation purposes.[3] In fact, the period under review probably did not have a developed state polity; efforts at hydraulic management appear to have been largely oriented towards individual or group efforts.

III

THE MAURYAN PERIOD

The political scenario considerably changed during the period from the sixth to the fourth century BCE, especially in the Ganga valley. For the first time in Indian history, territorial states (*mahajanapadas*) of both monarchical and non-monarchical types emerged, with a discernible concentration on the Ganga plains, the major theatre of political, socio-economic and cultural changes. The Kunala Jataka narrates a story of an impending clash between two non-monarchical clans, the Sakyas and the Koliyas, both located in north-eastern Bihar, close to the Nepalese terai region. The two neighbouring clans, according to the tale, amicably shared the water of the river Rohini for irrigational purposes. Intense rivalry developed between the two groups over the question of which clan would have the first use of the river. It was only with the intervention of Buddha himself that an actual war between the two parties could be averted. The famous grammarian Panini (*c.* fifth century BCE) mentions in the *Ashtadhyayi* not only different seasons, but also two rainy seasons, obviously implying the south-west and the north-east monsoons, and their beneficial role in agriculture. It is likely, though not provable, that the simultaneous development of territorial polity and urban society in the Ganga valley was a direct outcome of the generation and realization of the crucial agricultural surplus which could have hardly been possible but for adequate hydraulic advantages.

The rise of the Mauryas (*c.* 324-187 BCE) is a landmark in Indian history in that a nearly pan-Indian empire was created, thanks largely to the efforts of Chandragupta (*c.* 324-300 BCE) and Asoka (*c.* 272-233 BCE). The Mauryas are credited with establishing a well-organized administrative system with a large number of functionaries and a strong army. The material and political conditions under the Mauryan rule are better known than the previous ones as there is diverse and more or less reliable evidence. The *Indica* of the Greek ambassador Megasthenes to the Mauryan court—now lost and preserved only in the form of quotations, excerpts and summaries in later European classical accounts—speaks eloquently of the profusion of crops in India. The classical authors attributed this to two factors: the role of the life-giving streams of India and the two monsoons, the latter ensuring 'double cropping'.[4] The Classical authors correctly perceived the importance of the hydraulic endowments in sustaining the material life of the people. The highly fertile land ensured the generation of a surplus and its realization through an effective administrative machinery. The Greek authors further refer to a particular category of royal officials, the Agronomoi, who were in charge of rural areas. Among other things, their diverse functions included supervision of the sluices on the rivers, so that agriculturists received an adequate share of water for cultivation. This is one of the earliest impressions of a political power's interest in caring for and maintaining irrigation projects.

This impression seems to correspond to the prescriptions in Kautilya's *Arthashastra*, the celebrated treatise on statecraft and polity, the earliest portions of which are ascribed to the third century BCE and, hence, contemporary to the Mauryan period. Kautilya discussed embankments and irrigation projects under the broad category of *setu*. The *setu* is of two types: one with a natural source of water (*sahodaka*) and the other which is fed by water brought from elsewhere (*aharyodaka*). The latter type was technologically a more complex system than the first and possibly required channels to carry the water into a reservoir from a relatively distant source. The *aharyodaka* type of reservoir probably received water from a riverine source through a canal or a network of channels. It corresponds to the account of Megasthenes regarding the devices on the river for the distribution of irrigation water under some degree of official supervision. Kautilya, however, preferred a reservoir with a natural source of water to an artificially constructed hydraulic project, as the former was obviously easier to maintain with less financial and administrative involvement of the state authority.

The most striking recommendation of the theoretical treatise is the description of such reservoirs (*setus*) as sources of revenue. No Indian author prior to Kautilya viewed hydraulic projects as having revenue-yielding potentials. Kautilya identified seven heads of revenue from where the Samahartta (officer-in-charge of revenue collection) should collect taxes. One of the seven heads of revenue is the *setu*.[5] His recommendations were based on the theoretical premise that the ruler was the lord of the soil (including mines and mineral resources beneath the soil) and water, a position subsequently echoed in the *Manusamhita* (*raja bhumeradhipati udakasyacha*). The ruler, according to the *Arthashastra*, was therefore entitled to a water-cess (*udakabhaga*) from the cultivators who were provided with irrigation facilities by using various devices and technologies. He recommended the levy of this cess on a graduated scale and not at a flat rate: the more complex the device used to draw water for irrigation, the higher would be the rate of the *udakabhaga*. The levy ranged from one-fifth of the produce to as high as one-third. The highest cess would be imposed when the cultivator used a mechanical device set on streams to regulate the flow of water (*srotoyantra*). This recommendation immediately suggests a close parallel to the descriptions of the classical texts about the sluices set on rivers.

The combined testimony of the *Arthashastra* and the European classical texts points to the possible involvement of the Mauryan government in launching and maintaining river-based hydraulic projects which could have served a fairly large area. The Mauryan empire was the first imperial power of India that exercised political control over the two most important river systems of north India, i.e. the Indus and the Ganga systems.[6] This would have created conditions conducive to the launching of river-based irrigation projects. These were presumably supra-local hydraulic projects, different from and more complex than, small-scale local level hydraulic endowments like a well (*kupa*) or a tank (*tadaga*). The latter also belong to the category of *setu*, and it is very unlikely that all the tanks and wells in the vast Mauryan Empire were initiated, constructed and maintained by the state. These were probably constructed by individual and group efforts. Yet, the state expressed its theoretical prerogative over all types of hydraulic projects. When a new rural settlement was created, according to Kautilya, green vegetables, fish and reptiles grown therein should go to the ruler (*matsyaplavaharitapanyanam setushu svamyam gachhet*, *Arthasastra*, book II, chap. 1). In other words, Kautilya advocated that even the by-products of the *setu* should be taxed by the ruler on the ground of his being considered the ultimate master of hydraulic resources. Moreover, Kautilya was fully aware of the importance of rains for agriculture. That is why he laid down that some sort of rain gauge should be set up under the supervision of the Director of Agriculture (Sitadhyaksa, *Arthashastra*, book II, chap. 24).

To what extent were these prescriptions put into practice? The image of state monopoly over hydraulic resources and the state's demand for an irrigation cess in the *Arthashastra* can be used to argue in favour of the monolithic and unitary character of the Mauryan state, a portrayal strongly present in the historiography of the Maurya. Recent studies of this period, however, question the possibilities of a unitary state under the Mauryas which, however, did develop elements of centripetality.[7] The Mauryan realm consisted of three distinct regions: (*a*) the metropolitan state around Magadha in south Bihar, (*b*) the core areas mainly in the extensive Ganga plains, and (*c*) peripheral areas. Mauryan control manifested itself more in the metropolitan area and was not uniform over the other regions. It is against this background that the actual instances of the Mauryan interest in the management of hydraulic endowments should be examined. The best known relevant case is the construction of the famous reservoir Sudarsana (literally, of beautiful look) in Girinagara (Girnar, Kathiawar, Gujarat). The *setu* was initiated during the time of Chandragupta Maurya by his provincial governor, Pushyagupta. Asoka, the grandson of Chandragupta, later maintained this reservoir, and his provincial governor, Yavanaraja Tushaspha, added conduits to it.[8] This is, indeed, a supra-local hydraulic project launched and maintained by the Mauryans. The same setu or irrigation project was repaired by the Saka King Rudradaman I in CE 150 after it had been badly damaged by a storm. Nearly three centuries later the same irrigation project was damaged and repaired once more by Skandagupta (*c.* CE 454-66), the ruler of the Gupta dynasty.[9] In other words, the lake Sudarsana received sustained politico-administrative attention spanning from about the fourth century BCE to the middle of the fifth century CE.

Excavations at Vidisa (near Bhopal) in Central India, moreover, bring to light the remains of a large canal (185 × 7 × 5 ft.) which is dated to *c.* 300 BCE, i.e. belonging to Mauryan times.[10] It is unlikely that such a large canal could have been constructed by individual or group effort. Instead, this supra-local hydraulic project appears to have reflected Mauryan initiatives in providing irrigation facilities. Barring these two instances of supra-local irrigation projects, there is no direct evidence that the Mauryan administration exercised monopoly authority and control over all hydraulic resources, especially wells and tanks, in their vast realm.

The writers of the early Dharmasastra texts (*c.* 200 BCE to CE 300) agree with Kautilya that the ruler was theoretically the master of all hydraulic projects (*setus*). On the other hand, the same texts highly laud the construction of a well and/or excavation of a tank by an individual. Such acts, generally called *istapurta*, earned merit (*punya*) for the patron. For the first time around late centuries BCE donative inscriptions began to appear in different parts of the subcontinent, many of which recorded the gift of wells and tanks by individuals or by groups of individuals.[11] For example, Vasisuga excavated a well in *c.* 4-3 BCE in the north-western part of the subcontinent. Another person, Krisakavi, is also credited with a similar meritorious act.[12] In about CE 10 an officer in the finance department of the Kshatrapa ruler Sodasa at Mathura recorded in an inscription that he was responsible for the excavation of a tank, construction of an embankment around another tank, and also the digging of a well.[13] From Taxila are known similar instances of donation of tanks and wells by non-Indian individuals in CE 56 and CE 119 respectively.[14] A well-known Saka ruler of the western Deccan, Nahapana, and his son-in-law are lauded in inscriptions for excavating many tanks.[15] The same achievements are also attributed to Skandasvati, a high ranking officer (*amatya*) in Vaijayanti in northern Karnataka.

IV

CLIMATIC CHANGE IN ANCIENT AND MEDIEVAL INDIA

The profusion and diversity of agricultural crops in India is indicative of the extent of awareness among Indians from remote antiquity about climate and its interaction with soil and water. They accorded importance to variations in rainfall patterns in different regions of the vast subcontinent, where the success or failure of agriculture is largely dependent on the distribution of rains borne by the monsoon winds—the massive south-west monsoon from June to September and the north-east monsoon affecting peninsular India from October to February.

Though the traditional Indian scheme divides the year into six seasons each consisting of two months (possibly attempting an impression of a neat symmetry), there is also an alternative system of dividing the twelve months into three dominant seasons, each spanning over four months—summer (*grishma*), the rainy season (*varsha*) and winter (*hemanta/sita*). The latter tripartite division is mainly mentioned in inscriptions of the late centuries BCE and early centuries of the Christian era. This scheme clearly highlights the importance of the heavy rains brought by the south-west monsoon, the reality of which is experienced in India for nearly four months

(June to September). These rains, however, are not only unevenly distributed, but also uncertain and can enhance or doom agrarian production. The uncertainty of the monsoons lays the ground for the emphasis on irrigation systems which would provide support to the cultivator especially during lean seasons. The storage and distribution of water is a precondition everywhere for the growth and spread of sedentary agricultural settlements.[16] It is significant to note that an early medieval text, the *Brihatkalpasutrabhashya* (123a), reveals a remarkable awareness of the variability of hydraulic endowments and, therefore, the diversity of storage systems and irrigation mechanisms in disparate regions of the subcontinent. The text in question discusses the dependence of Lata (southern Gujarat) entirely on rain, of Sindhu (lower Indus valley and the Indus delta) on rivers, of the Dravida country (far south India) on reservoirs and of Uttarapatha (generally north India, but also denoting the area in modern Haryana and Punjab) on wells.[17] This statement is to be understood in the context of various irrigation practices across different regions of India which received varying degrees of precipitation.

The most striking feature of the climate of South Asia is the more or less predictable alteration of the monsoon winds which bring heavy rains to South Asia, especially to present-day India, Sri Lanka and Bangladesh. This particular natural phenomenon has not only engaged the attention of geographers and climatologists, but also captured the attention of early writers. As early as the fourth and third century BCE, Megasthenes noted in the *Indika* that the agrarian prosperity of India was largely due to two rainy seasons, facilitating a double crop.[18] Chakrapanidatta, the eleventh-century author of the medical treatise *Sabdapradipa*, was not only aware of the monsoons, but also provided a twofold division of the rainy season. This consisted of the season of the outburst of rain (*pravrish*) and profuse rainfall (*varsha*). His perceptions about the twin divisions of the monsoons, by which he understood the south-western monsoon system, are rooted in the southern part of the Ganga basin.[19]

Further discussion on the monsoons and their bearing on the possible rainfall pattern in the eleventh century may be in order at this juncture. The historian is particularly indebted to the work of earth scientists for unravelling the long range history of the monsoons. The monsoon wind system affects not only the climate of the Indian subcontinent, but also that of north-east Africa and the coastal areas of East Africa.[20] According to earth scientists, the almost clockwork precision of the monsoon has a close relation to the seasonal cycle of the sun's track across the sky. Yet, there can be considerable variation in the patterns of precipitation during a certain period, bringing in phases of relative lack or abundance of rainfall in wide areas of eastern Africa and South Asia. In other words, geographers underline that the pattern of precipitation in South Asia cannot be studied in isolation, but should be linked to the situation in eastern Africa.

The monsoon fluctuations over large and disparate areas of Africa and South Asia show striking affinity. This results in the onset of droughts in both Africa and South Asia at certain common time frames and demonstrates that the African monsoon decade-scale fluctuations share certain similarities with the changes in rainfall on the Indian subcontinent.[21] While the variability in the rainfall patterns in the Indian context is available only from the 1840s onwards—thanks to the pioneering efforts of Gilbert Walker who prepared rain gauge records—historical evidence of the annual rhythm of the monsoon from a remoter antiquity is available for the Nile river system. On the basis of his meticulous study of the Nile river flood data, Omar Tousson (1925) pushed back the evidence to CE 622.[22] Since that date to recent times the highest and the lowest levels of the Nile flood were measured every year with the help of a gauge, called Nilometer, located at Roda Islands near Cairo.

A high level of the Nile flood closely corresponds to regular and heavy monsoonal rains in East Africa and on the Indian subcontinent. A low Nile flood is an indicator of a weak monsoon regime for a particular year or period. Gilbert Walker used the Nile flood water data of more than a millennium (622-1925) to infer possible variability in the Indian monsoons. He noted the 'tolerably close correspondence between the abundance of the Nile floods and that of the monsoon rains of north-western India'. The *Imperial*

Gazetteer of India (vol. 1) stated, 'it is now fully established that years of drought in western or north-western India are almost invariably years of low Nile flood. The relation is further confirmed by the fact that years of heavier rain than usual in western India are also years of high Nile flood.'[23] No less significant is the observation of geographers that the years of low Nile flood correspond to cooler periods in Western Europe where long range meteorological data have been more precisely recorded. The chief significance of this exercise of examining the rainfall pattern in the Nile catchments area and the cool and warm phases in Western Europe lies in the fact that these have distinct bearings on the rainfall pattern on the Indian subcontinent.

Tousson's presentation of the Nile flood data from 622 to 1522 yields important insights into the rainfall pattern on the Indian subcontinent. The period of 377 years that elapsed between 622 and 999 witnessed 105 years of weak Nile flood (27.8 per cent weak flood years). This implies a corresponding low rainfall during those years in the Indian subcontinent and a cool period in Western Europe. Only 23 years of low Nile flood are noticeable in the rainfall computations for 290 years from 1000 to 1290 (8 per cent weak flood years). During the subsequent period of 231 years (1291-1522), the total number of low Nile flood years was 50 (21.60 per cent weak flood years). The least percentage of weak Nile flood, therefore, was in the first three centuries of the second millennium.[24] The possible years of weak Nile flood and hence low monsoon rains in the subcontinent during the eleventh century CE, according to the table prepared by Quinn,[25] were 1007, 1008, 1023, 1036, 1037, 1057, 1066, 1072, 1085 and 1096: a total of 10 years of low monsoon rains in India during the eleventh century. One may cogently argue that the onset of the eleventh century, the principal chronological concern in this instance, brought about greater precipitation in India than the preceding two or three centuries. It is likely that during the eleventh century the climate on the subcontinent was more moist than during the previous century, and this could have considerably enhanced the hydraulic resources in this century compared to the previous ones.[26] Such an environmental scenario could have been conducive to the spread of agrarian settlements in India in the eleventh century. The early medieval period in Indian history (*c.* CE 500-1300) and especially the period since CE 1000 looms large in the economic historiography of early India as one of unprecedented rural expansion which would have been barely possible without sustainable hydraulic resources.

V

HYDRAULIC SYSTEMS AND RURAL SETTLEMENTS

These observations pave the way for the discussion on the early Indian understanding of human habitations. In most literary presentations, the forest (*aranya*) was conceived as an arena for wild beasts, dangerous robbers, and fierce demons (*rakshasa*) defiling the sacred sacrifices of sages and forest hermits whose hermitages (*ashrama*) were in the forest. The forest was thus perceived as a space in contrast to the settled environment of the village.[27] Sanskrit sources describe a settlement area with multiple villages as a territory (*rashtra*) or a *janapada*, the latter literally referring to the feet (*pada*) of the people (*jana*). More specifically, these terms distinguished agricultural settlement areas from both city (*pura*/ *nagara*) and fortified capital (*durga*). The ideal *janapada* would naturally have arable tracts (*kshetra*), habitation areas (*vastu*) and uncultivated fallow land (*khila*).[28] The area intervening between the *janapada* and the forest was generally earmarked as pasture grounds (*vraja*/*gocara*).[29] The spread of sedentary agricultural settlements around 1000 involved changes in fallow, pasture and forest tracts.

Insightful analyses of the early medieval copper-plate charters during the last decade reveal that rural settlements were neither undifferentiated nor isolated, thereby negating the well-entrenched notion of the self-sufficient, stagnant and enclosed village in traditional India. One therefore needs a model of agricultural expansion that describes activities taking place in multiple villages. One cannot evaluate settlement expansion and the enhanced use of natural resources, including hydraulic reserves, merely according to the *Arthashastra* model, which recommended an active and predominant role of the political authority in the creation of fresh *janapadas*.[30]

The *Arthashastra* measures are often portrayed by historians as a uniform and standard method for creating new settlements irrespective of time and space, through intense involvement of the royal administration. It is suggested here instead, that the clue to settlement expansion lies in the creation of revenue-free land grants largely in favour of religious donees.

VI

A REGIONAL SURVEY OF AGRICULTURAL REGIMES

A closer investigation of regional traditions of water management may prove elusive. At first the agricultural and hydraulic situation in the north-east should be investigated. One inscription from Bangladesh refers to the largest known Brahmanical colonization programme in north India planned and designed by a political authority: an extensive settlement created in the tenth century in Srihatta (Sylhet area in north-eastern Bangladesh). The impressive size of the settlement, probably created out of fallow tracts (*bhumicchidranyayena*), is evident from the considerable administrative restructuring required to assemble a contiguous tract, involving the merging of three districts (*vishayas*). This area had extensive forest and marshy lands as revealed by descriptions on copper-plates from the seventh and eighth centuries. In CE 930, it became a *brahmapura* with 6,000 Brahmins and their families, a large number of craftsmen, and service groups as residents. The record mentions the presence of outsiders (*desantariya*) in Srihatta and of people from Vangala (*vangaladesiya* [Vangala = Barishal, Bakharganj areas in Bangladesh]), indicating that this area was populated by people brought from elsewhere.[31] Though the immigrants propitiated the same deities (Mahakala, Jaimini, Yogesvara and Agni), they required two separate monastic establishments (*mathas*); this is indeed a unique event in early medieval Indian history.[32] This entire complex was sustained by agricultural resources obtained by bringing hitherto uncultivated tracts under the plough.

An interesting variation is visible in the Varendri region, the very heartland of the Pala dynasty (*c.* CE 750-1200). Varendri (corresponding to Rajshahi, Bogra and Dinajpur districts in modern

Bangladesh) had been a flourishing, settled area for centuries, and was the ancestral home of the Pala kings,[33] when they temporarily lost control because of an internal rebellion in *c.* CE 1070. Royal control was restored under Ramapala (1072-1127), the last great ruler of the dynasty and the hero of the celebrated Sanskrit text, the *Ramacharitam* of Sandhyakaranandin. After narrating how the Palas re-established their political authority in Varendri by supplanting the rebel, the text describes the efforts made to improve the war-ravaged agrarian economy. Besides reviving regular cultivation, Ramapala is credited with the construction of 'public works of great utility in the shape of large lakes with tall palm trees and lines of hillocks on their border, so as to make them look like veritable seas'. These artificial water bodies were certainly larger and more impressive than ordinary tanks (*tadaga*) and ponds (*pushkarini*) and represent an amplification of hydraulic resources. No less significant is the description of the levy of moderate taxes, obviously to ensure that the local human resources did not desert the war-torn territory.

The greater parts of the Ganga river valley and the Ganga delta were watered by perennial rivers of glacial origin and well nourished by rains. This region, including Bengal, belonged to the category of *devamatrika* (area with profuse rainfall) and *nadimatrika* (riverine) tracts. Within this environment, hydraulic resources and facilities were important landmarks of rural space. The eleventh-century charters from Bengal and Bihar contain regular references to rivers, streams (*srotosvini*), rivulets (*ganginika*), dikes (*khata/kulya*) and embankments (*ali/brihadali*). Aside from the panegyric of Ramapala's interventions, there is little indication of the construction of large, supra-local hydraulic projects by politico-administrative authorities in this region.[34]

It is pertinent to discuss here the more arid region of western India, especially Rajasthan and Gujarat, the latter being famous for its agrarian economy which included cereals and cash crops like cotton, oilseeds, indigo and sugar cane. Agricultural prosperity is evident from indigenous sources and also from prominent references in Arabic, Persian and Chinese accounts. One source describes the transformation of an uncultivated highland (*uddhakhilabhumi*) into an arable tract by farmers who came from outside (*navyasamayatakutumbikaih*).[35] Hemachandra (1088-1172), the famous Jaina writer from Gujarat, was probably aware of the effects of growth on agrarian settlements, when he suggested in his *Parisishtaparvan* that many villages had assumed the character of towns (*gramascha purasannibha*; *Parisishtaparvan*, I.8).[36] Agrarian growth was due in part to improved iron technology, since Hemachandra was aware of the regular use of iron implements for agriculture. No less instrumental was the introduction of technology to utilize hydraulic resources for transforming undeveloped (*akrita*) into developed (*krita*) agricultural tracts.

Reservoirs were used for irrigation (*sechanartham*) and for moistening sown seeds (*siktam bijam*), as mentioned in the Jaina text, the *Upamitibhavaprapanchakatha* (906). Besides the usual local level irrigation projects like tanks and wells (*kupa*), new irrigation devices like the *araghatta/arahatta* and the *vapi*, particularly suitable for lifting water from great depths, began to figure in texts describing technology. While the *araghatta* is a type of waterwheel in wide use,[37] the *vapi* (a term derived from the Sanskrit root *vap*, meaning to sow) describes the step-wells (*baolis*) which abound in Gujarat to this day. The device *araghatta* demands close scrutiny. The *Gathasaptasati* of Hala (*c.* early centuries CE) offers one of the earliest accounts of the device under the name *rahattagadiya* (equivalent to Sanskrit *araghattaghatika*), or a wheel fitted with pots. The earliest epigraphic mention of the device goes back to CE 532 in the Mandasore prasasti of Yasodharman.[38] An essential part of the *araghatta* was the *ghatiyantra* or the device with pitchers, usually mounted on the wheel, but not attached to its rim. The *ghatiyantra* as an irrigation device is, therefore, often described as a 'pot-garland'. The *Upamitabhavaprapanchakatha* of Siddharshi (906) offers the most elaborate account of the *araghatta*. The water available through the *araghatta* irrigated (*sikta*) the seeds which would blossom into luxuriant crops. The *araghatta*, according to the text, draw water from a reservoir which in turn received water from an irrigation (*sechanartham*) well. The well was so deep that its bottom was invisible. The text unmistakably highlights two of its salient features: the spokes (*arakas*) of the wheel which was a revolving apparatus (*satatabhrama*).[39] This waterwheel, however, did not have pots/pitchers attached to its rim, but the chain of pots was instead mounted on the wheel which was clearly separate from the pot-garland. The text does not refer to any gearing mechanism enabling the conversion of horizontal to a vertical rotary motion. The latter feature became visible in India from the fourteenth century onwards and, as has rightly been suggested by Irfan Habib, belonged to the typical Persian wheel or the *saqia*.[40] The prevalence of *araghatta* as a hydraulic machine is best demonstrated by an eleventh-century panel from Mandor (Pali district, Rajasthan). From the left to the right, the panel presents a group of warriors, the waterwheel with pots (*araghatta*), the operator of the device and an animal. The six spokes of the wheel are clearly visible and there were possibly other spokes as well which cannot be seen. 'The pots with pronounced and flaring mouth are mounted on the outer rim of wheel with ropes at regular intervals. The position of the wheel and the direction of the pots unmistakably indicate the rotary motion of the wheel in the anti-clockwise direction.'[41]

The *vapi* refers to another type of irrigation mechanism which figured prominently since the early medieval times. As mentioned earlier, it is derived from the root *vap*, therefore, its close association with irrigating cultivated tracts is beyond any doubt. It is widely found in the arid regions of Gujarat and Rajasthan and is similar to the *baoli* of modern times. Its importance as a step-well for tapping the groundwater at considerable depth can hardly be overestimated. In sharp contrast to the stray references to the *vapi* in the tenth-century, texts like the *Samaranganasutradhara* of Bhoja and the *Aparajitapriccha* of Bhuvanadeva devote a full and elaborate chapter (chap. 74) to local level irrigation devices including the *vapi*.[42]

The security provided by a branch of the Chalukyas in Gujarat as dominant regional rulers gave a boost to the construction of storage tanks and the initiation of other irrigation projects. Thus, Mularaja (CE 941-96) directed his officers to dig wells and tanks and construct *vapis*. The tank excavated at Anahilapataka (Patan, Gujarat) was named after Durlabharaja (regnal period 1010-24). Similarly, the two tanks commissioned by King Karna (1066-94) were named after him (Karnasagara); the same ruler is credited with the construction of a *vapi* at Davad. In 1099, the Chalukya King Siddharaja endowed a piece of land for the maintenance of a step-well that had been constructed by the son of a minister (*amatya*) in northern Gujarat. In some instances, the kings were directly involved in the construction of irrigation facilities; in most cases, they interacted with subordinates who took the initiative in consultation with the local leaders.[43]

In Rajasthan, a region with less rainfall than Gujarat, inscriptions from the eleventh century reveal that the introduction of irrigation technologies resulted in the production of diverse crops even in this arid area. *Vapis* and *araghattas* appear more frequently as important landmarks in rural areas in Rajasthani inscriptions of the eleventh century than in those of ninth and tenth centuries. In 1059, another *araghatta* was constructed with reference to a rice field. Even more interesting information is furnished by an inscription of 1110 from Sevadi (Pali district), recording the construction of an *araghatta* for a double-cropped field yielding both summer and winter crops, described as *saradiyagraishmakakshetra*.[44] There is little doubt that the introduction of the *araghatta* and the *vapi* considerably benefited agricultural production, especially because they were largely adopted in the relatively arid regions of western India. But it is unlikely that the common peasants would have been able to afford them. Only rich peasants and landlords had the adequate means and resources to invest in these new hydraulic technologies and devices. In eighth-century Bodhgaya (in Bihar, under the rule of the Pala King Dharmapala), the cost of excavating a tank and designing four divine images in a temple near that tank was 3,000 *drammas* (silver coins).[45] Whether and how far the state authority directly invested in the development of these new technologies is difficult to determine. But they were indeed far outnumbered by the ubiquitous unpaved (*kachcha*) wells which the ordinary and poor peasants could afford and had access to.

As already stated, the administration's role in water management is in general apparent in the case of large-scale supra-local irrigation projects, often based on rivers. The most outstanding example of this comes from ninth-century Kashmir. Immortalized by Kalhana who in his *Rajatarangini* presented the history of Kashmir with remarkable accuracy, the text graphically describes the vagaries of the Vitasta (modern river Jhelum) annually flooding the valley. During the reign of Avantivarman (*c.* 836-55), Suyya who had mastered hydraulic technology, designed measures to present the flooding of the Vitasta. There was a conscious attempt to divert the course of the Vitasta and to deepen the river bed by desilting it. Suyya regulated the Vitasta by constructing several irrigation channels. According to Kalhana,

> After examining the different classes of land he (Suyya) procured a supply of water for the villages, which were thus no longer dependent only on rainfall. After watering all the village (lands), he took from (each) village (some) soil, ascertained by observing the time it took to dry up, the period within which irrigation would be required (for each soil, respectively). He (then) arranged (accordingly) on a permanent basis for the size and distribution of the water course for each village and by (using for irrigation) the Anula and other streams, embellished all regions with an abundance of irrigated fields.[46]

Kalhana eloquently praised these efforts which averted the devastating annual flood of the Vitasta. Not only did this lead to a rich harvest, but also the price of paddy, which grew in abundance, came down.

Peninsular India, an area that is not as arid as Rajasthan, has its own uncertainties of rainfall and the attendant need to conserve hydraulic resources. The south-western monsoon brings in abundant orographic rainfall on the Western Ghat mountain ranges, but as winds pass on to the interiors of Maharashtra and Karnataka they drop much less precipitation. The region around the Ratnagiri district in Maharashtra is known as a rain shadow and drought-prone region. The north-eastern monsoon brings some rains, mainly confined to Andhra Pradesh and eastern parts of Tamil Nadu. All the rivers in peninsular India are entirely rain-fed; water is thus a precious natural resource, conserved and controlled from a remote antiquity.

Karnataka especially witnessed a countrywide rise in land grant issuance. A record from 904 describes the activities of a petty ruler: he founded a village within a forest tract, paddy fields lay along the riverside and an excavated tank situated within the village. The following year, a Brahmin donor established a rural settlement for immigrant Brahmins, a huge tank fed by three streams from a nearby forest adequately served the newly established settlement, which may have grown after the clearing of a part of the forest.[47] In the eleventh century, a merchant (*sreshthi*) cleared a forest tract in Sorab taluk near a previously established *agrahara*, excavated a tank, and laid out paddy fields.[48] These cases point to a process that must have occurred continually in the tenth and eleventh centuries. One of the results of these initiatives was demographic growth (*janodaya*).

Throughout Karnataka, the main form of local level irrigation was an artificial lake or tank, a category of public works designated as bunds aligned with the natural sources of water (*sahodaka setu*) designed to trap run-off from rainfall. After CE 1000, observations reveal the construction of tanks with channels that were connected to rivers, described as bunds which were artificially fed (*aharyodaka setu*). Water managers regularly used sluices to control the inward and outward flow of water for these tanks. As early as 890, an inscription mentions a tank with four sluices. The reference to the 'Northern' sluice in another inscription of 1090 suggests the existence of more than one sluice on other sides of the tank. There are many epigraphic references to regular inspections and repairs of tanks and sluices. Boats were often used to dredge the tanks, in order to maintain and increase their capacity to hold water.[49] Though tanks were the principal means of storage of water in peninsular India, a special and individual feature of tanks in Karnataka was that most of them formed a chain. The chain tank irrigation system ensured the filling up of tanks at a lower reach with the excess and overflowing water in tanks at a higher level. The natural contours and physiography of the land in the plateau region of western Deccan was thus integrated into hydraulic projects. An excellent example of this is available in the 'Big Tank' at Kattageri (Badami taluk, Karnataka) during the reign of Vikramaditya VI (1076-1126), the greatest ruler of the western Chalukya dynasty. The method of draining excess water from a tank at a higher level was applied successfully here to fill up the tank at a lower level.[50]

An outcome of these efforts to ensure improved hydraulic resources was agrarian expansion and growth in Karnataka. A clear illustration of this is seen in the perception of the *kanguda* variety of paddy. Kanguda type of paddy had earlier been regarded as an inferior type, while the *Manasollasa* of Somesvara III (twelfth century) considered the same variety as an excellent paddy (*sutandula*), fit to be included in the royal dietary practices.[51]

VII

CONCLUSION

The discussion presented here offers only an outline of the problem, a few glimpses and gleanings, at the most, of the interlocking between hydraulic resources/projects and political interests in early India. The evidence presented and the observations arising thereof by no means argue for the presence of a hydraulic society in which is embedded the formulation of 'Oriental Despotism' by Karl August Wittfogel.[52] The inapplicability and the inappropriateness of Wittfogel's model in the Indian context have been amply demonstrated both on conceptual and empirical grounds.[53] Contrary to the static nature of the state under Oriental Despotism, historians have ably established the changing facets of state development and the processual nature of the state in India.[54] In spite of the Dharmasastra norm that the king was the lord of water (along with land), irrigation projects were not a state prerogative and did not constitute a state monopoly in early India. The involvement of the political authority in the construction and maintenance of hydraulic projects was evident only in the case of large-scale, supra-local projects based on riverine sources. Such projects were few in number *vis-à-vis* the apparent numerical superiority of local level irrigation projects, such as wells, tanks and ponds which were mostly undertaken and maintained by individual and/or group initiative at the rural and locality levels. Even in the cases of the royal tanks built by the Pallava and Chola rulers, these projects were certainly initiated and funded by the apex political authority, but their maintenance was assigned to the village assemblies. These local self-government bodies in south India had a unique subcommittee of annually elected representatives which looked after these tanks.[55] The village assemblies received donations and endowments in cash and kind which generated resources for the future maintenance of these royal tanks. Thus, the royal tanks as hydraulic projects did not yield any special political power to the apex authority. Last but not the least, the scant evidence and meagre practice of imposing water cess by the state authority upon the vast multitude of peasants precludes the possibility of a state controlled irrigation system or the utilization of hydraulic resource as a lever to extract political mileage in early India.

NOTES

1. See S. Jeyaseela Stephen, 'Water Resources and Management in the Rural Setting of Medieval South India', in the present volume.
2. For a general introduction to the Harappan civilization see B. and R. Allchin, *The Rise of Civilization in India and Pakistan*, Cambridge, 1982. D.K. Chakrabarti, *India. An Archaeological History*, New Delhi, 1999. S. Ratnagar, *Understanding Harappa*, New Delhi, 2001. For the gabarbands see B. Allchin, ed., *Living Traditions. Studies in the Ethnoarchaeology of South Asia,* New Delhi, 1994. The excellent website www.harappa.com designed by J.M. Kenoyer offers many photographs of Harappan wells and the Great Bath at Mohenjo-Daro.
3. R.T.H Griffith, tr., *The Hymns of the Rigveda*, vol. 2, 3rd edn., Varanasi, 1926, pp. 490-1. The extract has also been quoted in N. Ray, B.D. Chattopadhyaya, R. Chakravarti and V.R. Mani, *A Sourcebook of Indian Civilization*, Hyderabad, 2000, pp. 4-5. A.A. McDonnell and A.B. Keith, *Vedic Index of Names and Subjects*, 2 vols., London, 1912 for terms related to water bodies, hydraulic resources and the monsoon. L. Gopal, 'Agriculture', in *History of Technology in India*, vol. 1, ed. A.K. Bag, New Delhi, 1997, pp. 391-436, presents an overview of irrigation practices and early Indian understanding of hydraulic endowments.
4. The classical accounts of India, largely based on Megasthenes' *Indica*, give a description of the sevenfold classification of Indian people. The first group, the philosophers (sophists), made forecasts at the

beginning of each year, among other things, about drought and wet weather (J. McCrindle, tr., *Ancient India as Described by Megasthenes and Arrian*, Calcutta, 1921, p. 40). This mentions the importance attached to rainfall or the lack of it in India. See also R. Thapar, *Asoka and the Decline of the Mauryas*, 2nd edn, New Delhi, 1996.

5. R.P. Kangle, ed. and tr., *The Kautiliya Arthashastra*, 3 vols., Bombay, 1966-72. For Samahartta, see vol. 2, p. 12.
6. For the historical and political geography of India under the Mauryas, see the excellent maps in I. Habib, *The Mauryan Age*, New Delhi, 2005.
7. R. Thapar, *The Mauryas Revisited*, Calcutta, 1987. G. Fussman, 'Central and Provincial Administration in Ancient India. The Problem of the Maurya Empire', *Indian Historical Review*, vol. 11, 1987-8, pp. 43-72.
8. See D.C. Sircar, *Select Inscriptions Bearing on Indian History and Civilization*, vol. 1, Calcutta, 1965, pp. 75-80, 307-16 for the two Junagarh inscriptions that mention the lake Sudarsana.
9. A.M. Shastri drew attention to the Ramtek inscription (of the time of the Vakataka Queen Prabhavatigupta) which records the excavation of a tank named Sudarsana which was donated to a temple. This tank was situated in Central India. The name Sudarsana is likely to have been borrowed from its more illustrious counterpart in Kathiawad which had already been conquered by Prabhavatigupta's father, Candragupta II. Such a possibility is strengthened by the christening of another hydraulic project in the Vakataka realm as Sudarsana. The Hisse-Borala inscription of CE 458 mentions the construction of Sudarsana lake somewhere in the vicinity of modern Wasim (Akola district, Maharashtra), by one Svamilladeva, the ajnakara of the Vakataka King Devasena (of the Vatsagulma branch). The record also mentions a supervisor of the construction work (*karmopadeshtri*), named Bappa. See A.M. Sastri, ed., *The Age of the Vakatakas*, Delhi, 1992. R. Chakravarti, 'Politics and Society in India (300-1000)', in *Life, Thought and Culture in India*, ed. K. Satchidananda Murty, New Delhi, 2002, p. 77.
10. The area must have been incorporated in the Mauryan realm as Asoka's inscriptions have been found in Sanchi which lies in close proximity to Vidisa.
11. For an overview of *ihtapurta* in the Puranas and the Dharmasastras see P.V. Kane, *History of Dharmasastra*, vol. 2, Poona, 1962.
12. R.S. Sharma, 'Irrigation in the North', in *Perspectives in the Social and Economic History of Early India*, ed. id., New Delhi, 1983.

13. Sircar, *Select Inscriptions*, vol. 1, p. 121. The recommendations of the law books have been compiled by Kane, *History of Dharmasastras*, vol. 2.
14. Sharma, 'Irrigation in the North'.
15. See the Nasik inscription of Nahapana, in Sircar, *Select Inscriptions*, vol. 1, pp. 167-8.
16. O.H.K. Spate and A.T.A. Learmonth, *India and Pakistan: A General and Regional Geography*, 3rd edn, London, 1967. Traditional Indian understanding of the seasons led to the formulation of *rituvijnana* which L. Gopal considers to be 'climatology' that 'developed along with astronomy'. See Gopal, 'Agriculture', p. 419.
17. Cited by Gopal, 'Agriculture', p. 421. See also R. Chakravarti, 'Natural Resources and Human Settlements. Perceiving the Environment in India', in *The World in the Year 1000*, ed. J. Heitzman and S. Schenkluhn, New York, 2004, pp. 48-66.
18. R.C. Majumdar, *The Classical Accounts of India*, Calcutta, 1960.
19. F. Zimmermann, 'Monsoon in Traditional Culture', in *Monsoons*, ed. J.S. Fein and P.L. Stephens, New York, 1987, pp. 51-75. It is significant that Ibn Majid, the greatest navigator in the western Indian Ocean in the fifteenth century, was fully aware that the fury of the sea swelled with the typical summer monsoons and recommended voyages across the western Indian Ocean only with the gradual slackening of the south-west monsoon after late August. He termed the rainy season as 'vishkal', obviously derived from the Sanskrit term *varshakala*. See G.A.R. Tibbett, *Arab Navigation in the Indian Ocean Before the Coming of the Portuguese*, London, 1971.
20. Fein and Stephens, eds., *Monsoons*. H.F. Diaz and V. Markgraf, eds., *El Nino. Historical and Palaeoclimatic Aspects of the Southern Oscillation*, Cambridge, 1992.
21. J.E. Kutzbach, 'The Changing Pulse of the Monsoon', in *Monsoons*, ed. Fein and Stephens, pp. 247-68. W.H. Quinn, 'A Study of Southern Oscillation: Related Climatic Activity for 622-1900 Incorporating Nile River Flood Data', in *El Nino*, ed. Diaz and Markgraf, pp. 119-49.
22. O. Tousson, *Memoire sur L'Historie du Nil*, Cairo, 1925.
23. Quoted in Quinn, *Study of Southern Oscillation*, p. 125.
24. Quinn, *Study of Southern Oscillation*, p. 143, demonstrated that the period from 1000 to 1290 represented the Little Climatic Optimum (LCO),

and the subsequent 1291-1522 phase was an interim period between the LCO and the Little Ice Age (LIA), and 1694-1899 was located in the LIA. See particularly Table 6.7 in his study.

25. Ibid., pp. 140-1.

26. Utilizing the Nile flood data, M.K. Dhavalikar talked of a long period of relative lack of rain and consequent aridity in India from the seventh century onwards. This, in his opinion, adversely affected human settlements in India during the post-Gupta period (*c.* CE 600-1200). Drawing on various literary sources, Dhavalikar suggested an environmental change during this period leading to frequent outbreaks of famine. He argued that the lack of monsoonal rain and relative aridity contributed to the decline of many flourishing urban centres of pre-CE 600. He highlighted the environmental factor in the assumed urban decay of India during the post-Gupta period. See M.K. Dhavalikar, 'The Golden Age and After. Perspectives in Historical Archaeology', General President's address, in *Proceedings of Indian History Congress* (Calicut session), New Delhi, 2000. While his suggestions of a long period of relative aridity in India after CE 600 are supported by data on Nile flood and increasing cold climate in Western Europe, it is difficult to subscribe to his thesis of wholesale and widespread decay of urban centres in India after CE 600. He based his interpretation on the concept of 'urban anaemia' propounded by R.S. Sharma, *Urban Decay in India AD 300-1000*, New Delhi, 1987. The perspective of an overall urban decline in the entire subcontinent has been questioned on both empirical and conceptual grounds. See B.D. Chattopadhyaya, *The Making of Early Medieval India*, Delhi, 1994; id., 'State and Economy in North India. Fourth to Twelfth Century', in *Recent Perspectives of Early Indian History*, ed. R. Thapar, Bombay, 1995. See also R. Champakalakshmi, 'State and Economy in South India. Fourth to Twelfth Centuries', in *Recent Perspectives of Early Indian History*, ed. R. Thapar. R. Champakalakshmi, *Trade, Ideology and Urbanization of Early South India, 300 BC to AD 1300*, New Delhi, 1996. A recent critique of the concepts of declining trade and urban contraction is available in Chakravarti, ed., *Trade in Early India*, New Delhi, 2001. R. Chakravarti, Review of D.N. Jha, ed., 'The Feudal Social Order', *The Medieval History Journal*, vol. 5, no. 1, pp. 161-71.

27. C. Malamoud, *Cooking the World. Ritual and Thought in Ancient India*, Delhi/New York, 1998.

28. In royal charters, rural settlements figure with high and low lands

(*satala-soddesa*), saline areas with pits (*sagarttoshara*), dry and wet tracts (*sajalasthala*), shrubs and bushes (*sajhatavitapa*), dumping grounds (*avaskara*) and grasslands for the grazing of cattle extending to the end of the village (*sasimatrinaputigo-charaparyanta*).

29. R. Chakravarti, 'The Creation and Expansion of Settlements and Management of Hydraulic Resources in Ancient India', in *Nature and the Orient. The Environmental History of South and South-East Asia*, ed. R. Grove, V. Damodaran and S. Sangwan, Delhi/New York, 1998, pp. 87-105.
30. See the treatment of *janapada* creation (*janapadanivesa*) in Kautilya, *Arthashastra*, vol. 2, chap. 1.
31. One may assume that the sharp difference between the *desantariya* and the *vangaladesiya* in the newly created 'brahmana city' could signal their unequal access to resources in this area. See Ray, Chattoapdhyaya, Chakravarti and Mani, *A Sourcebook of Indian Civilization*, pp. 634-5. Also B.D. Chattopadhyaya, *Aspects of Rural Settlements and Rural Society in Early Medieval India*, Calcutta, 1990.
32. Sircar, *Select Inscriptions*, vol. 2, New Delhi, 1983, pp. 92-4.
33. Northern Bengal had a complex and developed economy with a strong agricultural foundation as early as the third century BCE, as illustrated by the fragmentary Mahasthangarh stone plaque inscription. This record mentions the cultivation of paddy and sesamum, a royal granary and the well-planned, prosperous city of Pundranagara (Mahasthan in Bangladesh, now a major excavated site), the earliest known urban centre of Bengal. The region's prosperity continued in the Gupta age (fourth to sixth century) and during the reign of Sasanka (*c.* CE 600 to 619 if not up to 637). Varendra or Varendri, in the heartland of north Bengal, was described as the ancestral home (*janakabhu*) of the Pala kings in the *Ramacaritam*. See H.P. Shastri, ed., *Ramacaritam of Sandhyakaranandin*, Calcutta, 1969.
34. The only exception to this general pattern is the unique practice of levying a water cess (*jalakara*) in the twelfth-century Gahadhavala realm around Kanyakubja (modern Kanauj in Uttar Pradesh). See D.C. Sircar, *Indian Epigraphical Glossary*, Delhi, 1966.
35. Indian texts and copper-plate charters seem to differentiate a hitherto uncultivated tract (*khila*) from an arable plot deliberately left or kept fallow (*khilakshetra*). It is a common and traditional agrarian practice that arable plots are occasionally kept fallow for a period to restore their fertility. In a thirteenth-century copper-plate from south-eastern

Bangladesh, administrative abbreviations were used to suggest such different categories of fallow tracts. Thus, *mu-ti* (*mundatikkara*) meant a tract kept fallow while *chi-khi-mu-ti* (*chirakhilamundatikkara*) denoted a tract never before brought under the plough. See Sircar, *Indian Epigraphical Glossary*.

36. This description provides a counterpoint to the account of towns in the *Brihannaradiya Purana*, according to which towns were beginning to wear the look of villages (*nayarani gamabhuyani hohinti*). On the basis of the *Brihannaradiya Purana*, B.N.S. Yadava (*Society and Culture in Northern India in the Twelfth Century*, Allahabad, 1973) impressed upon the urban decay and ruralization in the wake of a decline in trade and crafts. Contrary evidence that agrarian prosperity and expansion of agriculture could transform a village into a node for local level grain exchange comes from an epigraphic reference to Naddula, a village in Rajasthan. See Chattopadhyaya, *Making of Early Medieval India*. R. Chakravarti, *Trade and Traders in Early Indian Society*, Delhi, 2002. Located in close proximity to twelve villages, it gradually became a local level market centre (*mandapika*), then a city (*nagara*), and finally the political seat of the Nadole Chahamana kings. B.D. Chattopdhyaya, *Aspects of Rural Settlements and Rural Society in Early Medieval India*, has illuminated the history of a village named Kalikatti in twelfth-century Karnataka, which grew from an ordinary village into an outstanding or most prosperous village and finally assumed a nearly urban profile.

37. The term *araghatta* is also explained in lexicons as a deep well. The term is occasionally mentioned along with another irrigation device, the *ghatiyantra* or a pot-garland. Such a device consisted of a number of pots tied to a rope, probably set on a deep well and moved with the help of a pulley. The *araghatta* and the *ghatiyantra* were particularly useful in dry and arid regions where groundwater could be tapped only at a considerable depth. The term *araghatta* is often translated as the Persian wheel. Irfan Habib, however, has argued that the Persian wheel (*saqia*) was not in regular use in Indian agriculture prior to the thirteenth or fourteenth century. He differentiates it from *noria*, i.e. a waterwheel carrying pots or buckets fixed on its rim. The *noria*, used from the ninth to tenth century onwards, however, did not have a chain to carry pots nor did it have a gearing mechanism, typical of the *saqia*. See Irfan Habib, Presidential address, Section 2, Indian History Congress (Varanasi session), 1969. It is, therefore, better to employ the

term *araghatta* in the generic sense of a waterwheel. That *araghattas* were widely used as a hydraulic mechanism is evident from its use as a *simili* in Jaina literature. Merutunga, the author of the *Prabandhachintamani*, compared the fickleness of fortune with the circular rotation of buckets on the waterwheel (*ghatijalayantra cakre*). Quoted in Jain, *Trade and Traders in Western India*, p. 29. For a different interpretation of *araghatta* see L. Gopal, *Aspects of History of Agriculture in Ancient India*, Varanasi, 1980.

38. L. Gopal, 'Agriculture', p. 427.
39. Ibid., pp. 427-8.
40. I. Habib, Presidential address, Medieval India Section, Indian History Congress (Varanasi session), 1969.
41. The sculptured panel was first noticed by R.C. Agrawala, 'Persian Wheel in a Rajasthani Sculpture', *MAI*, vol. 16, 1966, pp. 87-8. A photograph of it is available in *India at Work*, published by the Centre of Advanced Study, Department of History, Aligarh Muslim University, on the occasion of the Indian History Congress, 1994. The quotation here is from T.M. Srinivasan, 'Irrigation and Irrigation Works', in *History of Technology in India*, vol. 1, ed. A.K. Bag, New Delhi, 1997, p. 587.
42. P.A. Mankad, ed., *Aparajitaprccha of Bhuvanadeva*, Baroda, 1950.
43. V.K. Jain, *Trade and Traders in Western India 1000-1300*, New Delhi, 1989, pp. 24-34.
44. Chattopadhyaya, *Aspects of Rural Settlements;* id., *Making of Early Medieval India.*
45. The Bodhgaya inscription of the time of Dharmapala, regnal year 26. For the text and translation see, R.R. Mukherjee and S.K. Maity, *A Corpus of Inscriptions of Bengal*, Calcutta, 1967.
46. M.A. Stein, tr., *Kalhana's Rajatarangini*, vol. 1, Westminster, 1900, p. 200.
47. *Epigraphia Carnatica*, vol. 10, Goribidnur taluk, 47.
48. Ibid., vol 8, Sorab taluk, 317.
49. R.N. Nandi, 'Agrarian Growth and Social Conflicts in Early India', in *The Feudal Order*, ed. D.N. Jha, New Delhi, 2000, pp. 303-44.
50. Srinivasan, 'Irrigation and Irrigation Works', p. 566.
51. *Manasollasa*, 3, 1373-4. Quoted in Nandi, 'Agrarian Growth', pp. 325-6.
52. K.A. Wittfogel, *Oriental Despotism: A Study in Total Power*, New Haven, 1957 .

53. R.S. Sharma, 'Irrigation in the North', in id., *Perspectives in the Social and Economic History of Early India.*

54. R. Thapar, *From Lineage to State*, Bombay, 1984. R.S. Sharma, *Aspects of Political Ideas and Institution in Ancient India*, 3rd edn, New Delhi, 1996. H. Kulke, ed., *The State in India 1000-1700*, New Delhi, 1994. See *Studies in History*, vol. 4, 1982, for several essays on the nature of the state in early India, with a particular thrust on the formation of the state in early medieval south India. R. Thapar, *Early India from the Origins to c.* AD *1300*, London 2002.

55. K.A.N. Sastri, *The Cōlas*, Madras, 1955.

CHAPTER 4

Water Resources and Management in the Rural Setting of Medieval South India

S. JEYASEELA STEPHEN

INTRODUCTION

Investigations in environmental history in general, and human interaction with nature in particular, cannot be ignored within the context of historical research in medieval south India one needs to focus on surface and groundwater resources and management which greatly depended on the abundant monsoonal rains. During this period, agriculture and human settlements expanded dramatically because of the availability of water storage and irrigation systems. The role of surface water is especially important, because rivers such as the Tambraparni, Vaigai, Kaveri, Pennai and Palar feed the plains of south India. The lands around these rivers served as the nucleus of several powers such as the Pandyas, the Cholas, the Samburvarayas and the Vijayanagara rulers.

This paper explores the role of water resources and management within the context of agriculture in south India from the mid-tenth century to the end of the seventeenth century. It is obvious that the central powers of the Cholas at Thanjavur, the Pandyas at Madurai, the Samburvarayas at Thiruvannamalai or the Vijayanagara rulers at Hampi and most ruling elites in the provinces exercised only little influence on water management. Major decisions were often made within a local framework. Accordingly, a major purpose of this paper is to dispute Wittfogel's model on 'Hydraulic Despotism' and to demonstrate that his theory is not valid in the context of south India.[1]

The present exposé gleans important insights from several medieval inscriptions, mostly sales deeds, revenue grants and royal orders found in Tamil, Telugu and Kannada-speaking regions. These materials reveal much about the nature of major water resources such as rivers, dams and lakes. Among the minor water resources, there are references to rain-fed and river-fed tanks or ponds together with canals, channels and sluices. Further, details on water rights, water supply, water lift works, water management, settlement of water disputes, unprecedented floods, relief measures undertaken by individuals or institutions are also mentioned.

II

HEAVY RAINFALLS, UNPRECEDENTED FLOODS AND THE FAILURE OF MONSOONS

According to medieval sources, heavy and sometimes unprecedented rains flooded regions across south India. Since the time of Rajendra Chola I (CE 1012-44), land and crops were considerably damaged by floods. The Srirangam records dating from the period of Kulottunga Chola[2] and Vikrama Chola[3] during the late eleventh and early twelfth century mention devastating floods along the Kaveri river. Inscriptions confirm that vast tracts of land were periodically laid to waste. Silt deposited by the floods of the Kaveri could destroy paddy fields and reduce crop yields for many years.[4]

Further, flooding of the Kollidam river washed away boundary stones and subsequently unleashed enduring strife over the precise course of property boundaries. An inscription dating from the twenty-ninth regnal year of Kulottunga Chola confirms that the boundary between lands owned by two temples at Srirangam and Thiruvanaikaval remained a subject of dispute.[5] Another piece of evidence of 1125 from Thiruvottur reports major flooding in north Arcot which had already been devastated by floods in 1004 and again in 1071.[6] According to this inscription, the floods destroyed the village and crops, and the villagers were unable to pay their taxes and had to settle their arrears by selling off some of their wetland. In 1126, they were compelled to dispose of their dry land as well as raise funds for the payment of their taxes.[7] Heavy rains are mentioned in the Somangalam inscription of Kulottunga Chola III for the Chingleput region during the years 1190 and 1191.[8]

Apart from unprecedented heavy rainfall during the Middle Ages, monsoons sometimes failed. During the reign of Rajendra Chola I, crops failed in 1019 in Thirukarugavur in the Thanjavur region.[9] Another record mentions that due to the failure of the monsoon in 1121, the Jaganathaperaru and Paranthakaperaru rivers dried up and led to a severe drought and crop failure.[10] Stone inscriptions describe the failure of monsoon rains in Panjai and Thirukadaiyur in the Thanjavur region during the months of *avani* and *puratassi* (August, September and October) in 1160, and the ensuing drought that destroyed the crops.[11] Similar conditions were observed in Thirukkachur in the Chingleput region in 1188.[12] Thirteenth-century records mention the failure of monsoon rains in 1201, 1202, 1208, 1215 and 1239 in certain parts of Thanjavur, Thiruvannamalai, Ayyampattai and Thirukachur.[13] Portuguese documents confirm famines in the Tamil country in 1520, 1531, 1532 as well as between 1535 and 1540. Due to inadequate rainfall in 1646, the region was ravaged by food shortages for two years.[14] The monsoons also failed in 1660 and 1672, causing famines in Thiruchirapalli and Thanjavur.[15]

Medieval sources, however, do not have much to say about relief measures. When the Jaganathaperaru and Paranthakaperaru rivers dried up due to drought in 1121, the people living along these rivers seized the initiative and raised funds for irrigation works. To this end the assembly of Jaganatha Chaturvedimangalam donated jewels belonging to a local temple in exchange for communal land earmarked for irrigation.[16] Records also refer to the munificence of private individuals. During a famine in Thiruvannamalai, two persons initiated relief works by constructing an embankment along the Palar river. In 1202, they constructed a freshwater tank with a sluice and paid the workers in gold, paddy and other means from their personal resources.[17]

One may conclude that the role of central authorities in mitigating disaster caused by unprecedented floods or drought is often not an issue. Evidently, the rulers of medieval south India did not organize relief efforts. Instead, the extraordinary conditions of flood or drought made the locals realize the power of water and the vital significance of storing it. They were prepared to take the initiative to solve their problems by constructing reservoirs for water resource management. This paper first addresses the various dams built on the rivers as well as the engineering works introduced in medieval south India.

III

DAMS

Irrigation and flood control in south India, and specifically the control of water from the Kaveri river, dates back to the third century CE. An inscription from Tiruvaduturai dating from the reign of Parakesari Karikala Chola mentions the construction of a monumental barrage on the banks of the Kaveri. This was known as the Grand Anicut that measured up to 18 ft. in height, 16 ft. in breadth and 1000 ft. in length.[18] The project was completed by 12,000 persons enslaved during a campaign in Sri Lanka.[19] Irrigation by the Kaveri is also mentioned in the great Tamil epic, *Silappadikaram*.[20] Karikala Chola constructed around 160 km. of embankment along the Kaveri. This diverted water into a network of irrigational canals about 17 miles east of present-day Thiruchirapalli.[21] Before the rise of the Vijayanagara rulers in the fifteenth century, the Grand Anicut was the only dam project mentioned. How much importance people attached to water is best expressed in a verse from an inscription of 14 October 1389. This verse describes water as the life of all living beings and a manifestation of god (*toy-atma*).[22] A later inscription dated 11 February 1410 uses the metaphors of motherliness and sentimentality, to describe how Lakshmidhara-Amatya, a minister of Harihara II, instilled values of public welfare into the child Lakshmidhara. She exhorts: 'construct a tank, dig a well, build a temple and free the helpless from miseries'.[23]

An attempt was made during the Vijayanagara rule to tap the water of the Kaveri in the Kannada region. An inscription of 14 August

1465 informs that during the reign of Virupaksha II, Devaraja, the son of Simgana Odeya of Nagamangala, constructed a dam on the Kaveri at Sitapura in Madhya district. He also dug a canal and diverted water to Sitapura. Later, the *mahajanas* (village assembly) of neighbouring Haruru asked him to extend the canal to their area as well. Devaraja agreed, and in return they gave him a large tract of land (Yajamana-Bhagaa) that was irrigated by waters of the new canal.[24]

After having fully exploited the water of the Kaveri, measures were taken to harness other rivers as well. An inscription dated 30 November 1416 mentions that the village assembly of Katari-yaghalli ordered that repair work of the dam Araliya Anai on the Palar river in the Katariyaghalli region was to be carried out. This had been in ruins for a long time. An inscription of 3 November 1434 mentions another dam on the river Haridara in the vicinity of Harihar. At the behest of Devaraya I, this dam was constructed and funded by the village assembly of Haridara as well as by the residents of Harharaksetra taluk in Davanagere district. In addition to the dam, an irrigation canal was extended to Harihar, and the benefits of this development were shared—two-thirds for the temple of Harihareshvara and one-third for the people. In course of time, the dam collapsed and caused havoc to the people and the temple.

In Telugu country, a dam was built across the Musi river. A stone inscription of 1554 from Panugallu mentions repair works near the village Namalli in Indupura Sima, located in modern Ramannapeta and Nalgonda taluks. Portuguese missionary accounts throw additional light on the construction of a dam by the Muslim governor at Aanaikaraipalayam in Tamil country in 1679.[25] Inscriptional refer-ences to a dam at Suralur in Coimbatore lack details and are inconclusive.[26]

During the Vijayanagara period many village assemblies undertook the construction of major dams for storing irrigation water. These village assemblies acknowledged the need to construct dams as a means of mitigating the hardship of the local people. Some dams were also constructed and repaired by local individuals. They took into account topographical features such as hillocks that offered suitable conditions for the construction of riverine dams. Details of these dams, such as their maximum water level, dead storage level, length of spillway, total length of masonry and top or base width are however not mentioned in the inscriptions.

IV

LAKES, TANKS AND SLUICES

In the absence of rivers (*arus*) and tributaries (*sittarus*), the only means of developing agriculture in south India was artificial lakes (*eris*). Royal initiative and individual sponsorship played a very important role in this context. During the Middle Ages, several large lakes were constructed for storing rainwater, such as the Vairamegha-tataka of Uttiramerur, the Chola-varishi of Sholingur, the Kaliyan eri near Annaimalai in Madurai, the Periya eri of Bahur near Pondicherry and the Rajendra Cholap-Periya at Punganur.[27] As early as the seventh century, the Pallava ruler Mahendravarman I constructed a large lake and the cost was borne by the royal exchequer. Named after him, it was known as the Mahendra tataka.[28]

In medieval times, the responsibility for maintaining these man-made lakes was entrusted to local authorities. The creation of local committees known as *eri variyam* reveals the special interest of the local villagers in managing these freshwater resources. The primary concern of the village assembly was to remove silt behind the dam wall every year before the onset of the monsoons. This measure was primarily aimed at ensuring that sufficient water would be stored for the following dry season.[29]

Special endowments were set up to safeguard the infrastructural integrity of these artificial lakes from neglect or the penury of village authorities. Periodic repairs were financed by a special cess, known as the *eri-ayam*, which was imposed on the peasants. One such example is found in the Bahur and Tirubhuvanai region of Pondicherry.[30] An inscription mentions that in 1010 the village assembly (*sabha*) of Nemili in South Arcot set aside *eri-ayam* for the maintenance of a local lake.[31] Another record states that *irai kaval*, that is a collected tax, was used to finance the *eri*.[32] Each village also set aside plots of land so as to finance the lakes and tank irrigation works. These lands were known as the *vettaparru*, i.e. 'tenure for the vetti'.[33]

Water tanks also played a major role in irrigation. The Nagarjunakonda inscription of Abhira Vasusena mentions that two rain-fed tanks (*kulams*) were dug in south India as early as CE 278. One of these was located at Setagiri and the other at Nuvera.[34] During the Middle Ages, several rulers took a personal interest in having dry tanks.[35] Rajendra Chola I constructed the Cholaganga tank together with a nearby system of canals that is no longer functional. This was done to ensure water supply for a large area north of the Kollidam river and also for his new capital Gangaikonda Cholapuram and its immediate surroundings.

Village headmen and local officers evinced a keen interest in the construction and renovation of lakes and tanks in the Pandya country during the Middle Ages.[36] A system of 'donor's share' (*vittavan vilukadu*) was adopted under which one-fourth of the sacred foodstuffs offered at the temple was given to the person who invested in the improvement of the temple's irrigational resources.[37] A Tamil inscription mentions a deed called *silasasanam*. This was issued by the temple's *sthanathar* in favour of the Mallapa *nayaka* of Nedungunram. The assignment was valid for all generations, 'as long as the sun and the moon existed'.[38] This procedure probably enhanced regular trade in sacred food (*prasadam*).[39]

Water was supplied to the fields through the construction of sluices which had two granite pillars of varying height, depending on the depth of the reservoirs.[40] The sluice mouth could be opened by lifting a rod. The sluice pit (*kumili*) was another system for regulating the flow of water from the reservoir. In the case of *kumili*, water from the reservoir flowed into the sluice from above. In many places small ponds (*kuttai*) were also constructed for irrigation purposes, and sluices formed a part of this system.[41]

The Chinnakollaipatti inscription of 819 mentions Etti Saathan, the *kilavan* of Iluppakkati, as the renovator of some bunds and sluices. He rebuilt in granite the collapsed *madai* (bund) on Arasaiyur Kal Perumkulam in Sattur. In the same place, two other bunds,

Ponnan madai and Punkuni madai, as well as the *sennir madai* (rainfall bund) on Pudukulam were rebuilt in brick.[42]

Sluice construction technology was already highly developed in medieval times. The use of chiselled blocks of stone instead of rubble as well as a string line to set the stone were the two most significant developments during this period.[43] The *tumpu* was a single valve system operated without any devices for mechanical advantage. In the case of tumpu, water from the reservoir flowed into the sluice from the side. The water lift was worked by bulls.

Since well technology was not highly developed in the Middle Ages, *kinarus* (wells) were not a major source of water for irrigation purposes. In general, well construction was not widespread in dry areas with no nearby river access. Records such as the Dalavaypuram plates show that individual plots of land were irrigated by wells.[44] These only became a major source of artificial irrigation in some areas under the rule of the *nayakas*. Under Nayniappa nayaka, for example, lands became cultivable, because wells were dug at various places in the South Arcot district[45] as well as at Devikapuran in the North Arcot district.[46]

V

CANALS AND CHANNELS

Long canals (*kal* or *vaykkals*) were constructed and used for irrigation purposes—often by the local elites—to carry water from a river, lake or tank between villages.[47] In 720, an irrigation canal (*kal*) was excavated at the Vaigai river. The Pandya King Centan Arikesari constructed a sluice which was named after him (Arikesariyan). The area watered by the new canal belonged to Paruttikuttinadu (Aruppukottai).[48] Other canals diverted water from the Kaveri, Pennai or Musi rivers.[49]

Each agrarian unit at the village level had a network of channels to supply water to every field, leading from the village tank (*ur kulam*) or 'channel of the locality' (*nattu perumkal*) to other lakes and tanks. In Thiruvayppadi village in the Thanjavur region fallow lands were sold in the fifteenth year of Rajaraja Chola II to enable the construction of a bund and channel for the irrigation of arable land.[50]

Olukkai was a branch channel from a main canal that watered specific fields or small plots of land. An inscription of Vijayanarayanam refers to a channel—*paramesvara vayakkal*—which passed through the brahamadeya, Vijayanarayana chaturvedimangalam.[51] Two inscriptions of Sucindram mention three main channels—Alaikkal, Marutakuna vaykkal and Thiruvenkata vaykkal—that carried water to the *devadana* lands of Nripasekhara valanallur in the Pandya country.[52] Rajaraja Chola I (985-1013) had the Uyyakondan irrigational channel constructed in the Thiruchirapalli region.[53] The Tiruvalangadu plates of Rajendra Chola I mention new canals dug during 1012-14 that fed other minor irrigation channels.[54] Saluva Thirumalideva Maharaya not only constructed two canals, but also created the biggest network of channels in the Tirumalarayanpattinam area.[55]

VI

TAXES, WATER RIGHTS AND DISPUTES

Irrigation taxes (*nir kuli*) were introduced by the rulers in the sixteenth century. These were mainly collected by the local officers. The irrigation tax levied on wet, dry as well as garden lands and groves varied. This was done in accordance with the different types of land classification. The *nayakas* in Chandragiri and Chittoor adopted similar schemes of taxation, and revenues from some taxes were gifted to the local temples.[56]

Water rights attached to particular plots of land were frequently mentioned in south India since lands often changed hands following a sale or gift. Inscriptions refer to the freedom to dig wells, canals or channels but equally admonish against wasting rainwater and at the same time encourage villagers to store it for irrigation purposes.

Whoever financed or executed the construction of irrigation works had a right to receive a portion of the crop, but the bulk of the harvest clearly belonged to the cultivators.[57] This right known as the *dasavanda*, was personal, heritable and transferable.[58] Stone records mention that a piece of rent-free land was granted for the building or repair of a tank on the condition that one-tenth of the crop was shared.[59] The nayakas' motivation for constructing irrigation works thus derived partly from such rights to gain and partly from the religious merit such deeds were believed to yield, ensuring one's happiness in the next world.[60]

An inscription from Rachapeta in the Nalgonda district mentions that in 1529 chief Masand Yeli Kutub Khan Zmuluk Odeyalu permitted his son-in-law Keman Muluk to construct a tank in Empuru village for which one share of the yield was given to the officer and the balance three shares remained with the farmers. The officer took one of the farmers' shares as his salary and in payment for incidental charges for maintaining (*dasavanda*) the tank and its channels. According to most scholars, the portion of the crop surrendered amounted as a rule of thumb to 10 per cent, but in medieval south India this figure varied considerably.[61]

Irrigational networks linking more than one village were managed collectively, but this arrangement often led to water disputes. One such conflict broke out between a temple and the local residents when an irrigational channel was dug in Tirupati. The dispute was resolved due to the efforts of an officer named Yagnarasar who intervened on behalf of the nayaka.[62] Mallar Ayyangar who had been appointed by the *nayakas* settled a dispute between the Srirangam and Jambukeswaram temples. The resolution contained an instruction that the Srirangam temple could use water from the tank at Sembiyanallur.[63] Similar sources also describe an irrigation agreement reached between the trustees and treasurers of the Shiva and Vishnu temples of Perumbakkam. It permitted the authorities of the Shiva temple to dig a channel within the town limits to supply water to the tank at Tiruvamattur. It received in compensation 300 *kuzhi* of wetland in Vedampattu village.[64]

VII

CONCLUSION

South India has depended on seasonal rains since ancient times, but the construction of extensive waterworks—with few exceptions—was undertaken only during the reign of the Pallavas between the seventh and ninth centuries. The Pallava rulers exercised administrative control over irrigation networks by imposing fines on individuals who diverted water from rivers and tanks without authorization. A tax on excessive water consumption was paid by each tenant or landowner to the Pallava king. However, the situation changed when successive kingdoms and states were disinclined to invest in large projects and instead encouraged private enterprise or initiative.

The first major expansion of dam irrigation was witnessed only during the Vijayanagara period (mid-fourteenth to mid-seventeenth century). Dams were constructed, for example, along the Pennai, Musi, Mandavya and Kaveri rivers. The prosperity of agriculture depended to a large extent on the facilities provided by the *nayakas* for irrigation and more specifically by the village assemblies. A department of waterworks (*varigripakarna*) was established, and water engineers (*jalasutri*) played a crucial role in the construction of dams. It was chiefly the village assemblies that were interested in irrigation facilities and constructed lakes and tanks of varying capacity. The dams constructed during the Vijayanagara period expanded irrigated areas, increased yields of major food crops and contributed towards economic development. Dams also helped in flood control. Individual financiers obtained *dasavanda* rights in the share of the produce for their investment in irrigation.

Since rainfall was the central regulator of agricultural activity in south India, the people focused on reorganizing production but the central authorities did not exercise direct control over the land. While the rulers sometimes initiated or financed the construction of major irrigational systems, state control hardly existed under the Chola, the Pandyas and the Vijayanagara rulers, and the concept of 'Hydraulic Despotism' has fundamentally no relevance in the context of south India.

NOTES

1. The theory of 'Hydraulic Despotism' was formulated by K.A. Wittfogel. K.A. Wittfogel, *Oriental Despotism: A Comparative Study of Total Power*, New Haven, 1957. For criticisms see I. Habib, 'An Examination of Wittfogel's Theory of Oriental Despotism', *Enquiry* (Old Series),

no. 6, 1962, pp. 54-73. I. Habib, 'An Examination of Wittfogel's Theory of Oriental Despotism', in *Studies in Asian History*, ed. K.S. Lal, Delhi, 1969, pp. 378-92.

2. *Annual Report on Epigraphy* (*ARE*) (including Indian and South Indian Epigraphy, published by the Government of India since 1881) 123 of 1938-9. *ARE* 108, 112, 113, 118, 119, 121, 130, 131 of 1947-8. *ARE* 8, 10 of 1948-9.
3. *ARE* 38 of 1948-9.
4. *ARE* 64 of 1892. *ARE* 375 of 1903. *ARE* 158 of 1937-8. *ARE* 125 of 1938-9. *ARE* 108, 112, 113, 118, 119, 121, 130, 131 of 1947-8. *ARE* 8, 10, 38 of 1948-9. *ARE* 308 of 1935-6.
5. *ARE* 113 of 1938-9.
6. Archaeological Survey of India, ed., *South Indian Inscriptions* (*SII*) Madras/New Delhi, 1890-1990, vol. 7, no. 96. *ARE* 322 of 1906. *ARE* 428 of 1905.
7. *SII*, vol. 7, no. 96. *ARE* 87 of 1900, pt. 2, para 24. *ARE* 88 of 1900, pt. 2, para 24. *SII*, vol. 7, no. 97.
8. *SII*, vol. 7, no. 193. *ARE* 183 of 1901. *Epigraphia Indica* (*EI*), vol. 7, Calcutta, New Delhi, 1900, p. 6.
9. *ARE* 404 of 1961-2.
10. *ARE* 521 of 1920. *ARE* 1921, pt. 2, para 35.
11. *ARE* 191 of 1925. *ARE* 258 of 1925.
12. *ARE* 274 of 1909. *ARE* 279 of 1909.
13. *ARE* 86 of 1911. *ARE* 560 of 1902. *ARE* 114 of 1927-8. *ARE* 1910, pt. 2, para 29. *ARE* 225 of 1927, pt. 2, para 30.
14. J. Thekkedath, *History of Christianity in India from the Mid-16th Century to the End of the 17th Century, 1542-1700*, vol. 2, Bangalore, 1982, p. 225.
15. S. Jeyaseela Stephen, *The Coromandel Coast and Its Hinterland. Economy, Society and Political System, 1500-1600*, New Delhi, 1997, pp. 143, 158, 195. Ibid., *Letters of the Portuguese Jesuits from Tamil Countryside, 1666-1688*, Pondicherry, 2001. For specific years see the respective annual letters.
16. *ARE* 521 of 1920. *ARE* 1921, pt. 2, para 35.
17. *ARE* 560 of 1902. During famines a tax called *panchanvara* was levied to provide against famines (*panjams*). See K.A.N. Sastri, *Studies of Cola History and Administration*, Madras, 1932, pp. 142-3.
18. *ARE* 110 of 1925.

19. Sastri, *The Colas*, Madras, 1937, p. 262.
20. The text runs as follows:

    'But finding her (Kaveri) movement arrested by the barrier the anaicut with its doorway she noisily leaps beyond it in the sportive mood natural to her finest freshes. No sound other than this can be heard. We can hear there neither the sound of the bucket nor of water lift neither the usually loud "Pecottah" nor the palm leaf basket used in irrigation.'

    See H. Chakarabarti, 'History of Irrigation in Ancient India', *Proceedings of the Indian History Congress*, Jabalpur, 1970, Delhi, 1971.
21. F.E. Morgan, *Irrigation in Southern India*, ed. S. Payne, London, 1914-15, p. 285.
22. *Epigraphia Carnatica* (*EC*) (Old Edition), vol. 10, 6, Madras. *ARE* 1978-9, no. B. 167, Kalludi, Giribidanur taluk, Kolar district.
23. S. Ritti and B.R. Gopal, eds., *Inscriptions of the Rulers of the Sangama Dynasty* (*1336-1485*), 5 vols., New Delhi, 2004, no. 423. See also Marur inscription of Devaraya I, in *EC* (Old Edition), vol. 8, SC 8.
24. *Inscriptions of the Rulers of the Sangama Dynasty*, no. 778.
25. S. Jeyaseela Stephen, 'Most Buried Treasure. Letters of the Portuguese Jesuits from Tamil Country in South India During the 17th Century', *Hispanic Horizon*, vol. 18, no. 20, 2001, p. 79.
26. *ARE*, 304 of 1909.
27. Sastri, *The Colas*, rpt., Madras, 1984, p. 303. Kallathan eri is mentioned in line 6 in *ARE* 183 of 1895. Marai perari yean nam peral vetti kulathukkum is found in *ARE* 122 of 1894. Eri katti is recorded in *ARE* 122 of 1894.
28. *EI*, vol. 4, pp. 152-3.
29. *ARE* 322 of 1923.
30. *ARE* 178 of 1902. *ARE* 192 of 1909.
31. *ARE* 156 of 1942-3.
32. *SII*, vol. 2, pt. 3, no. 106.
33. Y. Subbarayulu, *Studies in Cola History*, Chennai, 2001, pp. 93-4. Various inscriptional terms are mentioned such as irrigation labour dues, necessary for the supply of water to the agricultural fields. Vettis specifically called work on rivers and canals in *ARE* 368 of 1909. Kaverrikulai kulai kappu (protection of banks), Kulai vetti (bank labour), Kurampu (dam or causeway), Nir amanci (water labour), Cennir amanci (pure water labour), Eri amanci (lake labour), Al amanci

(manual labour), Nir vilai kuli (work on hydraulic irrigation), Ilai kulam (new bank). See J. Heitzman, *Gifts of Power. Lordship in an Early Indian State*, Oxford/Delhi, 1998, p. 177. *Vetti mutal* (forced labour) is mentioned in *SII*, vol. 7, no. 411.

34. *EI*, vol. 34, pp. 197-8.
35. Pullakulam is mentioned in line 6 in *ARE* 183 of 1895, Vettuvitha kulamum in *ARE* 122 of 1894, and Pandtha perari ennum peral kulamum vetti is mentioned in *ARE* 122 of 1894.
36. *SII*, vol. 14, nos. 43-4, 78, 91.
37. T.N. Subramanyam, *South Indian Temple Inscriptions* (*SITI*), Madras, 1953-5, vol. 1, pp. 342 (1542), 339 (1541). The Kanchipuram inscriptional text runs 'vittavan vilukkadu nallil onrukku'.
38. S. Subramaya Sastry, *Tirumala Tirupati Devasthanam Epigraphical Series* (*TTDES*), 6 vols., Madras, 1931-8, vol. 4, pp. 264-5.
39. In one instance such sale reached 4,600 panams actually resulting in ploughing back the returns. *TTDES*, vol. 4, nos. 72, 74, 93; vol. 5, no. 88; vol. 3, no. 157, 159.
40. Gurukkal, *Agrarian System*, p. 160.
41. Ibid.
42. Ibid.
43. *SII*, vol. 14, no. 26; vol. 14, no. 44.
44. *Pandiyar Seppedugal Patthu,* ed. T.N. Sbramanyam, Madras, 1967, pp. 95-115, 212-13, 219.
45. *ARE* 388 of 1912.
46. *ARE* 387 of 1912.
47. Purushothaman vaykkal (line 3 in *ARE* 183 of 1895). Sri mahdhava vaykkal (line 3, in *ARE* 183 of 1895). Parameswara vayakkal (in *ARE* 186 of 1895). Kothukula vayakkal, iruumudichola vayakkal ponngal vayakkal chandrasekaara vayakal are mentioned in *ARE* 173 of 1895.
48. Vaigai bed inscription in *EI*, vol. 38, pt. 1, pp. 27-32.
49. *SII*, vol. 13, no. 13; vol. 13, no. 163. *ARE* 200 of 1934-5. *Inscriptions of the Rulers of the Sangama Dynasty*, no. 371. *Inscriptions of Andhra Pradesh*, Nalgonda dt., no. 36.
50. *ARE* 88 of 1931-2.
51. *SII*, vol. 14, no. 17. Another main channel of the village also finds mention in another record. See *SII*, vol. 14, no. 400.
52. *Kanyakumari Kalvettugal*, Madras, 1968, nos. 212, 224.

53. R. Sewell, *List of Antiquities in Madras Presidency*, vol. 1, Madras, p. 269.
54. *SII*, vol. 8, pt. 3, p. 437.
55. Stephen, *The Coromandel Coast and Its Hinterland*. See the section on Tirumalarayanpattinam.
56. *ARE* 54 of 1934-5 (1507). *ARE* 119 of 1931 (1588). *ARE* 251 of 1904. *ARE* 177 of 1941. *SITI*, vol. 1, pp. 43-4.
57. M. Rama Rao, *Telugu Inscriptions of Andhradesa*, Tirupati, 1969, vol. 1, pt. 1, no. 891 (1592). *ARE* 388 of 1916 (b).
58. B. Stein, *Peasant State and Society in Medieval South India*, Delhi, 1980, p. 426.
59. *ARE* 179 of 1913 (1533). *ARE* 94 of 1913. *ARE* 388 of 1916 (b).
60. One of the seven *satantakas* mentioned in literary sources such as Rayavacakamu is the excavation of a tank. See N. Venkataramanayya, *Further Sources of Vijayanagar History*, vol. 3, Madras, 1946, p. 140. Meritorious activity for those donors contributing to the construction of a tank is referred to as *dharman*, an act of religious merit in the inscriptions. See *ARE* 72 of 1935-6.
61. P.V. Parabrahma Sastry, 'Irrigation, Land Reclamation and Tenancy in Late Medieval Andhra', in *Agrarian Conditions in Andhradesa. 17th & 18th Centuries*, ed. R. Soma Reddy, Hyderabad, 1996, p. 170.
62. *TTDES*, vol. 1, no. 224.
63. *ARE* 16 of 1938-9 (1533).
64. *ARE* 9 of 1922.

CHAPTER 5

Dams in India between the British Territorial Expansion and the 'Green Revolution'

MARTIN KRIEGER

INTRODUCTION

The construction of large dams in India has been a heavily discussed and disputed issue during the last decades within the country and abroad. On the one hand, the subcontinent lacks sufficient water resources and fossil fuels and is forced to import oil and other sources of energy. Despite that, people struggle with frequent brownouts, high energy prices and in many cases an inferior quality of potable water. On the other hand, erecting dams and creating large water reservoirs usually demands the resettlement of thousands of people, very often of tribal origin. This in itself can act as a catalyst for new serious social problems. As the major initiator of dam projects, the state is caught between the interests of tribal and subaltern groups on the one side, and the pressures of modernization including large-scale agriculture, industry and global markets on the other.

The current discussion on dams in India tends to neglect that the relevant technologies have a very long history in India and that, since the Middle Ages, people were well aware of their risks and benefits. Different today, perhaps, are only issues surrounding the magnitude of the projects. Whilst the pre-colonial period mainly witnessed the construction of small dams, the British introduced the technology for developing large infrastructural projects. The latter, of course, was developed further in independent India.

Karl August Wittfogel has argued that water played an eminent role in the foundation of society and state (especially in the east), and that the construction of dams was mainly a task of the ruling elites and contributed meaningfully to the further concentration and centralization of political power.[1] Accordingly, the construction of dams is perceived as a cornerstone in the emergence of the so-called 'Oriental Despotism'. Today, such theories are carefully scrutinized by scholars including Clifford Geertz (for Bali), who postulated that it may very well have been the ruling elites who originally constructed dams, but it is the local population or communal co-operatives who maintain them democratically.[2] Even if Wittfogel's theory is gradually marginalized, if not rendered obsolete, one must give him credit for first emphasizing the interdependence of water, state or communal power and for initiating an enduring discussion on the broader subject.

This paper investigates the relation between dams and state power in colonial and independent India. It specifically questions if and when changes may have occurred. Was it the British who introduced large dam projects to India, or was India just an experimental platform for developing new technologies? If an independent India surpassed the British in terms of technology, one may legitimately enquire whether the functions of a dam (for example, for mere irrigation or storage) remain in place. Or, do dams today serve very different purposes? In order to gain a fuller appreciation of the overall historic context, some brief remarks on pre-colonial dams merit further enquiry.

II

DAMS IN PRE-COLONIAL INDIA

Small dams have been constructed all over India since ancient times, even if the more distant past remains murky. Little is known about the techniques and situation of these early dams. Certain regions are deemed particularly suited for the construction of small dams such as valleys with a low gradient and irregular water flow. In such cases dams not only regulate water for irrigation purposes, but also serve as reservoirs during the dry season. They especially enable the farmers to plant wheat or rice in semi-arid or arid regions that would otherwise not be suited for growing such crops. In this context, south Bihar with its many tributaries of the Ganges, regions south-east of Surat, together with the mountain regions of Tamil Nadu merit special mention.

It does not seem likely that small dams were already built during the earlier, pre-urban periods of the Indus civilization. More likely, agriculture depended on the higher rains in winter.[3] The early Harappan period witnessed the construction of small field embankments that filled field enclosures during the annual floods. The first canals were probably constructed only during the mature Harappan period. The bulk of agricultural production, however, depended evidently on winter and summer rainfall in north-west India that in the previous centuries was almost certainly higher than today. Water management was chiefly done through canals, wells and tanks.[4]

Large artificial lakes partially maintained by dams first appeared during the Mauryan period, such as lake Sudarsana in the fourth century BCE. Irrigational practice supplements scholarly studies on agriculture and reservoir building. An example is set by the contemporary sage Kashyapa, who exhaustively studied the impact of land gradients, soil composition and the preparation of mortar for the construction of dams. He also examined the flora and fauna of the surrounding lands.[5] Kautilya's *Arthashastra* explains the interdependence between irrigation and the state and outlines the ruler's duties for the first time.[6]

In south India, early irrigational projects were introduced during the first centuries CE. It was probably the regional kings in the Tamil country who constructed canals and dams, but local chiefs or temples made arrangements for their maintenance. The first major project by the Chola rulers was the Grand Anicut, a barrage across the Kaveri river dating from about the second century CE, that was developed to irrigate vast tracts of land along the waterway. This prompted Sir Arthur Cotton to undertake projects some one and a half millennia later. Subsequent centuries witnessed the creation of sizeable reservoirs in the south held by earthen dams. For example, Rajendra Chola's Viranam tank dating from the eleventh century measured more than 10 miles in length and 3.5 miles breadth.[7] Between the thirteenth and the beginning of the sixteenth century, the Delhi Sultanate sponsored several large irrigational projects in the north. Here, streams were frequently blocked by barrages (bunds), while water was diverted into canals for irrigation. The elites profited by an increasing state income.[8] Such a policy of state initiative was also pursued by the early modern rulers of Vijayanagara, Golkonda or the Marathas—be they Hindu or Muslim.

Smaller dams could also have been maintained by the local village communities without any interference by the elites, such as in Travancore in south India, where the wealthy farmers employed workers for performing physical labour on such projects. Even during the beginning of British colonial expansion it was not the colonial state that organized minor works, but, as in the case of south Bihar, often the local zamindaris who recruited human labour from the lower castes. In this case one cannot possibly speak of 'Oriental Despotism' on a large scale, but rather of mandatory labour in a strictly local context.

III

DAMS IN COLONIAL INDIA

Since at least two millennia, India had created a vast theoretical and practical knowledge on irrigation and on the construction of dams. The first Portuguese travellers to India observed and described dam constructions and publicized these in Europe. Long before British territorial expansion took place, an enormous exchange of knowledge occurred in both directions, i.e. Europeans studied Indian irrigational systems and—even more—European knowledge was brought to India.

Especially during the eighteenth century, European—mainly Spanish—technology was brought to India and found its way to the as yet independent states. This fact especially applies to the Meer Allum dam near Hyderabad which was constructed between *c.* 1790 and 1810. The buttress construction of this enduring dam with its several arches clearly resembles its Spanish counterpart described by Don Pedro Bernardo Villarreal de Berriz in the 1730s.[9]

The attitudes of the British towards the traditional, indigenous irrigation systems were ambiguous until the first half of the nineteenth century, even if they were well aware of the high profits reaped from such irrigation systems. Local techniques were adapted in some places, while traditional irrigation networks were neglected in others. There was no uniformity across British India. It appears as if many decisions on water management were made at a regional level and depended on the personal ambitions as well as interests of the colonial authorities.

As a rule the British favoured the maintenance and adoption of traditional large diversion schemes but neglected minor structures in more remote areas.[10] Large dams enabled the colonial authorities to reap higher revenue from the rural population because larger areas could be supplied with water. The taxes levied by the British on irrigated land were substantial. Arthur Cotton, one of the leading architects of canals and dams in India, observed: 'Water in India is more valuable than Gold of Australia'.[11] Proverbially this may very well be true, not because water is an indispensable sustainer of life, but because Cotton almost certainly had an eye on fiscal revenue as well. These mercantile biases were underscored intellectually by delving into details and amassing knowledge, as the British themselves had little experience with irrigation works. During the initial phase of territorial expansion, the British endeavoured to collect information deemed suitable for subsequent application in India. In 1818, Paolo Frisi's eminent study on 'Del modo di regolare i fiumi e i torrenti' of 1762 was translated into English at the government's expense. In 1850, the Honourable East India Company instructed Captain R. Baird-Smith to conduct field studies in Italy so as to examine the classical irrigation systems on the peninsula. Further expeditions to Italy, France and Spain followed in the 1860s.[12]

It seems, however, that many of the smaller indigenous irrigation and dam systems collapsed throughout India during the nineteenth century. This observation, for example, applies to the Sahyadri mountains studied by David Hardiman.[13] For centuries, several hundred small dams in the valleys of this mountain range had been managed by the local communities with sporadic support from the ruling elites, such as by the eighteenth-century Peshwas. Financial and logistical aid was entirely withdrawn after the British assumed control of the region in 1818. The Resident Collector explained that assistance by the authorities 'must depend on the expected increase of revenue desirable from those repairs whether or not the Government would undertake to sink so much money' into a project.[14] According to colonial discourses, smaller projects would not yield a sufficient tax income to attract British support. The result was a staggering decline in the number of dams in the Sahyadris during the period of British supremacy. During the 1920s, the Tatas made plans to construct a number of substantial dams in this region, notably with the support of the British authorities but without compensating farmers for their confiscated land. These plans were thwarted by stiff resistance from the local population.[15]

While neglecting the traditional smaller irrigation systems, the British emphasized since the beginning the paramount significance of maintaining larger indigenous constructions. The period between *c.* 1810 and 1830 may be seen as a turning-point in British civil engineering and dam construction in India. An early example of how local techniques were adopted on a wide scale is seen in the construction of the Coleroon dam under the auspices of Arthur Cotton. Since the second century CE, the masonry barrage of the Grand Anicut had dammed the Kaveri river near its mouth at the Bay of Bengal at a width of 1,080 ft. In the nineteenth century, this dam and the adjoining canals silted up, causing the water to be diverted from the main branch of the Kaveri to the Coleroon. The latter is a substantial branch of the river that passes through the temple town of Chidambaram. In 1836, Cotton undertook the construction of a new dam across the Coleroon. Drawing lessons from the old dam, he adopted the technique of constructing masonry work over a foundation laid in the weak alluvial bed of the river. The dam partially collapsed the following year, and although it was repaired, it remained weak until it was completely reconstructed at the end of the nineteenth century.[16] Similar observations hold true for large canal systems. In 1817, reconstruction works were begun on the dilapidated Jamuna canals that had been excavated after the fourteenth century by the Sultans of Delhi and subsequently by the Mughals.[17] This observation illustrates how the colonial authorities, at least initially, sought to build on the know-how of their predecessors, but did so with an eye on large water management projects.

Examples like the Coleroon dam underscore the failure of the British to work closely with the local people and elites, or even to utilize extant expertise. Existing structures were sometimes modified without adequately understanding their different functions. Colonial discourses of the period may explain British attitudes. European biases of the nineteenth century created something of a 'hydrological dichotomy'. British civil engineering is set apart from the natural environment and the local communities. The latter were regarded as bearers of inferior technology and, therefore, as an insignificant source of knowledge.[18] Nevertheless, the initial British projects dating from the first half of the nineteenth century were successful in that they raised ample revenues and also prevented famine in some regions.[19]

Between the 1830s and 1860s—during the so-called 'Period of Classical Works'—the British launched their own, newly invented projects featuring modern technology. India served as an experimental platform, and technologies developed here were transferred in many instances to other British colonial possessions. One stimulus can be found in the severe famine that swept across India between 1832 and 1833. In the 1850s, Arthur Cotton was enjoined to develop entirely new irrigation systems along the Godavari, Krishna and Mahanadi rivers with the aim of preventing future famines. In the north, large canal and dam projects along the Ganges and in Punjab were launched that borrowed heavily from Italian and French technology.[20] This period also witnessed a major change in the administration of water management. Until the 1850s, the responsibility for maintaining irrigation infrastructure was entrusted to the Military Board, but in subsequent years, it was successfully transferred to the civil works departments.[21]

Before the 1860s, diversion schemes remained the focus of attention, but the remaining decades of the nineteenth century witnessed a visible shift toward storage systems. A growing population heightened the demand for water along seasonal rivers, especially in arid areas such as west Punjab or Sind. As a result, colonial policy concentrated on the construction of large dams for storage and irrigation purposes. Many of these irrigation schemes yielded huge revenue for the government.[22] The first major storage dam was the Poona dam that was started in 1868 and features a height of 98 ft. This was followed by the Tansa, Bhatgur and Betwa dams in the 1890s. The first dam built of concrete was constructed across the Periyar river in the southern Westghats and completed in 1898. Plans for such a project had been underway since 1808.[23]

The major beneficiaries were the colonial rulers themselves. Irrigation infrastructure initially yielded a net return of around 4-5 per cent annually, but this increased to nearly 10 per cent by the 1940s.[24] Apart from the British, the zamindars and other landlords reaped considerable benefits, not least because they were allocated rights along minor irrigation canals. While the peasants had exercised greater control over the distribution of water in pre-colonial times, they were now reduced to the status of mere consumers.[25]

Technical progress led to the proliferation of hydroelectric generation projects by the end of the nineteenth century. Experience with hydroelectric driven flour mills led to the construction of a plant near Darjeeling in 1897 that was expected to supply electricity to the municipal authority for street lighting. Other hill stations followed in the 1920s. In 1910, the Tata Hydro-Electric Power Supply Company was founded which supplied electricity to Bombay. Hydroelectric technology, however, was not much developed, not least because industrialization was not a feature of the British policy in India. Only some industries that supplied military facilities necessitated the construction of larger hydropower projects.

After the First World War, when the new technology of reinforced concrete was well established, the British developed plans for large-scale dams. It was only during the 1930s that the new technology was introduced to meet the demands of large-scale dam construction and hydroelectric generation, for example, the Mettur dam (210 ft. high) across the Kaveri river.

Large-scale dams were far more resistant to damage by the forces of nature, such as heavy rainfall, storm or erosion and as a result they did not require continuous repair works as in the case of the smaller, traditional dams. They equally enabled the colonial authorities to expand the land under irrigation, attract zamindars as well as new farmers and helped forge loyalty between the colonial masters and the population. New varieties of grains were introduced in some regions. During the British period, therefore, irrigational dam projects transformed not only agrarian society, but also its relation to the local elites and the colonial government.

IV

DAM PROJECTS IN INDEPENDENT INDIA

The construction of large dams was an art developed to a significant extent during the colonial period. The construction of large dams or hydroelectric power generation projects, however, was not very significant before 1947. After Independence India recognized the need to pursue these technologies, mainly to give a fillip to national progress on a broader scale. Plans for large-scale dams were underway as early as 1938 by the 'National Planning Committee' and later by Jawaharlal Nehru, who, in sharp contrast to Gandhi, was in favour of industrialization. The large projects discussed by the 'National Planning Committee' became an important instrument of modernization and capital intensive industrialization in post-colonial India. This programme was principally organized and financed by the public sector. It was argued that the goal of sustained national development would be realized by economic growth, the creation of agricultural surpluses and the pursuit of large-scale projects like dam construction.[26]

Immediately after Independence in 1947, the Government of India initiated several projects along major rivers with the aim of solving the most urgent problems, including food crises and the shortfall of electricity. Dams acquired a highly symbolic meaning in the context of modernization as Nehru dubbed them the 'secular temples of modern India'.[27] The government, it should be underscored, was prepared to pay the social and ecological costs of dams.

During the 1950s, however, the construction of dams for agricultural purposes gradually assumed a subordinate role to other mega projects. Hard currency reserves and foreign aid enabled the government to launch ambitious industrial projects such as the steel works at Rourkela. The price of agricultural produce was kept low and emphasis was placed instead on the stimulation of industrial production. This 'mercantilist' policy deprived farmers of a chance to reap higher profits and in turn increase their investment in mechanized agricultural production. It was hoped that a growing industry would push agriculture to a higher level of productivity.[28]

The severe drought of 1965-6 and the food crisis that ensued finally led to the formulation of a new policy known as the 'Green Revolution'. Its principal objective was to decouple or shield Indian agriculture from climatic imponderabilities and—in order to meet the needs of an ever-growing population—expand agricultural production to semi-arid and arid regions. High-yielding varieties of grain (HYVs), the production and distribution of industrial fertilizers and the expansion of irrigated lands by wells, canals and large dams helped overcome initial obstacles.[29] Up to 10 per cent of state expenditure was earmarked for the construction and maintenance of dams. Before 1900, a total of 42 large dams built in India, there were 251 dams for the half century between 1901 and 1950, 234 during the 1950s, 461 during the 1960s and 1190 during the 1970s.[30]

While the north-west benefited from a tremendous increase in the production of wheat and the south-east from rice cultivation, several states such as Orissa and Bihar did not show any noteworthy improvement.[31] In Maharashtra, powerful pressure groups formed by cotton and sugar cane producers successfully lobbied for the construction of dams that mainly served their own ends. Between

1952 and 1979, 341 dams were constructed in Maharashtra alone. This accounts for more than one-third of all dam projects in India for that period.[32] Nevertheless, the 'Green Revolution' failed to mitigate glaring social inequalities, because it was chiefly the landowners who reaped the benefits of the new irrigation projects, and not the swelling number of agricultural labourers.

The growing number of large dams is not just a manifestation of the 'Green Revolution', but also of the enhanced demand for electricity in a country that has sparse resources of oil and gas. Since the 1960s, the government has abandoned the British legacy of overemphasizing irrigation projects and balanced these more prudently in favour of hydroelectric power generation. Modern power plants have been attached to older dam projects, such as to the Periyar dam (1965), but more recent developments feature integrated power generation facilities.[33] While India produced 575 MW of hydroelectric power in 1951, this output rose to 1,917 MW in 1960-1 and further to 19,370 MW in 1991-2.[34] These new projects face their own distinct sets of problems. The demand for irrigation water reaches its peak in the weeks immediately preceding the arrival of the first rains, while industry and households consume maximum electricity during the hot season a few months before that. Accordingly, large dams find it difficult to balance both the needs of agriculture and patterns of electricity consumption. When additional factors such as profitability are introduced into the picture, it is clear that water management authorities prefer hydroelectric power generation simply because the margins in this industry are higher. Not to be omitted in this calculation is the fact that hydroelectric power projects greatly exacerbate environmental hurdles. As a rule, hydroelectric power generation requires the flooding of far larger areas as compared to projects that strictly serve irrigational ends.[35]

The legacy of the 1947 Partition of British India was the formation of two independent states, India and Pakistan. The Ravi, Sutlej and Jhelum, all tributaries of the Indus, were interconnected before Partition through the 'Triple Canal Project' in west Punjab. Its purpose was to ensure better irrigation facilities and expand the lands under irrigation. After 1947, the Indo-Pakistan border divided this irrigational system in two. Initially, the canals were diverted to comply with the new borders. Eventually, however, both countries decided to construct new large-scale storage dams to manage their respective water resources in this region.[36]

Under colonial rule, and especially after Independence, large-scale dam projects came under severe scrutiny. Not only the high social cost of resettling vast numbers of displaced persons was questioned, but also the tangible benefits accruing from the completion of the project. Attention was drawn in this context to the imbalance of cost and benefit. Despite the acknowledged advantages for agriculture, industry and electrification, these mega projects created new problems that were previously unknown, or were less pressing. Apart from the issues of resettlement, there were problems resulting from salinity, silting and flooding. Earthquakes became a new matter of concern. For example, on 11 December 1967, an earthquake measuring 6.5-7.0 on the Richter Scale rocked the area east of Bombay. The Koyna dam suffered serious damage in the process. Although the dam did not burst, the damage was considerable and around 200 people associated with the power project lost their lives, many of them employees and their families.[37]

The authorities had underestimated not only the ecological impact, but also the social cost. The construction of dams and the creation of artificial water reservoirs displaced millions of people. It has been estimated that anywhere between 10 and 50 million persons were displaced between the 1940s and the 1980s, a fairly substantial proportion of India's total population. The highest figures for an individual dam project are estimated at 150,000. The high numbers may have less to do with the magnitude of a particular project than with the affected region's population density. A significant proportion (in some cases up to 90-100 per cent) may be tribals or the scheduled castes.

There is still no nationwide formula for compensation. When and where compensation was even forthcoming, it usually consisted of cash. These funds were frequently spent on consumer goods and not used for the acquisition of new landholdings. The hopelessly outdated Land Acquisition Act of 1894 was rarely, if ever, invoked, and scant attention was paid to issues of gender.[38] It almost goes without saying that large-scale dam projects often failed to meet the overoptimistic targets of the authorities.

Taking all costs into consideration, including the social and ecological ones, it remains doubtful whether large dams are ultimately profitable. Since the beginning of the 1980s, investment costs have increased sharply, and correspondingly, the prospects of a project ever becoming profitable have declined, if not whittled away entirely.[39]

V

CONCLUSION

In the course of investigating the continuities and discontinuities in the history of dam building and management in modern India, one needs to take into account major shifts in technology and politics. Both evolved more or less independent from one another. With specific regard to the transfer of European construction technology to India, two distinct phases may be distinguished. The first began in the late 1700s and the second with the advent of the twentieth century. The first period was characterized by the introduction of buttress dams in line with the Spanish model. This enabled the construction of storage dams together with simple irrigational facilities. Local rulers extended their support to these projects such as in the case of the Meer Allum dam. The second period witnessed the introduction of advanced building materials, such as the use of steel reinforced concrete, or the deployment of modern technology for hydroelectric power generation. Their introduction, however, did not immediately create major discontinuities in policy formulation. Half a century elapsed before the British applied the buttress technology on a wider scale (i.e. in the 1830s). Also, hydroelectric power generation aroused little enthusiasm among the colonial authorities. At the level of policy formulation, it was not until the 1960s that priorities shifted away from simple irrigation and water storage to power generation projects.

The policy underlying dam construction in India between colonial rule and Independence is surprisingly consistent. For the period under review, the entire system of water management can only be deemed 'conservative'. Also consistent are the principal beneficiaries of the dam projects. The political elite benefits in the form of fees and taxes, and the landed elite is empowered to expand agricultural production. The lower strata of society bear the brunt of the adverse side effects, either by eking out a living as landless labourers, or worse still, are forced to cope with displacement and resettlement.

NOTES

1. 'The hydraulic state is not checked by a Beggar's Democracy. Nor is it checked by any other effective constitutional, societal, or cultural counterweights. Clearly it is despotic.' See K.A. Wittfogel, *Oriental Despotism: A Comparative Study of Total Power*, 3rd edn, New Haven, 1959, p. 126.
2. Some general objections against Wittfogel's models are mentioned in J.H. Steward, 'Initiation of a Research Trend. Wittfogel's Irrigation Hypothesis', in *Society and History. Essays in Honor of Karl August Wittfogel*, ed. G.L. Ulmen, The Hague/Paris/New York, 1978, pp. 3-14. C. Geertz, 'Organization of the Balinese "Subak"', in *Irrigation and Agricultural Development in Asia*, ed. W. Coward, Ithaca, 1980, pp. 72 ff.
3. B. Allchin and R. Allchin, *Origins of a Civilization: The Prehistory and Early Archaeology of South Asia*, New Delhi, 1997, p. 135.
4. Ibid., pp. 147 ff., 169 ff. B. Allchin and R. Allchin, *The Birth of Indian Civilization*, Harmondsworth, 1968, p. 258.
5. S. Singh, *Taming the Waters. The Political Economy of Large Dams in India*, 2nd edn, New Delhi, 2002, p. 26.
6. Ibid., p. 27. S. Bhattacharya, 'Land, Soil, Rainfall, Irrigation. Some Aspects of the Backdrop of Agrarian Life in the Arthasastra of Kautilya', *The Indian Economic and Social History Review*, vol. 15, no. 2, 1987, pp. 211-20. See also Ranabir Chakravarti's contribution in this volume.
7. Singh, *Taming the Waters*, p. 28.
8. Ibid., p. 30.
9. Don Pedro Bernardo Villarreal de Berriz, *Maquinas Hydraulicas de Molinos y Herreiras, y Govierno de los Arboles y Montes de Vizcaya*, Madrid, 1736.

10. D. Ludden, *Peasant History of South India*, Princeton, 1985, p. 15.
11. Singh, *Taming the Waters.*
12. N. Smith, *Man and Water: A History of Hydro-Technology*, London, 1971, p. 46.
13. D. Hardiman, 'Small-Dam Systems of the Sahyadris', in *Nature, Culture, Imperialism. Essays on Environmental History of South Asia*, ed. D. Arnold and R. Guha, 3rd edn, New Delhi, 1999, pp. 185-209.
14. Ibid., p. 204.
15. M.S.S. Pandian, *The Political Economy of Agrarian Change: Nanchilnadu 1880-1939*, New Delhi, 1990, pp. 105 ff.
16. N. Smith, *A History of Dams*, London, 1971, p. 189.
17. Smith, *Man and Water*, pp. 47 ff.
18. D. Gilmartin, 'Models of the Hydraulic Environment: Colonial Irrigation, State Power and Community in the Indus Basin', in *Nature, Culture, Imperialism*, p. 214.
19. Smith, *Man and Water*, p. 48.
20. See Salvatore Ciriacono's contribution in this volume.
21. Singh, *Taming the Waters*, p. 38.
22. Smith, *A History of Dams*, p. 189.
23. Ibid., pp. 200 ff.
24. Singh, *Taming the Waters*, p. 36.
25. Ibid., p. 41.
26. Singh, *Taming the Waters.*
27. Ibid.
28. D. Rothermund, ed., *Indien. Kultur, Geschichte, Politik, Wirtschaft, Umwelt. Ein Handbuch*, Munich, 1995, pp. 475 ff., 492.
29. Ibid., p. 492.
30. C.V.J. Varma, A.R.G. Rao and E. Sundaraiya, eds., *Typical Dams in India*, New Delhi, p. 282.
31. Singh, *Taming the Waters*, pp. 76-80.
32. Ibid., p. 82.
33. Varma, Rao and Sundaraiya, eds., *Typical Dams in India*, p. 305.
34. Singh, *Taming the Waters*, p. 92.
35. Ibid., p. 94.
36. R. Ghosh and S.B. Sen Sarma, *Surface Water Resources Development and Dams in India*, New Delhi, 1982, p. 146. Gilmartin, 'Models

of the Hydraulic Environment', passim. Smith, *A History of Dams*, pp. 229 ff.

37. Ghosh and Sen Sarma, *Surface Water Resources Development*, pp. 220 ff. Varma, Rao and Sundaraiya, eds., *Typical Dams in India*, p. 282.
38. Singh, *Taming the Waters*, pp. 182-203.
39. S. Singh and P. Banerji, eds., *Large Dams in India. Environmental, Social and Economic Impacts*, New Delhi, 2002, p. 291.

CHAPTER 6

Water and Polity in Pre-colonial South-East Asia— A Preliminary Historiography

MAITRII AUNG-THWIN

GLOBAL STUDIES AND HYDRAULIC HISTORY

Recent scholarship in South-East Asian studies has produced exciting and provocative findings, reasserting the importance of considering regionally-based histories in a global context beyond dichotomous renderings.[1] After several decades of sustained and arduous work in specifically defined fields of research (a response that sought to counter the presumptions and paradigms of colonial and nationalist historiography), area specialists have returned to the stage of world history armed with new empirical data, methods and insights. This trend is actually a dialogue within a longer scholarly conversation, where specialists of Asia have attempted to redress the works of earlier scholars (Montesquieu, Hegel, Marx and Weber) who constructed the region(s) on its lack of European traits.[2] This paradigm, as Victor Lieberman explored in great detail, generated a genealogy of scholarship that was determined to address these concerns, yet all along succumbed to the notion of difference between the two cultural zones.[3] In the American academe, scholars such as Kenneth Pomeranz and R. Bin Wong, have attempted to reintegrate the histories of Asia (mostly in reference to Chinese history) with Europe while challenging some of the long-standing assumptions and barriers separating and constricting what has been approached as two separate fields.[4]

In South-East Asian studies, the banner of global studies continued from a post-colonial perspective: in comparative colonialism Ann Laura Stoler comes to mind; in peasant studies, resistance and the study of the state, the inspirational James Scott is a notable case; in the study of nationalism Benedict Anderson's *Imagined Communities* is essential reading; and in anthropology the elegant writings of Clifford Geertz have provided many broad and important connections linking seemingly disparate cultural fields, methods and data alike.[5] Until recently, however, very little work had been done towards linking pre-colonial South-East Asian history with patterns and processes in other regions while providing a new theoretical framework in which to engage such pursuits. Due in part to the rather late arrival of South-East Asian studies as a field of inquiry, scholarship in the twentieth century was devoted to charting the narrative structures, learning the languages, defining the region's character and constructing 'country-based' histories that were as much a part of the nation building process as they were about the trends in scholarship.[6] In short, scholarly emphasis was on constructing the uniqueness of South-East Asia and the varieties of local cultures that lay within, rather than engaging in how these characteristics might be considered in a broader, global context.[7]

In a series of articles, an edited volume, as well as in his seminal work, *Strange Parallels: Southeast Asia in Global Context, c. 800-1830*, vol. 1, Victor Lieberman accomplished for the region and for global history what has not been adequately attempted before by providing a conceptual and methodological framework for assessing South-East Asian history within a global context that transcends the peculiarities and provincialities of data, location, time and scholarly method. His combined work addresses the continuing legacy of viewing Asia through the prism of Europe and in particular problematizes the view that Asian history is characterized by its perceived historical stasis. Though recent scholarship has vigorously sought to correct this interpretation, Lieberman has departed from these efforts as many continue to evaluate their data based on the original paradigm of 'European exceptionalism'.[8] As many of these studies were initiated in response to the general assumption that the histories of Asia and Europe were incomparable, scholars since the 1960s have directed their attention to illustrating Asia's dynamism while some have even suggested Asia's superiority to Europe.[9] While the pendulum of emphasis has certainly swung, the pendulum and the fundamental categories of this conversation have nonetheless remained intact. In other words, the basic framework for analysis and the fundamental indices for comparison continue to be borrowed from Europe, structuring (and prescribing) the very conceptualization of global history. Proposing a third way, Lieberman has called for a comparison of early history (800-1830) based on the processes of integration as they relate to state, cultural and territorial formation. In his comprehensive and exhaustive project (*Mainland Mirrors: Russia, France, Japan, and the Islands*, vol. 2, is in press) Lieberman has shown that in 'ostensibly disparate' parts of the globe, on the 'outer rims' of Eurasia, various polities between the ninth and nineteenth century (in roughly four cycles) demonstrated a synchronic pattern of consolidation, fragmentation and re-consolidation. Broadly speaking, Lieberman's work traces the 'trajectories and dynamics' of mainland South-East Asian history and compares it to Russia, France, Japan, China and India while specifically addressing the nature of these parallel processes, the mechanisms underlying these patterns of political, cultural and territorial consolidation, and the features connecting the Eurasian continent. It is within this framework that a comparative history of Eurasian hydraulic polities may be considered.

II

HYDRAULIC HISTORIOGRAPHY IN SOUTH-EAST ASIA

Scholarly interest in South-East Asian water management, irrigation works, temples, agriculture and its archaeology originated with and was pursued by colonial administrators who were charged with decoding and reconstructing indigenous systems of labour, revenue extraction and land reform in order to help formulate and initiate economic, legal and social policies of governance.[10] Irrigation and other forms of hydraulic technology were seen, along with temple structures, language, literature and art as possible conduits for information about the South-East Asian past that could not only inform and improve the nature of colonial rule, but also provide scholar-officials with the *raison d'être* for colonialism itself.[11] South-East Asia's material past, especially its temples and water technology, was viewed as representing the pre-colonial state in all of its distant and now absent glory. Specifically, these material remains were seen as part of South-East Asia's lost past, the result of a declining and degenerate monarchical system that did not have the desire or capability of maintaining this ancient knowledge. Many doyens of the field (who were once colonial administrators themselves) saw the temples of Angkor, Pagan, Sukothai and Majapahit as the physical expression of 'Oriental Despotism' and the absolute authority of the state.[12] Kings who were eulogized as 'universal conquerors' or 'future-Buddhas' in their chronicles or inscriptions were described as tyrants and megalomaniacs, relegating the material record as evidence of their self-glorification.[13] Thus, while temples were thought to ensure and establish the near-divinity of monarchs, irrigation works such as the great reservoirs of Angkor were considered along utilitarian lines as part of their centralized state, fusing the despotic interpretation of early South-East Asian states with the 'liberating' rhetoric of colonial administrators.[14] To early officials, who codified these findings in surveys and reports, the representation of hydraulic technology as being directly administered by the state enabled them to present their policies as resurrecting the practices of a 'lost past' while at the same time, entrench the idea that pre-colonial agricultural societies and their irrigation works were controlled and managed by the state.[15] One result of this approach by colonial scholar-officials was to encapsulate the study of hydraulic works within the scope of kingship and despotic authority, which reflected colonial perceptions of the pre-modern state within their own political values about the South-East Asian past.[16]

In reaction to the tropes of colonial scholarship, native scholars writing at the time of Independence reacted to these interpretations by merely changing the final assessment of what were essentially colonial narratives.[17] Kings were no longer seen as weak, despotic, or tyrannical, but innovative, far-sighted and benevolent in their rule.

Irrigation canals, weirs, tanks and other hydraulic works were seen as remnants of the polities that would serve as the foundations for the modern nation state and were thus viewed as being a part of a national past.[18] Archaeological surveys continued to map and chart hydraulic works in order to demonstrate the extent and sophisticated manner in which these systems operated, a reminder of the nation's past and a celebration of its unifying qualities. Where once colonial scholars viewed irrigation technology as a means to understand and construct economic policy (which indirectly justified its existence as an authority) so, too, would the study of hydraulic works serve to bolster the image and idea of the new nation state. The nationalization of ancient monuments and the linking of pre-colonial hydraulic works to the present created an understanding of the past that positioned the nation as the inheritor of its greatness, much in the same way colonial powers hoped to establish a similar association. Creating a common history through print media, expositions, popular culture and education was designed to integrate the variety of ethnic groups, religions and patron-client relationships that characterized South-East Asia.[19] Fundamentally, however, the paradigm of hydraulic technology and its relationship to the state remained the same: irrigation enabled and was enabled by the mechanics of the central authority which allowed kings to manage agricultural production and the economic welfare of kingdoms. Though the narrative was presented in a different light, the story of hydraulic history remained more or less unchanged in its 'nationalist' rendition.

This slight departure did not impress scholars trained in the 1960s who sought an alternative to the way in which South-East Asian history may be interpreted; something fundamentally different from the colonial and nationalist interpretations. John Smail's seminal work, 'On the Possibility of an Autonomous History of Modern Southeast Asia' urged just that—it argued that the shift by nationalist historians had not really corrected the external perspective of South-East Asia, which often privileged European narratives, categories and themes to make sense of the region's history.[20] Smail argued that nationalist historiography had only shifted the 'moral perspective' (in reference to how a historian represented in a positive or negative light the culture, institutions and individuals within the narrative) and that such interpretations unintentionally maintained the adage that modernity could only be defined in terms of European criteria.[21] What was needed was a writing of South-East Asian history that was based on its own periodization, its own themes of analysis, and one that put the South-East Asia in the foreground of academic scrutiny. Thus, the writing of 'modern' South-East Asian history that began as a chapter in the settler history of Europe was viewed as insufficient in favour of a South-East Asian history with a 'European' chapter. This reposition of focus and the effects of this calling altered significantly the way in which hydraulic works (especially in Angkor) began to be seen.[22]

Scholars who examined indigenous texts, chronicles and inscriptions began to construct a sense of what constituted the South-East Asian conceptual universe, by interpreting religious references not as a sign of 'history immobile' but as a sign of continuity within the South-East Asian conceptual world.[23] The study of kingship was now studied for what it could reveal about conceptions of leadership and how it may reflect indigenous values and concerns. These sorts of departures led scholars to connect the maintenance and renovation of irrigation technology (in the case of Angkor) to ritual and symbolic interpretations of hydraulic systems. Major irrigation reservoirs, pools and moats were considered for their symbolic connections to the Hindu-Buddhist cosmology while local irrigation systems revealed much about the communities involved in their maintenance.[24] Local stories, myths, legends, and folktales began to be translated and analysed for what they revealed about the conceptions of water as it pertained to religion, social behaviour and relations at the rural level.[25] In short, the history of hydraulics took a different course and emphasis under the rubric of the 'autonomous history' school, water technology and its management was examined for what it revealed about South-East Asian culture and for the terms in which those ideas were expressed. The emphasis on the conceptual and anthropological aspects of water moved the narrative of hydraulic works in South-East Asia towards a new binary framing, which questioned whether they served a utilitarian function or if they were merely symbolic.[26] Within these two poles continued the debate and the uncertainty of whether or not irrigation technology was dependent on the state's centralizing mechanisms.[27]

More recently, post-colonial historians have begun to decolonize the epistemology of South-East Asia and have concentrated on reconstructing the role of colonial knowledge in their understandings of the region.[28] It is through the questioning of the context in which many sources were produced that has led to the study of how archaeological surveys, ethnographic reports and the comprehensive gazetteers reflect power politics, cultural assumptions and administrative agendas of colonial officials of the time. In one's reappraisals, one may look back to the reports on irrigation to see what they have to say about the concerns of the colonial state as well as their perception of history and culture. For instance, scholars are well aware that colonial observers were as much inventors of tradition as they were investigators of it.[29] In Bali, for instance, Dutch officials who were eager to understand, control and manage the agricultural production of the island needed to 'find' evidence that the pre-colonial state did indeed control local irrigation works.[30] This would not only reinforce Dutch self-images that they were preserving an important feature of the Balinese past (which the Balinese were incapable of doing themselves), but it would also justify by means of precedence, authority of the Dutch.[31] Thus, post-colonial approaches are now considering hydraulics as a means to studying the anthropology of colonialism, its effects on our understanding of South-East Asia and its effect on subsequent scholarship. The debate on whether hydraulic works represent state authority or local initiative still continues but the use of colonial sources and its corresponding scholarship is under greater scrutiny. Although these approaches have been considered for the hydraulic history of Bali (though not extensively), it is in the mainland agrarian states where these considerations could best be applied.

III

HYDRAULIC HISTORY IN BURMA

In contrast to the maritime world of South-East Asia (and with the exception of agrarian Java and Bali), the agrarian states of classical South-East Asia (ninth to fourteenth century) and their successor states relied extensively on various forms of hydraulic technology. Much of the research has been conducted by scholars of Cambodia, where the most obvious structures and beleaguering questions continue to challenge the field. However, recent important work has been done by scholars of Burmese history, though not as voluminous as in Cambodia or even Thailand. In the context of Burmese history, studies of irrigation, though few, have been extremely important as they have revealed the complex nature of the pre-modern state, especially with regard to ideology, economy and infrastructure. An understanding of hydraulic technology in early Burmese history has been possible through socio-economic studies of the pre-colonial state, exemplifying the continuing paradigm and assumption of central maintenance of irrigation works. In short, irrigation continues to be assessed within the overarching emphasis on its utilitarian qualities.

For much of its history, the cultural, ideological and political centre of the Burmese polity lay in Upper Burma, the emotional and economic heartland of the country, where, predictably, the best irrigated lands were located.[32] Other than a brief interlude in the sixteenth century when the monarchy shifted to the coast (in order to take advantage of the booming maritime trade), all capitals of Burma were set up nearest to its economic 'breadbasket', the river valleys of Upper Burma. It is here where the pre-classical civilizations of the Pyu and the classical state of Pagan emerged, setting the charter for subsequent successor states.[33] As Pagan was to British Burma what Angkor was to French Indo-China, British officials focused their efforts on decoding the workings and mechanisms of the pre-colonial state in order to shape their policies.

The data scholars rely on in their study of hydraulic works in Burma are predominantly based upon findings in the archaeological records and colonial documents.[34] As mentioned earlier, the majority of this literature was written in order to facilitate colonial policy as British Burma became an important world supplier of rice. Early surveys and censuses charted the nature of irrigation in colonial Burma with the intent of making it a revenue generating enterprise. Most of the early accounts of irrigation describe the nature and extent of irrigation works, focusing primarily on its utilitarian features.[35] These sources emphasized the material connections and functions of irrigation, entrenching the way in which scholars would consider hydraulic technology in Burma. As a result, current understanding of irrigation in Burma has remained closely linked to essentially two reoccurring analytical perspectives: its relationship to the socio-economic apparatus of the pre-modern state, and the symbolic dimensions of water as it reveals the ideological underpinnings of the state. In short, the conceptualization of hydraulic history has remained closely viewed within the framework of the state.

Michael Aung-Thwin's *Irrigation in the Heartland of Burma: Foundations of the Pre-Colonial Burmese State* (1990) is arguably the most comprehensive study to date on the Burmese hydraulic history. In a careful synthesis of indigenous language sources, colonial reports and archaeological findings, Aung-Thwin has investigated the nature of irrigation in pre-colonial Burma and explained its relevance to both the early Burmese state as well as to understanding Burmese history. Unlike earlier colonial reports and histories which discussed irrigation in terms of water management, productivity and engineering, Aung-Thwin has located the study of irrigation squarely within the context of Burma's institutional, ecological and social history. Irrigation is considered not merely in the context of state infrastructure, it is seen as a necessary result of the geographic and climatic fixtures characteristic of Upper Burma's dry zone. Burma's north-south mountain ranges, its major rivers that run parallel to them and its limited rainfall have created environmental conditions necessary for irrigated rice production. With the exception of one dynasty, the capitals of the monarchies were in Upper Burma since the most vital resources (people and rice lands) were located in this region. Thus, irrigation in Aung-Thwin's view is one of the fundamental mechanisms of Burmese history, it is implicated in the growth and consolidation of the pre-colonial state and it explains how its agrarian-based economy created the conditions for its ideological orientation to the interior.

The work describes the nature of Upper Burma's irrigation system, focusing on the 'breadbasket' region consisting of the Kyaukse, Minbu, Mu Valley, Tonplon (Mandalay) and Yamethin divisions. In contrast to Angkor, which may have used its huge reservoirs for irrigation, Burmese hydraulics were based on harnessing the output of perennial rivers that continued to water the plains after the annual flood waters had subsided. Canals, weirs and tanks diverted the water of mountain rivers to the plains where water was less abundant. Soil types, rice strains and technical details are all considered with the patterns of Burma's socio-economic history. The predictability and stability of agricultural output, augmented by a sophisticated irrigation network promoted social and cultural stability as well as, according to Michael Aung-Thwin, institutions that reflected the intimate and sensitive relationship between it and other eco-demographic factors such as scarce labour and plentiful land. In short, irrigation is placed within the context of Burmese history, stretched and considered within the broader historical context that emphasized the unique internal forces affecting the nature of state development.

Many of these approaches were adopted and applied by Janice Stargardt in her study of the Pyu, the early urbanized civilization that preceded the emergence of the classical Pagan.[36] Though a more comprehensive study that sought to understand urbanization in Burma, Stargardt applied aerial photography and art history in her analysis of irrigation and its role in polity formation. She traced and analysed the characteristic association of canals and tanks with urban spaces, noting significant technological changes in the hydraulic systems, and considered their implications for agrarian production and population dispersal. While Aung-Thwin focused on the relationship between state institutional irrigation networks, Stargardt argued that in an earlier period, the 'main technological discoveries as well as the management of water took place at the village level'.[37] Yet far more provocative are the connections she identifies in terms of symbolism and the role of water in the construction of cities. Like capital cities during the monarchical period that used canals and moats to represent the cosmic ocean that circles Mt. Meru, the axis of the world, so did Pyu cities use water to draw attention to these ideological underpinnings.[38] In addition, Pyu cities and their hydraulic works were fashioned like a moving wheel in reference to the sacred *cakka* which has key symbolic significance in Vedic, Hindu, and Buddhist literature. According to Stargardt, the cities (in this case Sri Ksetra) were organized and structured along the design of the *cakka* in order to indicate that their leader was a *cakkavartin* or universal conqueror.[39] Her research reveals that even water was channelled to flow in an auspicious clockwise motion like the Wheel of Law.[40] While Stargardt's conclusions on this issue have elicited mixed reactions from archaeologists, the important point is how hydraulic works may be interpreted in both an urban context, as in the case of the Pyu capital cities, and a rural context, as in the case of the classical kingdom of Pagan. Both works maintain a strong materialist orientation though the role of the state differs: in the Pyu cities, local initiative played a role in technological improvements in that authority was limited in the countryside, while Pagan hydraulic works were believed to be managed and administered by the apparatus of state/church institutions.

Though certainly not exhaustive, the brief survey of research on pre-colonial irrigation works indicates that the general trends directing South-East Asian studies as a whole has influenced the interpretation of hydraulics in early Burma. While several studies of irrigation have focused on the 100 odd years of colonial rice production in Lower Burma, over 1,000 years of history point to irrigated rice production in Upper Burma, providing insight into the nature of Burmese institutional history. In sum, these works have considered the role of water infrastructure within the context of pre-colonial, country-based studies, with an emphasis on top-bottom organizational strategies of wet rice cultivation. The need for local, rural and village-based studies in the context of Burmese history remains an area in which anthropologists in Bali have already made much progress.

IV

TOWARDS AN ANTHROPOLOGY OF WATER

While historians have predominantly focused on the role of hydraulic technology as it related to the pre-colonial state's economic and administrative capacity, anthropologists have approached irrigation works in island South-East Asia as a means of exploring social organization. Significant findings in Bali by Clifford Geertz, Mark Hobart and J. Stephen Lansing have demonstrated that the study of symbolic, ritual and calendrical roles of 'water temples' is important for an understanding of irrigation and social organization.[41] Responding to Marx and Wittfogel, whose theories related the centralization of power to the management of hydraulic works, many scholars have argued that Balinese irrigation was oriented towards and managed by local authorities. Farmers, organized in *subaks* or agricultural associations, administed their irrigation works according to local concerns and schedules.[42] Since reservoirs or other forms of water storage were not used in Bali, the nature of water management was dependent on a closely monitored dispersal of water and assessment of the flow, timing and needs of farmers downstream. Responding to these challenges, Clifford Geertz's study of these associations noted that agricultural rituals were a part of the schedule for the dispersal of water, adding another level of meaning to the role of irrigation.[43] Geertz proposed that a 'complex ecological order was both reflected in and shaped by an equally complex ritual order, which at once grew out of it and was imposed by it'.[44] Further studies that both extended and departed from Geertz described the different types of calendars involved in determining the timing of water dispersal which was connected to the different stages of rice cultivation. Central to the nature of irrigation management and its relation to ritual is the role of the water temple, explored in detail by Lansing.

Lansing's research has convincingly shown that water temple networks played a discernible role in hydraulic management outside the sphere of centralized royal authority.[45] This provocative finding has provided yet another context in which to consider the role of hydraulic technology within local societies that operated in conjunction with, but not necessarily under the authority of, more broad based, kingdomwide initiatives.[46] Lansing's work focuses on the relationships formed through the control and management of water irrigation. Water temples were erected along the course of water with the central and most important temple situated at the source of water. Lansing and other scholars have demonstrated how each temple was hierarchically connected to the temple that supplied it with water upstream, connecting it both in terms of its water and the spiritual purity that was associated with water.[47] Farmers built a small shrine at the point where a temple's water first entered his fields, normally at the 'upstream' end of his fields. These shrines were connected to larger temples where collective rites and meetings took place. These were linked to a regional temple, where a major canal first entered a group of terraces. Finally, major springs, lakes or headwaters of rivers had a major temple, to which all others were connected. Temple administrators met seasonally according to particular calendars connecting the harvests with the dispersal of water, so that agriculture production could be managed and timed according to the specific needs and concerns of all the communities involved. Each temple planned its stage of planting and harvesting one stage ahead of the temple downstream, so that crops could be controlled and water consumption administered. The water temple served as an organizational unit across village communities, organizing farmers into temple associations based on religious as well as economic ties.

The importance of their work lies in the fact that it has presented an alternate case where irrigation was not the sole prerogative of the state, but was managed by local leaders and communities. In addition, it has provided an interesting methodological approach that challenges the way in which hydraulic technology has been viewed and studied. Irrigation was important to integration as much as it was instrumental to agricultural production. The management of water, the relationship between water temple communities, and the symbolic dimensions associated with water itself offer a glimpse into the conceptual world of the Balinese, providing an interesting avenue of comparison in Eurasian history. Hydraulic technology in

South-East Asia can thus be viewed as being varied in accordance with locality and geographic specificity. In some cases irrigation works were managed closely by the state while in others, the local communities were in charge. What remains to be explored in the South-East Asian context is whether these patterns of central or local integration necessarily operated separately or worked together simultaneously.

V

CONCLUSION: TOWARDS A HISTORY OF IRRIGATION AND INTEGRATION IN EUROPE AND ASIA

The study of hydraulic technology in the South-East Asian context has been guided by a fairly consistent paradigm. Scholars have investigated irrigation technology in order to study the nature and centrality of state power and influence. Others have argued that irrigation could also be considered within a local context, outside the parameters of state involvement. This centre-periphery debate appears to be related in part to the types of sources and theoretical frameworks used, notably colonial sources and the seminal studies by Marx and Wittfogel, who pushed and defined the agenda of the field. Where historians and archaeologists have been enthusiastically following this calling, ethnologists and cultural anthropologists have focused on different questions related to hydraulic technology, demonstrating the potential of studying these networks in order to understand the South-East Asian conceptual world. Interestingly, these studies lie within the original binary context of whether or not the state was involved in irrigation, a useful but not as broadly conceived a framework for applying to Eurasian history.

Lieberman's approach to using integration as a category in which to engage a comparative history of Asia and Europe may be a more suitable framework for studying the sub-field of hydraulic history. The role of irrigation and water technology is undeniably an important link that transcends geographical and cultural boundaries, making it an attractive category of analysis. Irrigation and its relation to integration provides a unique opportunity to extend the analyses of Eurasian studies beyond the relationship between water and the state. Specific case studies, important for their detail, may be more illuminating if considered within the wider framework of integration, which addresses cultural and social history as much as political and economic developments. It is towards these issues that the future of comparative research in hydraulic history lies.

NOTES

1. V. Lieberman, *Strange Parallels: Southeast Asia in Global Context, c. 800-1830*, Cambridge, 2003.
2. Ibid., p. 66.
3. This paper does not attempt to reconstruct this historiography which has been cogently presented by Lieberman, ibid., pp. 66-84.
4. K. Pomeranz, *The Great Divergence*, Princeton, 2000. R. Bin Wong, *China Transformed*, Ithaca, 1997. 'AHR Forum: Asia and Europe in the World Economy', *The American Historical Review*, vol. 107, no. 2, April 2002, pp. 419-80. For an exhaustive analysis of this historiography see Lieberman, *Strange Parallels*.
5. A.L. Stoler and F. Cooper, eds., *Tensions of Empire. Colonial Cultures in a Bourgeois World*, Berkeley, 1997. J.C. Scott, *Seeing Like a State. How Certain Schemes to Improve the Human Condition have Failed*, New Haven, 1998. B. Anderson, *Imagined Communities*, London, 1983. C. Geertz, *The Interpretation of Cultures*, London, 1993.
6 J.D. Legge, 'The Writing of Southeast Asian History', in *The Cambridge History of Southeast Asia*, vol. 1, ed. N. Tarling, Cambridge, 1992. C. Reynolds, 'A New Look at Old Southeast Asia', *Journal of Asian History*, vol. 54, no. 2, 1995, pp. 419-66.
7. J.C. van Leur, *Indonesian Trade and Society*, The Hague, 1955. J.R.W. Smail, 'On the Possibility of an Autonomous History of Modern Southeast Asia', *Journal of South-East Asian History*, vol. 2, 1961, pp. 72-102. H.J. Benda, 'The Structure of Southeast Asian History: Some Preliminary Observations', *Journal of South-East Asian History*, vol. 3, 1962, pp. 159-68. O.W. Wolters, *History, Culture, and Region in Southeast Asian Perspectives*, Ithaca, 1999.
8. Lieberman, *Strange Parallels*, pp. 66-73. He notes that scholars were compelled to 'find' examples of European historical patterns in the Asian context as an early attempt to address externalist views of the region while comparativists reinforced these differences by pointing to a unique tradition of 'fragmented political structures' that promoted

'legal traditions, property rights, urban autonomy and contractual government'.

9. Ibid.
10. For studies of colonial modes of rule and their influence on knowledge production, see B.S. Cohn, *Colonialism and Its Forms of Knowledge: The British in India*, Princeton, 1996. R. Mrazek, *Engineers of Happy Land. Technology and Nationalism in a Colony*, Princeton, 2002. N. Dirks, ed., *Colonialism and Culture*, Ann Arbor, 1992. P. Pels and O. Salemink, *Colonial Subjects: Essays on the Practical History of Anthropology*, Ann Arbor, 2000.
11. South-East Asian civilizations were seen to have sunk into decline, only to be rediscovered by European surveyors and explorers. See Legge's discussion of these trends in *Cambridge History of Southeast Asia*, vol. I, pp. 11-14.
12. For examples in Burmese historiography see G.E. Harvey, *A History of Burma*, London, 1925; D.G.E. Hall, *Early English Intercourse with Burma 1587-1743*, London, 1928.
13. Ibid.
14. See B. Groslier, *Indochina*, London, 1966. He suggested that the success of Angkor's kingdom was due to the highly centralized state structure which managed the all-important hydraulic works.
15. J.S. Lansing, *Priests and Programmers. Technologies of Power in the Engineered Landscape of Bali*, Princeton, 1991, pp. 35-6.
16. This debate, a response to Wittfogel, questioned whether central authority was a necessary requirement for the successful management of hydraulic technology. This body of scholarship offered alternative interpretations in the case of Angkor, that posited more symbolic uses for the great reservoirs and tanks than utilitarian, economic purposes. See E. Moore, 'Water Management in Early Cambodia', *The Geographical Journal*, vol. 155, 1989, pp. 204-14. Moore, 'The Waters of Angkor', *Asian Art and Culture*, vol. 8, 1995, pp. 37-51. R. Acker, 'New Geographical Tests of the Hydraulic Thesis at Angkor', *South East Asian Research*, vol. 6, no. 1, 1998, pp. 5-47. Recent work by Pottier has reassessed this view and demonstrated that networks of canals did connect the great reservoirs to the rice fields, and that a combination of centrally organized and locally managed water works contributed to the agrarian state's agricultural output. See C. Pottier, 'Some Evidence of an Inter-relationship between Hydraulic Features and Rice Field Patterns

at Angkor During Ancient Times', *The Journal of Sophia Asian Studies*, vol. 18, 2000, pp. 99-119.

17. R. Heine-Geldern, 'Conceptions of State and Kingship in Southeast Asia', *Far Eastern Quarterly*, vol. 2, 1942, pp. 15-30.
18. C. Reynolds, 'A New Look at Old Southeast Asia', *Journal of Asian Studies*, vol. 54, no. 2, 1995, pp. 419-66.
19. Anderson, *Imagined Communities*, London, 1991.
20. Smail, 'On the Possibility of an Autonomous History of Modern Southeast Asia', *Journal of South-East Asian History*, no. 2, 1995, pp. 72-102.
21. This trend parallels similar interpretations by Asianists who sought to find parallels to European traits in order to make Asian history 'more positive'. See Lieberman, *Strange Parallels*, p. 67.
22. See Moore, 'Water Management', Acker, 'New Geographical Tests'.
23. See M. Aung-Thwin, *Pagan: The Origins of Modern Burma*, Honolulu, 1985. K. Taylor, *The Birth of Vietnam*, Berkeley, 1983. R.C. Ileto, *Payson and Revolution*, Quezon City, 1979.
24. E. Mannika, *Angkor Wat: Time, Space, and Kingship*, Honolulu, 1996.
25. J. Strong, *The Legend and Cult of Upagupta*, Princeton, 1992.
26. Moore, 'Water Management'. Acker, 'New Geographical Tests'.
27. Lieberman, *Strange Parallels*, pp. 228-9.
28. P. Pels and O. Salemink, *Colonial Subjects. Essays on the Practical History of Anthropology*, Ann Arbor, 2000. M. Aung-Thwin, *Myth and History in the Historiography of Early Burma*, Athens (Ohio), 1998.
29. See Pels and Salemink, *Colonial Subjects.* E. Hobsbawm, *The Invention of Traditions*, Cambridge, 1983.
30. Lansing, *Priests and Programmers*, pp. 35-6.
31. Ibid., p. 18.
32. M. Aung-Thwin, *Irrigation in the Heartland of Burma. Foundations of the Pre-Colonial Burmese State*, Singapore, 1990.
33. Ibid., pp. 1-4.
34. For instance, see references to irrigation in the Upper Burma Gazetteer, District Reports, Annual Reports of the Irrigation Department (Annual Reports of the Archaeological Survey) and Annual Reports, Archaeological Survey of India.
35. Aung-Thwin, *Irrigation in the Heartland of Burma*, p. 4.
36. J. Stargardt, *The Ancient Pyu of Burma*, vol. 1, Cambridge, 1990. See also A. Thaw, *Report on the Excavations at Beikthano*, Rangoon, 1970. G.H.

Luce, *Phases of Pre-Pagan Burma*, 2 vols, Oxford, 1985. R.L. Brown, 'Pyu Art: Looking East and West', *Orientations*, vol. 32, 2001. B. Hudson, N. Lwin and W. Maung, 'The Origins of Bagan', *Asian Perspectives*, vol. 40, 2001.

37. At the same time Stargardt seemed to support the idea of an integrated system between capital and rural communities, forming what she termed 'irrigation societies'. See Stargardt, *Ancient Pyu of Burma*, pp. 54-104.
38. See her discussion on the symbolic dimensions of water technology in chap. 3, pp. 105-44.
39. Stargardt argued that the citadel in the centre of the city was hydraulically, architecturally and ritually marked by the concentric moats and the 'radiating' canals that sprung from the citadel like spokes on a wheel. See Stargardt, *Ancient Pyu of Burma*, p. 106.
40. Ibid., pp. 106-11.
41. C. Geertz, 'The Wet and the Dry. Traditional Irrigation in Bali and Morocco', *Human Ecology*, vol. 1, 1972, pp. 34-9. J.S. Lansing, 'Balinese "Water Temples" and the Management of Irrigation', *American Anthropologist* (New Series), vol. 89, no. 2, 1987, pp. 326-41. M. Hobart, 'Padi, Puns, and the Attribution of Responsibility', in *Natural Symbols in Southeast Asia*, ed. G.B. Milner, Singapore, 1982, pp. 5-28.
42. Lansing, *Priests and Programmers*, p. 41.
43. Geertz, 'The Wet and the Dry', pp. 34-9.
44. Ibid.
45. Lansing, *Priests and Programmers*, pp. 51-72.
46. Ibid., pp. 33-5.
47. Ibid., pp. 55-9.

PART III

EUROPE: MARITIME POWERS

CHAPTER 7

The Hanseatic League as a European Maritime Power in the Late Middle Ages[1]

HORST WERNICKE

INTRODUCTION

Maritime power in Europe was not only maintained on the basis of territorial statehood, such as by the Dutch Republic or England, it could also be exerted by other structures of association. During the latter Middle Ages, this especially applied to the regions around the Baltic and the North Sea together with their vast economic hinterlands that were linked to the maritime trading world via their riverine networks. These regions were dominated by the Hanseatic League which is commonly regarded by modern historians as a mercantile community of interest or a corporate union.[2] Two phases of the League's history can be ascertained: during the first period, the Hanseatic merchant communities conducted trade that was privileged by several rulers. Individual merchants, and not towns and territories, gave the impulse for economic enterprise. Since the middle of the twelfth century, these enterprises were protected by the merchants' trading base or town of origin, but in practice protection proved to be worth very little. During the second period, beginning in the thirteenth century, the commercial initiatives of individual merchant communities lost their pre-eminent position and were subsequently replaced by political and military alliances forged by the participating towns with the aim of protecting their merchants. Mercantile success now depended to a large extent on the show of military might and on the diplomatic skills of a given Hanseatic town.[3] It is with regard to this second period, that the major question of statehood 'on the water' merits further exploration.

Defence of the merchants' rights was a principal concern of every single town of the League. The physical layout of the individual towns that evolved during the Middle Ages clearly reflects this attitude. Substantial fortifications were erected for military defence, and one could enter the town only through well-protected gates. High church towers enabled close monitoring of the surrounding countryside.[4] Besides, additional advantage was gained by exploiting the precise geographic setting of a town: rivers, lakes, swamps or islands and peninsulas were all taken into consideration in the planning and development of the town's defences. Outside the fortification, the authorities purchased land and constructed watchtowers to protect major routes leading in and out of the towns. Even if Hanseatic towns gave the impression of being closed off and self-sufficient, at least to the outsider, a closer scrutiny reveals a very different picture.[5]

This paper explores the history of the Hanseatic League with special reference to conflict management. Conflict management can be regarded as a broad indicator of statehood. In particular, this paper questions whether the military force exerted by the League aimed at establishing a maritime state power, or whether it was an attempt to secure trade and market shares.

II

LEGAL RIGHTS, PROTECTION AND MILITARY FORCE

In order to secure his livelihood and conduct trade, the Hanseatic merchant had to leave his well-protected home base. His major concern was to ensure the same kind of safety while at sea as he enjoyed at home. Outside towns, territorial power was exerted usually by local rulers who not only claimed rights of property to their estates, but also the right to use physical force, and if need be, violence, against persons trespassing on their lands. The Hanseatic merchant, thus, faced the might of arms from the beginning of his voyage and had to consequently secure his rights and personal safety outside the confines of his home town. When a town was subject to the authority of a given territorial ruler, personal safety may very well have been secured across the whole of his territory. Such a policy, however, succeeded only in rare instances. The Holy Roman Emperor, or ducal and clerical overlords often failed to lend protection to the towns. Accordingly, merchants and later even towns took matters into their own hands by forging agreements to respect and protect each others' properties abroad.[6]

The safeguarding of rights, liberties and privileges was a principal concern of the Hanseatic merchants and—since the thirteenth century—also of the Hanseatic towns across the region in which they conducted their business.[7] After the thirteenth century, the Hanseatic towns succeeded in strengthening their sea power through mercantile and nautical innovations. These include special forms of administration and capital management, as well as the introduction and development of new ships such as the cog. The introduction of the comparatively spacious cog facilitated a shift from trade in luxury goods to bulk goods. This process was also facilitated in the latter Middle Ages by establishing an intricate network of ports and factories that spanned across the Baltic region and Western Europe. This ensured ready access to marketplaces and productive regions together with institutional and legal support for trade.[8]

Hanseatic interests were, however, not only defended by peaceful enterprise but also by force at times. Recourse to military force was deemed permissible, but only for defence. Neighbouring dukes or noblemen often targeted these trading centres on account of their wealth. The desire to tap into the wealth of the Hanseatic towns often resulted in sieges or protracted legal tussles.[9] Such conditions and problems brought towns together for the purpose of common defence. When invoked, these agreements stipulated the number of troops to be marshalled by each contracting party.[10] Such defence pacts aimed at protecting towns from assaults by individual rulers, but they often proved woefully inadequate when territorial overlords launched joint offensives. One such case was King Eric Menved of Denmark in the fourteenth century.[11]

Defence was organized along different strata of society. The towns were always willing to meet threats by obliging their citizens to supply weapons and other materials from private estates, public buildings and arsenals. It should be noted, however, that since the middle of the fourteenth century, individual towns also had their own weapons and sometimes even large devices to break through city walls. Military exercises were conducted regularly for younger members of the citizenry and soldiers mustered from the lower strata of society. Since the fourteenth century, the towns increasingly relied on mercenaries who were often either noblemen or other persons from neighbouring territories and placed under the command of a local captain. In the event of war, all citizens were required to join the urban defence forces. This type of militia formed the backbone of military protection well into the early modern period.[12] When a conflict affected another Hanseatic town, urban communities raised troops to assist them. Since the fourteenth century, such direct military aid was frequently substituted by financial assistance. How much was paid depended on the duration of the war and the distance to the conflict zone. Often the towns were in a far better position than their enemies, not least because they were generally in a position to manufacture their own weapons and gunpowder.

The Hanseatic towns not only fought defensive wars, but some of them were offensive as well. Since the 1280s, the trade blockade backed by military force emerged as a means of advancing commercial interests. Such blockades, for instance, were imposed on Bruges in Flanders, Bergen in Norway and Nowgorod in Russia. Any trade connections interlinking these emporia with ports were completely severed by Hanseatic ships. The Hanseatic towns required their merchants to abandon factories in a blockaded port, whilst merchandise belonging to enemy nations or cities was confiscated. Blockade and boycott became a common means to secure market share, enhance the status of Hanseatic merchants abroad, and in the thirteenth century contributed meaningfully toward the establishment of a Hanseatic naval hegemony around the Baltic and the North Sea.[13]

III

PIRACY AND SAFETY OF SHIPPING ROUTES

The principal objective of Hanseatic policy was to secure shipping routes around the Baltic and north-west Europe. As most land routes were in a desperate and uncertain state, peaceful trading across the sea became the precondition for any commercial success. In this respect, merchants sought to secure long distance shipping rights, protection within ports as well as in adjacent waters. Against the backdrop of these concerns, it may be said that most wars were waged with the objective of securing safe passage from east to west, from the Baltic to the North Sea through the Danish Sound (the so-called *Ummelandfahrt*). It should be borne in mind that Hanseatic ships were not constructed as warships, but as trading vessels, so that, even in the event of war, a battle on the open sea was far less significant than the marine blockade and the stationing of land troops.[14]

A major threat to commerce was from illegal piracy or legalized privateering in times of war. Territorial overlords encouraged acts of privateering around the Baltic in times of conflict, mainly at the expense of Hanseatic trade.[15] Actual wars of attrition were waged on behalf of the kings of Sweden, Denmark, England and France, as well as the North German rulers of Mecklenburg and Pomerania. Toward the end of hostilities, the Hanseatic towns saw themselves compelled to combat piracy as well as freebooting by the enemy.

At the end of the fourteenth century, piracy became a serious safety issue, especially since it had been encouraged by Queen Margaret I during a war between Mecklenburg and the united crowns of Denmark–Norway–Sweden. In the initial phase, the Hanseatic towns benefited economically as a result of the hostilities because they delivered supplies for Mecklenburg to the occupied Swedish capital of Stockholm. When the hostilities escalated and began to threaten trading in the Baltic, the Hanseatic League changed course and began to crush piracy, a move half-heartedly supported by Queen Margaret. To this end, the Hanseatic towns assembled a military force with ships, troops and funds. The very composition and structure of this fleet testifies to the commitment of the

TABLE 7.1: COMPOSITION OF THE HANSEATIC FLEET AT THE END OF THE FOURTEENTH CENTURY[16]

Hanseatic Town	Number of Ships	Number of Crew
Lübeck	9	600
Stralsund	4	400
Anklam, Greifswald, Wolgast and Demmin	2	120
Stettin, Stargard, Golnow, Gartz, Greifenhagen, Damm and Cammin	2	200
Kolberg, Rügenwalde, Stolp Treptow, Greifenberg, and Wollin	2	80
Prussia (Teutonic Order)	10	1,000
Kampen	2 (and 4 riverboats)	300
Dordrecht, Amsterdam, Staveren, Harderwijk and Zuidersee	2	200
Zeeland	4	400
Livonia	2	200

various Hanseatic towns and the significance they attached to this enterprise (see Table 7.1).

The data clearly reveal the political and military significance of the Hanseatic towns and their interest in maintaining safety in the Baltic Sea. Lübeck constituted the principle town of the League and together with the Prussian towns contributed the largest number of ships. Of less importance was Stralsund followed by other Pomeranian towns, as well as the emporia of the Low Countries and Livonia. One needs to bear in mind that for every hundred mariners, an additional twenty marksmen had to be mustered and equipped. Even if the activities of the Hanseatic fleet had little overall impact, the capture of the island of Gotland in 1398 by Prussian troops destroyed the pirate's nests established on this island.

Later, the Hanseatic League was compelled to assemble a second fleet to fight piratical forces.

As can be gleaned from the data in Table 7.2, the structure and composition of the second Hanseatic fleet had changed compared

TABLE 7.2: SECOND HANSEATIC FLEET[17]

Hanseatic Town	Number of Ships	Number of Crew
Lübeck	2	200
Hamburg	1	50
Stralsund, Greifswald and Stettin	2	200
Prussian Towns	2	200
Livonian Towns	1	100

to the first. Atain, twenty soldiers served for every hundred mariners on board. In addition, each vessel had to carry ten large crossbows. Each large ship was under escort by a number of smaller vessels that could enter shallow coastal waters and inlets. The new composition demonstrates the enhanced military might of the fleet, despite comprising a lower number of ships than the first. The new strategy proved successful, and the Baltic Sea privateers were chased into the North Sea. In 1400, a North Sea fleet was formed that included 950 mariners dispersed over eleven ships, and two more vessels with 127 mariners were dispatched for the Baltic Sea (see Table 7.3).

Several towns of the Low Countries contributed toward this third naval force, but the collaborative effort did not last and degenerated into bitter rivalry.[18]

Apart from assembling such fleets, the League also engaged fast vessels for chasing away pirates and other hostile craft. They were

TABLE 7.3: THE HANSEATIC NORTH SEA FLEET OF 1400

Hanseatic Town	Number of Ships	Number of Crew
Lübeck	2	200
Hamburg	1	100
Bremen	1	50
Wismar	1	50
Rostock	1	50
Stralsund	1	100
Prussian Towns	3	300
Towns of the Low Countries	1	100

provisioned by individual towns or groups of towns, which seized the booty and shared the proceeds from the sale of confiscated assets. Yet another way of protecting Hanseatic ships was to hire soldiers who were stationed on board trading ships. Regulations passed by the municipal authorities of the League determined the number of soldiers to be stationed on board, together with the number of weapons. They also stipulated the days of departure from a given port, or the passage through dangerous waters, such as the Danish Sound. Trading fleets were composed of a minimum of ten and sometimes twenty vessels (1392/1404). The latter is true for Prussian towns. These and related regulations served to tighten the League from a loose association to a closely knit community of shared interests between the merchants and the Hanseatic towns.

IV

FOREIGN POLICY AND WAR

In many instances, it was not the pirates, but the territorial overlords who emerged as the enemy. Despite frequent military action against pirates, the Hanseatic League in the early years of its existence sought to remain politically uncommitted or neutral. Attempts on the part of France, England and Burgundy to forge a military alliance with the League during the Hundred Years' War were rebuffed. When the English impounded Hanseatic ships, the League did not respond. Before the middle of the fourteenth century, the seizure of Hanseatic ships by the King of Denmark also elicited no armed response. It was only during the wars waged by King Valdemar IV Atterdag of Denmark that comprehensive measures for defence were taken. This can be taken as a clear manifestation of tighter military structures and cooperation among the Hanseatic towns. The King of Denmark may very well have exerted power on land against Sweden, but the League was growing increasingly aware of its potential as a maritime force. When Denmark captured the town Visby on Gotland island in 1361, the Hanseatic League declared war and had the support of Sweden's ruler Magnus Eriksson and his Norwegian allies.[19] In this particular instance, a fleet was assembled, comprising six ships and other minor craft from Lübeck, together with warships from the Pomeranian towns of Stralsund, Greifswald, Kolberg and Stettin. Kiel also placed a ship at the League's disposal. The principal objective was to protect the waters in the northern Baltic around Gotland, and funds were raised to finance this fleet through customs duties (*Pfundzoll*) approved by a gathering of the Hanseatic towns (*Hansetag*) assembled in Greifswald in September 1361. It was also decided to boycott Danish trade. The imposts were levied on all commodities and collected from each ship. Any captain who resisted payment was barred from trading. The amounts raised in this way were quite impressive. At a meeting in Stralsund in 1364 a final tally was calculated (see Table 7.4).

However, the sums levied were not sufficient to meet the expenses and the shortfall was met through higher contributions from Rostock, Wismar, Greifswald and Kiel. It took many years to settle the accounts between the various towns, a process, incidentally, that was never fully concluded.

A cost-sharing formula was also applied to the war that ensued between the League and King Valdemar of Denmark from 1368 to 1369. Denmark was defeated, and Copenhagen was captured

TABLE 7.4: GAINS FROM THE PFUNDZOLL, 1361-64[20]

Hanseatic Town	Men	Duty Levied on Each Town (in Mark)	Amount Paid by Each Town (in Mark)
Lübeck	600	40,878	38,536
Rostock	400	27,252	32,303
Stralsund	400	27,252	25,980
Hamburg	200	13,626	12,000
Wismar	200	13,626	14,346
Greifswald	200	13,626	14,556
Stettin	200	13,626	13,143
Kolberg	100	6,813	6,534
Anklam	50	3,406	1,792
Stargard	50	3,406	1,792
Kiel	40	2,725	5,250

together with Elsinore and Helsingborg on the northern tip of the Danish Sound. The success of the coordinated military strategy of the League is particularly well illustrated by the capture of the latter two fortifications. Their fall ensured Hanseatic dominance of the Baltic until the towns were returned to Denmark by treaty some fifteen years later.[21] When the Peace of Stralsund was concluded in 1370, the Hanseatic League did not want to despoil the Danish monarchy, it simply wanted to assert its hegemony over the Baltic and have Denmark formally recognize and accept that supremacy.

In the aftermath of the wars, the Hanseatic towns found themselves steeped in debt and struggled to recoup the funds spent on provisioning ships and troops. Funds were collected chiefly from the proverbial pockets of the inhabitants and citizens of each town, mainly through extraordinary imposts and higher taxes on bread, beer or wine. Everyone was adversely affected by such measures. Tensions arose between the municipal authorities and the inhabitants, often reaching a breaking point and resulting in open revolt.

Despite all these problems, the League continued to advance as a leading mercantile and political power in the Baltic and North Sea. The Hanseatic merchants increased economic dependence of the coastal population and the vast hinterland of continental Europe. This observation is substantiated by the fact that in many instances the League was able to strengthen its privileged position at the expense of its competitors. The principal concern was to pacify maritime trade and also take precautions against possible disturbances by certain military forces and mercantile institutions. To ensure safety, a complex system of rules was devised. These regulated, amongst other things, the duration of mariners' contracts, shipbuilding standards, as well as the presence of foreign merchants in the Hanseatic towns.

The penetration of English merchants at the close of the fourteenth century, and of Dutch entrepreneurs into the Baltic since the 1420s seriously affected Hanseatic trade in the long run. The English merchants were chiefly engaged in bartering English textiles for grains, timber, ash, tar and copper, preferably in Prussia. But the major threat was from Dutch trade with its advanced technologies, larger cargo capacity and access to timber for shipbuilding. Eventually, the Hanseatic League lost out to Dutch competition. While war against the Danish Union before 1435 served to strengthen the position of the Hanseatic towns, a confrontation with the Dutch proved to be a serious challenge. This heightened competition is best reflected in the Dutch–Hanseatic War between 1438 and 1441. In the long term, the League lost its leading market position to its competitors from western Europe. During the sixteenth century, the Baltic came to be dominated by Dutch shipping.

V

CONCLUSION

The Hanseatic League jealously guarded its power on the seas. However, pursuit of maritime supremacy was never an end in itself. Naval power was an instrument of securing routes and market positions, and never aimed at territorial expansion or achieving statehood. The Hanseatic League, thus, cannot in any way be seen as a homogeneous and expansive state power based on water, but as a confederation of merchants and—during the second phase of its history—as an association of mercantile towns. Even if this structure often hampered concerted defence efforts, or hindered the raising of funds to finance the war effort, the League succeeded in securing its maritime supremacy in the Baltic and North Sea for centuries.

The Hanseatic League did not hesitate to exert military force to achieve certain political ends and its commercial supremacy on the seas. However, before any war was declared, it tried other avenues to achieve these ends, including diplomacy and threats. Peaceful trade required a protector, and the Hanseatic League was one of them.

NOTES

1. Translated from German by Peter Borschberg and Martin Krieger.
2. H. Wernicke, *Die Städtehanse. 1280-1418: Genesis-Strukturen-Funktionen*, Weimar, 1983.
3. See ibid., pp. 84 ff.

4. O. Borst, *Alltagsleben im Mittelalter*, Frankfurt (Main), 1983, pp. 184 ff.
5. Ibid.
6. This especially applies to the co-operative of the Gotland merchants as shown by D. Kattinger, *Die Gotländische Genosschenschaft. Der frühhansisch-gotländische Handel in Nord- und Westeuropa*, Cologne/Weimar, 1999.
7. H. Wernicke, 'Von Rechten, Freiheiten und Privilegien: Zum Wesen und Dynamik in der Hanse', in *Beiträge zur hansischen Kultur-, Verfassungs- und Schiffahrtsgeschichte*, ed. N. Jörn and H. Wernicke, Weimar, 1998, pp. 283 ff.
8. A.T. Mahan, *Einfluß der Seemacht auf die Geschichte*, Berlin, 1896, pp. 32 ff. See also R.W. Unger and A.T. Mahan, 'Ship Design, and the Evolution of Sea Power in the Late Middle Ages', *The International History Review*, vol. 19, no. 3, August 1997, pp. 518 ff.
9. H. Wernicke, 'Auseinandersetzungsformen der Städtehanse und der hansischen Städtemitglieder mit der feudaladligen Umwelt. Stufeneiner Klassenauseinandersetzung', *Wissenschaftliche Zeitschrift der Ernst-Moritz-Arndt-Universität Greifswald, Gesellschafts- und sprachwissen schaftliche Reihe*, vol. 30, nos. 1 and 2, pp. 21 ff.
10. E. Isenmann, *Die deutsche Stadt im Spätmittelalter*, Stuttgart, 1988, pp. 121 ff.
11. K. Fritze, *Die Hansestadt Stralsund. Die beiden ersten Jahrhunderte ihrer Geschichte*, Schwerin, 1961, pp. 93 ff.
12. Isenmann, *Die deutsche Stadt im Spätmittelalter*, pp. 148 ff.
13. Wernicke, *Städtehanse*, pp. 149 ff.
14. K. Fritze and G. Krause, *Seekriege der Hanse*, Berlin, 1989, pp. 220 ff.
15. Ibid., pp. 232 ff.
16. Verein für Hansische Geschichte, ed., *Hanserecesse* (hereafter *HR*), rpt., Cologne/Weimar, 1970 ff., see in particular *HR*, vol. 1, pt. 1, no. 7.
17. Ibid.
18. D. Siefert, *Kompagnons und Konkurrenten. Holland und die Hanse im späten Mittelalter*, Cologne/Weimar/Vienna, 1997, pp. 137 ff.
19. *HR*, vol. 1, pt. 1, nos. 262-3.
20. *HR*, vol. 1, pt. 1, no. 325, 22. *HR*, vol. 1, pt. 1, no. 354, 5. *HR*, vol. 1, pt. 1, nos. 393, 406.
21. N. Jörn, R.-G. Werlich and H. Wenicke, eds., *Der Stralsunder Frieden von 1370: Prosopographische Studien*, Cologne/Weimar/Vienna, 1998.

CHAPTER 8

Denmark as a Naval Power during the Fifteenth and Sixteenth Century

JENS E. OLESEN

INTRODUCTION

During an air attack on the city of Lübeck in the Second World War, a Danish flag hanging in the church of Saint Mary was consumed by fire. The flag had been taken from a Scandinavian vessel that attacked Holstein and the Hanseatic towns during the 1420s. Thanks to extant drawings, however, knowledge of the flag and its emblems have been preserved. Besides religious motifs, the flag depicted the three Danish lions, the Norwegian lion holding an axe, the three crowns of Sweden and the Pomeranian griffin. All this is very telling, for King Eric of Pomerania's fleet was indeed assisted in this war by ships and forces from across Scandinavia.[1]

Since the opening decades of the fifteenth century, Denmark gradually established a fleet that not only controlled and protected Danish waters, but also transported men and weapons to the front lines. In fulfilling this, the king depended, as in the Middle Ages, on his governors and bishops for support. The Danish fleet, however, remained relatively insubstantial until the sixteenth century. Defence was organized and financed by the state, a fact that can be taken as a clear indicator of modern statehood, and by the eve of the seventeenth century, Danish power and hegemony rested chiefly on the strength of its navy. Kings Christian IV (1588-1648) and Christian V (1670-99) recognized the importance of a strong naval force that was capable of protecting Danish and Norwegian positions, and particularly securing interests in the Skagerrak, the North Sea and in Baltic waters.[2]

During the Middle Ages, the Hanseatic League dominated the trading networks that spanned across Scandinavia and the Baltic. For a long time, this thwarted the Scandinavians' attempts to create their own naval capabilities. There is consensus among scholars that Denmark did not start building a fleet until well into the fifteenth century.[3] Against the backdrop of this evidence, this paper will argue that King Eric of Pomerania, who headed the Scandinavian Union, or the Union of Kalmar (1397-1520), between 1388/9 and 1439/40, launched a process of state modernization. This process was initiated during a war against Holstein in the early fifteenth century. This modernization subsequently exerted a deep influence on Danish maritime warfare. After 1452, strategic calculations generally included scenarios for armed confrontation at sea.[4] This paper also attempts to document that during the reigns of the Danish Kings Christian I, Hans, Christian II, Frederik I, Christian III and Frederik II, efforts were made to strengthen and expand the Danish fleet. By the sixteenth century this had evolved into a strong military force in the service of the early modern state. During the Nordic Seven Years' War (1563-70), the naval fleet of Denmark—that at the time also comprised Sweden—became particularly active in the Baltic.

II

THE KALMAR UNION AS A NAVAL POWER

During the first half of the fourteenth century, Denmark could hardly be called a state proper. No king ruled between 1332-40, and the crown lands were divided into several units or pawned fiefs. Various territories were controlled by German aristocrats. The kingdom of Denmark was, however, rebuilt after 1340 under the leadership of Valdemar Atterdag (died 1375) and later under his daughter Margaret (died 1412). Queen Margaret founded the Kalmar Union during the summer of 1397, after Valdemar had conquered Scania, Öland and Gotland from Sweden in 1360-1.

In the late fourteenth century, the Danish navy comprised at most ten ships. In the event of war, they were joined by additional vessels of the various governors, bishops and cities. The old feudal defence system was still in place. Queen Margaret and Eric of Pomerania hired mercenaries from England and commandeered ships belonging to merchants.[5]

Despite the consolidation of crown authority on land, control of the adjacent seas left much to be desired. Pirates and German privateers (the so-called 'Viktualian brethren') posed a serious threat to merchants at the end of the fourteenth century. The people of Mecklenburg were particularly active as pirates. They garrisoned Stockholm on several occasions, raided the Danish and Norwegian coastline, and inflicted substantial losses on Danish and Hanseatic ships. However, they were not alone in committing these or similar acts, as it was no secret that the King of Denmark and his men were engaged in acts of piracy in the Baltic.[6] Yet the king was also ready to fight pirates and secure maritime trade routes. In 1414 and 1417, for example, Eric of Pomerania sponsored 'peace-ships' that were mustered to assist the Hanseatic League in suppressing piracy. The Danish king gradually assumed the role of protecting maritime merchants. Towards the middle of the sixteenth century, Danish vessels regularly patrolled in the Belts, the Baltic, the North Sea as well as the Norwegian coast, with the aim of crushing piracy. If anyone had plans to rob merchants at sea, it was advised to do so only with the permission of the king's men.[7]

Around the same time, the king made efforts to secure the Danish coastline. As early as 1248 and 1308, Lübeck's fleet had succeeded in conquering and plundering Copenhagen, but a fresh attack in 1428 was successfully rebuffed. This Danish repulse is rather significant, for the region around the Sound (*Øresund*) witnessed growth during the opening decades of the fifteenth century, not least thanks to the enhanced trade between the Baltic region and Western Europe. Eric of Pomerania constructed a fortress in Malmö and founded the city of Landskrona in 1413 in the hope of attracting Dutch and English merchants. He also built Elsinore and upgraded the fortress Krogen, and in 1416 he took over the city of Copenhagen from the bishop of

Roskilde. The city became the new Danish capital and the principal harbour of the navy. The region around the Sound represented the dominant political and economic node of the Kalmar Union. Eric of Pomerania ruled the three kingdoms as a single entity, and hoped to consolidate inter-Scandinavian relations.[8]

In the wars against the Wendish towns of the Hanseatic League, naval craft were deployed to sever maritime trade networks, particularly in 1427. In July that year, the Danes overwhelmed a fleet of 36 trading vessels carrying a large cargo of salt, and in retaliation the Hanseatic towns under the command of Tidemann Steen launched an unsuccessful attack on Copenhagen. Later, a Scandinavian fleet comprising more than 70 vessels and 1,400 armed men successfully launched an attack on Stralsund, but a second offensive on the port city some days later resulted in heavy casualties numbering around 500-600 men. Among the prisoners of war taken by Stralsund were soldiers of the bishop of Roskilde. Although Rostock and Stralsund had negotiated for peace with Eric of Pomerania in 1428, a peace treaty was only signed in the summer of 1435. In the aftermath of the war, the Hanseatic towns continued to enjoy their privileges across Scandinavia.[9]

Contrary to existing research it should be underscored that the king's cousins, the dukes of Pomerania, helped him with ships and soldiers and were actively involved in the enduring war to secure control over Schleswig. As mentioned earlier, the Danish flag in Lübeck clearly depicted the four participating groups of vessels from the three Scandinavian countries and from Pomerania in the fleet of the Kalmar Union.

During his war with the Wendish Hanseatic cities, Eric had introduced the Sound Toll in 1429. Over time, the Danish kings earned considerable wealth from the international trade passing through the Sound. The Toll was a continuation of a small toll originally levied at Skanör-Falsterbo in Scania, and in some ways it foreshadowed new patterns of trade and exchange during the fifteenth and sixteenth centuries. The Sound Toll was to be paid at Helsingborg. As ships increased in size and tonnage, Eric demanded a toll of 1 silver nobel for each ship. After 1429, this was to be paid at the fortress of Elsinore (Krogen) located on the coast of Sealand across from Helsingborg. Both castles were placed under the command of the king's loyal governor, Peder Oxe. Ships belonging to the Wendish Hanseatic towns were, however, soon exempt from the tolls, but all other foreign vessels were required to pay. Over a long period, the Sound Tolls were raised on several occasions. The payment of these dues is well documented, and it transpires from surviving records that the Dutch came to dominate Baltic trade well before the end of the fifteenth century.[10]

Documents recording the development of the Danish royal fleet are extant, and ship lists have been preserved for the years 1471 and 1487. In the early spring of 1487, King John (Hans) convened his governors and bishops in Copenhagen together with ships and soldiers. Gotland was about to be claimed by Sweden, and pressure was exerted on the Danish governor, Iver Axelsson (Thott), to preserve the island for Denmark. The move was successful. Some ships in the king's fleet arrived from Danzig. Between 29 and 40 vessels (including the ships from Danzig) were mustered, of which at least four were Cravels (Kravellen), i.e. large craft built according to innovative standards.[11]

As the Union of Kalmar faced dissolution in the fifteenth century, the Swedes and Danes directed their naval forces to transport troops and also engage one another in combat. The conflict became endemic, and the king lost control of Sweden, but he retained control over Denmark and Norway. After the 1480s, a permanent Danish–Norwegian navy was established. It proved instrumental in the ensuing struggles against Sweden and Lübeck, as well as for imposing blockades, shuttling Danish troops between Denmark and Stockholm, or laying siege to places in Sweden as well as Finland, which was under Swedish control at the time. Maritime domination made it possible to sidestep the vast forests of southern Sweden. By the end of the fifteenth century, the king had begun to assert himself as the protector of Baltic shipping, an industry that was not in the hands of Scandinavians.[12]

During the reign of King John (Hans) (1481-1513), the royal fleet expanded to 28 ships. A naval war against Sweden was waged between early 1509 and 1512 and the Danish fleet emerged victorious on several occasions. Sweden, by contrast, launched a concerted effort in 1522 to crush Danish–Norwegian maritime dominance when it acquired an entire fleet from Lübeck. In that year, this Hanseatic town joined forces with Sweden until Christian II, the last monarch of the Union of Kalmar, took flight. His departure was a major setback for Denmark, not least because he retreated to the Netherlands with a substantial part of the Danish fleet. As a result the new king, Frederik I of Denmark and Norway, was compelled to build up a navy from scratch and by 1532 the Danish fleet comprised a mere five ships. Against the backdrop of this evidence, it is understandable why Christian III (1534-59) and Frederik II (1559-88) launched an intensive shipbuilding programme to expand the navy. By 1558, Denmark's navy comprised 35 vessels including 16 large ships. By that time, Denmark had re-emerged as a formidable naval power in Northern Europe, even surpassing Sweden's fleet in strength and numbers.[13]

III

THE DECLINE OF MEDIEVAL POWER STRUCTURES

On the basis of the evidence brought forward so far, an important question need be raised: What made it possible for both Denmark and Sweden to emerge as naval powers before the middle of the sixteenth century? The answer lies in the collapse of Baltic trade and power relations after *c.* 1500. Steeped in medieval institutions and practices, the Baltic had been sealed off from the rest of Europe. After 1397, the three Scandinavian kingdoms of Denmark, Norway and Sweden had shared a fate in a characteristically medieval union, that brought the territories closer together under the primacy of a Danish royal dynasty.[14]

One may be tempted to conclude that when the Union of Kalmar held sway (1397-1520), real political power in Scandinavia was exercised by the king and his royal councillors. But this was clearly not the case, even if Eric of Pomerania and his progeny evidently sought to expand Scandinavian interests. Political and economic power was, in fact, wielded by the Hanseatic League or to be more precise, by the great merchants of the Wendish Hanseatic towns with Lübeck as their unrivalled leader.[15]

The League clearly dominated trade across the Baltic. Large quantities of food and raw materials sourced from around the Baltic passed through Lübeck and from there were redistributed to other Western European markets. Of minor significance is the flow of goods in the opposite direction as only modest quantities of refined and manufactured wares were sold in the Baltic ports. The Hanseatic towns maintained a rigid political and economic stranglehold over the entire Baltic region, and they clearly perceived it as an exclusive trading preserve for their merchants. For this reason, the Baltic long remained closed to outside forces and developments. During the fifteenth century, however, the Wendish Hanseatic towns began to compete with ports in other parts of Europe, and especially in the Netherlands. This competition intensified to the extent that the Hanseatic towns waged a war against the Netherlands from 1438 until 1441. The Scandinavian monarchs were not unaware of this confrontation, and exploited it successfully with the aim of strengthening their access to markets and trading networks outside the Baltic.[16]

Further to the east of the Baltic—but of less importance for Denmark—another medieval institution held sway: the powerful Order of the Teutonic Knights, whose organizing influence spread from the centre in the present-day Baltic states to eastern Europe. This mighty feudal institution sealed off the Baltic in the east in much the same way as the Hanseatic League did in the south and west.[17]

For centuries, these two powerful medieval institutions held both the Baltic as well as the Scandinavian kingdoms tightly locked. It has been argued that the kings of the Kalmar Union did not rule by the grace of God, but with the consent of the Hanseatic League and the masters of the Teutonic Order. Relations between the Union and the Order remained tense for most of the fifteenth century, and especially after the great battle of Tannenberg/Grünwald in 1410. Eric of Pomerania sought until 1422 to regain territories in northern

Estonia that had been sold to the Order in 1346. A war erupted between the Prussian towns and the Order around the middle of the fifteenth century (1454-66).[18]

With the advent of the sixteenth century, the existing structures were doomed and certain to shake the foundations of the Scandinavian kingdoms, especially Denmark. It is next to impossible to pinpoint a specific cause for the decay of the medieval power structures after 1500. The collapse of both the Hanseatic League as well as the Teutonic Order may very well be regarded as a localized event within the context of broader European developments that included a crisis of the Roman Church and its challenge by the Protestant Reformation, as well as the weakening of the central authority enjoyed by the Holy Roman Emperor. What occurred, in short, was a breakdown of a united Western Christian world that had been sustained by the twin authorities of the Pope and the Emperor. Their pre-eminence and worldly authority were eventually supplanted by territorial states. The end of the Union of Kalmar, the Order of the Teutonic Knights, and the weakening economic stranglehold of the Hanseatic towns on the Baltic Sea and its surrounding regions can be taken as local manifestations in the broader meltdown of medieval norms and values. The old overland trading routes across central Europe lost ground and were replaced by networks of maritime trade that skirted the European Atlantic seaboard. The long-term outcome of these developments was a complete shift in Europe's economic and trading activity away from northern Italy and its centres such as Venice, Florence and Milan. The future now belonged to Western Europe's seafaring nations and their trading centres such as Lisbon, Antwerp, Amsterdam and London.[19]

As these cities and their hinterlands emerged as important nodes of trade, they became highly urbanized, and witnessed not only a growth in population, but also in power and wealth on a scale hitherto unseen in Europe. The rapidly growing, densely populated centres became increasingly dependent on imported foodstuffs as well as raw materials. The flow of bulk commodities including grain, ore and lumber grew significantly at the beginning of the sixteenth century. This development also spelt the end of the Hanseatic League's firm grip on the Baltic trade.

Neither Lübeck nor any of the other Hanseatic towns around the Baltic were capable of coping with the heightened volume of trade. In the course of just a few decades they had all been sidelined. The Dutch and English merchants assumed an ever increasing share of the Baltic trade. Captains and sailors from these nations were in a position to leverage on the significant improvements in marine technology that had been initiated chiefly in the Atlantic trading world. A growing number of commercial vessels (from the end of the fourteenth and the beginning of the fifteenth century) circumnavigated the north of Jutland, sailed to the Danish inner waters and then proceeded via the Sound to various Baltic destinations. This route emerged as the principal shipping artery and remained so for many centuries. The old route via Lübeck and north Germany lapsed into disuse. With these changed patterns of commercial activity, the character of the Baltic, too, changed from an area under almost exclusive Hanseatic control to an open sea, frequented freely by vessels from the principal Western seafaring nations. This remoulded network of trade and commercial interaction gave Denmark a new-found role as a maritime gateway.[20] With the collapse of the old powers, Denmark, much like its Swedish counterpart, was at liberty to establish its own niche in the new commercial trading system. This development, in fact, marked the beginning of a long and costly road to modern statehood.

The most visible symptom of the new political order was the aforementioned dissolution of the Kalmar Union following its protracted decline. The last Union king, Christian II (1513-23), sought to purge the Swedish elite in the Union with the so-called Bloodbath of Stockholm in 1520. This move proved to be a major faux pas and only served to accelerate the process of disintegration. Gustav I Eriksson (Vasa) emerged as the King of Sweden (1521/23-60) and founded a new dynasty.[21]

With the dissolution of the Union, two independent states emerged: on the one hand Vasa Sweden, and on the other the remains of the former Union, the dual monarchy of Denmark and

Norway. The struggle between these two state entities for mastery of the Baltic—known as the *Dominium Maris Baltici* or Dominium of the Baltic Sea—became the most pronounced objective of each player until the Great Northern War of 1720-1.[22]

In the wake of the crucial remoulding of international maritime trading patterns, Denmark found itself in a fortunate but unfamiliar position in the northern European political landscape. The Sound now functioned as the gateway to the Baltic, and Denmark controlled that passage entirely. Its role as gatekeeper was significantly enhanced and greatly underscored following the boom in Baltic trade.[23] It is important to emphasize that the balance of power in the Baltic was more than just an ephemeral issue of essentially regional significance. In the course of the sixteenth century, the Baltic emerged as a region of sensitive strategic importance that attracted and also affected many European powers, not just Denmark. It was imperative for Denmark to preserve and protect its interests with a powerful fleet.[24]

IV

DANISH MARITIME POWER AND THE NORDIC SEVEN YEARS WAR

In the early 1500s, innovations in shipbuilding and weaponry brought about many changes. Ships became bigger, faster, featured heavier artillery with greater firing power that enabled them to engage and destroy whole fleets. These changes prompted the Danish monarchs to assume control of shipyards and monitor shipbuilding. In 1509, King John (Hans) gave orders to build ships at a yard at Nakskov Fjord, and around at the same time, the first ships were built in Copenhagen (Bremerholm). Since the 1540s, the capital city emerged as the centre of the royal shipbuilding programme, employing carpenters and specialists from all over Denmark. Many Norwegians served as shipmates and crew.[25]

During the reign of King Christian III, a naval fleet was built that was comparable in size to the greatest fleets of Europe. The fleet was under the command of an admiral when operating in Danish and foreign waters. The governor of the castle of Copenhagen was entrusted with the administrative responsibility in all matters pertaining to the fleet. Though the cities and the nobility joined the war effort by sending their ships, there were fewer vessels belonging to nobles. The naval fleet of 1548 consisted of 11 big ships and 14 smaller craft. In 1558, the number of big ships had increased to 16. This expansion continued under the reign of Frederik II.[26]

In the beginning, the Danish king only controlled the coastal waters, particularly the waters near the Sound. But by the end of the sixteenth century he exercised control over almost the entire Baltic Sea. This was possible not only by securing trade and demanding toll for passage through the Sound, but also because he disposed over a large fleet and could demand respect for the Danish flag and laws of admiralty. The king, however, needed merchantmen to transport foodstuffs or building materials to Copenhagen, as well as to the more remote parts of his realm that included Iceland, the Faroe Islands, Norway, Gotland and the island of Oesel (1558-1645).[27]

Denmark's role as gatekeeper is enshrined in the maritime code of 1561. Though its provisions are modelled on Hanseatic and Dutch laws, it stands out as an independent work in its own right. Apart from regulating relations between the captain and the crew, the code clearly expresses the importance attached to the sea and seaborne trade by the King of Denmark.[28]

The Nordic Seven Years' War (1563-70) waged between Denmark and Sweden also saw the Danish fleet in action. King Frederik II hoped to ban foreign commerce from accessing Sweden. Using the navy to provide logistical support to the land troops proved difficult, but combat at sea proved decisive. This was because the Swedes based their tactics on firing power rather than on a boarding strategy preferred by the Danes and Lübeckers. Eventually, Sweden gained the upper hand in the conflict and successfully lifted the Danish blockade. In September 1563, the fleets were engaged in combat when a fierce battle broke out between Gotland and Medelsten. Even if the Swedes subsequently withdrew to Stockholm, the Danish–Lübeck fleet was simply too small to successfully impose a blockade. In October, Swedish vessels called at German ports without any difficulty.[29]

In a move to tighten the blockade, King Frederik together with

Lübeck and Poland vigorously lobbied the Hanseatic cities to discontinue their trade with Sweden. He was particularly preoccupied with measures that would accommodate the naval and commercial policies of Rostock and Stralsund toward Sweden. In May 1564, the Danes inflicted serious damage on the Swedes, but only at a high cost. Additional successes followed in August when the Swedish fleet withdrew and the blockade on Stockholm could be tightened. Only 36 ships called at Stockholm that year, resulting in a severe shortage of salt.[30]

The tide of fortune began to change, however. In 1565 and 1566, the Danish fleet was damaged by severe weather. Even if the Swedes were in a position to run the Danish blockade, they hardly had any authority over the Baltic Sea. Nevertheless, they managed to capture a Dutch fleet carrying salt and this success helped them tide over the crisis. King Frederik II of Denmark managed to reconstitute his fleet by the summer of 1567, but there was no confrontation at sea that year. A tight financial situation as well as the lack of manpower on both sides reduced hostile encounters to a minimum for the rest of the war.[31]

The Nordic Seven Years' War marked a significant change: never before in Scandinavia had sustained campaigns been carried out on such a large scale and for such a prolonged period of time. Also, both sides mobilized significant resources for naval warfare, further escalating the cost of the conflict. There were major confrontations at sea. While the fleets proved incapable of lending close support to the land-based war campaigns, the monarchs of Denmark and Sweden increasingly realized the importance of navies.

The war represents the first modern conflict between the two Scandinavian powers and was rooted in the desire of both sides to dominate the Baltic. The struggle resurfaced during the 1570s and many new naval craft were commissioned. With the easing of tensions in the 1580s, both sides reduced the size of their navies. The only exception was the sizeable but short-lived galley force built for Sweden's protracted war with Russia. The Swedish Civil War (1597-9) triggered a new naval race with Denmark, but during the first half of the seventeenth century, the two navies remained more or less static in terms of size and strength.[32]

V

CONCLUSION

Between 1410 and 1435 Eric of Pomerania fought the counts of Holstein to secure control over the Duchy of Schleswig, and from 1426 he also engaged the Wendish Hanseatic towns. To this end, he received military and naval support not only from Denmark, but also from Norway, Sweden–Finland and Pomerania. His navy featured the latest innovations in shipbuilding and navy tactics, and he no longer relied only on the feudal medieval defence system. The naval fleet adopted a common flag during the course of combat. This development, coupled with the king's policies and initiatives, generally portray the first decades of the fifteenth century as a period of transition and modernization in late medieval Scandinavia. Eric of Pomerania emerged as one of the founders of the Scandinavian and later Danish naval fleet.

The decline of the Hanseatic League and the Teutonic Order during the first decades of the sixteenth century paved the way for Denmark's role as the gateway to, and gatekeeper of, the Baltic Sea. The endemic struggle to bring Sweden back into the Union of Kalmar resulted in the etablishment of the first small Danish royal fleet built by King John (Hans) at the end of the fifteenth century. Over the next century, this fleet was expanded, and during the second half of the sixteenth century and especially during the Nordic Seven Years' War, the importance of Danish naval power in the Baltic became increasingly clear. During the 1580s, both Denmark and Sweden reduced the size of their fleets before a new naval race began at the end of the sixteenth century.

NOTES

1. See among several publications especially J. Steenstrup, K. Erslev et al., eds., *Danmarks Riges Historie*, vol. 2, Copenhagen, 1898-1905, p. 438.

2. E. Hornborg, *Kampen om Östersjön*, Stockholm, 1945, pp. 78 ff. L. Jespersen, 'The Macht staat in Seventeenth-Century Denmark', *Scandinavian Journal of History*, vol. 10, 1985, pp. 271-304.
3. W. Christensen, *Dansk Statsforvaltning i det 15. Aarhundrede*, rpt, Copenhagen, 1903, pp. 363-4. J.H. Barfod, *Flaadens fødsel*, Copenhagen, 1990, passim.
4. For the history of the Kalmar Union, see L.-O. Larsson, *Kalmarunionens tid från Drottning Margareta till Kristian II*, Falun, 1997. J.E. Olesen, *Rigsråd-Kongemagt-Union: Studier over det danske rigsråd og den nordiske kongemagts politik 1434-1449*, Aarhus, 1980. Christensen, *Dansk Statsforvaltning*, pp. 355-6, argues that Eric of Pomerania deployed more than old-fashioned feudal forces in his war against the counts of Holstein and the Wendish Hanseatic cities.
5. J. Bill, B. Poulsen, F. Rieck and O. Ventegodt, eds., *Dansk Søfarts Historie*, vol. 1, Copenhagen, 1997, p. 190. A. Tuck, 'Some Evidence for Anglo-Scandinavian Relations at the End of the Fourteenth Century', in *Medieval Scandinavia*, vol. 5, 1972, pp. 75-88.
6. Bill, Poulsen, Rieck and Ventegodt, *Dansk Søfarts Historie*, vol. 1, p. 189.
7. Ibid.
8. J.E. Olesen, 'Erich von Pommerns Alleinherrschaft 1412-1439/40', in "*huru thet war talet j kalmarn*". *Union und Zusammenarbeit in der Nordischen Geschichte. 600 Jahre Kalmarer Union (1397-1997)*, eds. D. Kattinger et al., Hamburg, 1997, pp. 215-16.
9. K. Fritze and G. Krause, *Seekriege der Hanse. Das erste Kapitel deutscher Seekriegsgeschichte*, Berlin, 1997, pp. 117-27.
10. K. Hørby, 'Øresundstolden og den skånske skibstold. Spørgsmålet om kontinuitet', in *Middelalderstudier. Tilegnede Aksel E. Christensen paa tresårsdagen 11. september 1966*, Copenhagen, 1966, pp. 245-72. M. Venge, *Fra åretold til toldetat. Middelalderen indtil 1660. Dansk Toldhistorie*, Copenhagen, 1987.
11. Bill, Poulsen, Rieck and Ventegodt, *Dansk Søfarts Historie*, vol. 1, pp. 208 ff. Christensen, *Statsforvaltning*, pp. 100-6.
12. J. Glete, *Navies and Nations. Warships, Navies and State Building in Europe and America, 1500-1860*, vol. 1, Stockholm, 1993, p. 137.
13. Bill, Poulsen, Rieck and Ventegodt, *Dansk Søfarts Historie*, vol. 1, pp. 190 ff. Glete, *Navies and Nations*, p. 137.
14. J.E. Olesen, 'Pommern, Skandinavien und der Ostseeraum in der ersten

Hälfte des 17. Jahrhunderts', in *Unter der schwedischen Krone. Pommern nach dem Westfälischen Frieden*, ed. I. Asmus, Greifswald, 1998, p. 13.

15. A. Grassmann, ed., *Lübeckische Geschichte*, 2nd edn, Lübeck, 1989.
16. B. Jørgensen, 'Københavnertraktaterne 1441 og deres tilblivelse', in *Middelalderstudier*, pp. 273-304.
17. See among other contributions W. Sonthofen, *Der Deutsche Orden*, Augsburg, 1955, passim.
18. J.E. Olesen, 'Norden og Livland i det 15. århundrede', *Nordisk Tidsskrift*, 1981, pp. 314-25.
19. J. Merriman, *A History of Modern Europe from the Renaissance to the Present*, New York/London, 1996, pp. 19, 181 ff.
20. K.J.V. Jespersen, *A History of Denmark*, Houndmills/New York, 2004, pp. 14 ff.
21. Larsson, *Kalmarunionens tid*, pp. 433 ff.
22. K.J.V. Jespersen, 'Rivalry without Victory. Denmark, Sweden and the Struggle for the Baltic, 1500-1720', in *In Quest of Trade and Security. The Baltic in Power Politics 1500-1990*, vol. 1 *(1500-1890)*, ed. G. Rystad, K.-R. Böhme and W. M. Carlgren, Lund, 1994, pp. 137-76.
23. Jespersen, *A History of Denmark*, p. 15.
24. Jespersen, 'The Machtstaat', passim.
25. Bill, Poulsen, Rieck and Ventegodt, *Dansk Søfarts Historie*, vol. 1, p. 190.
26. J.H. Barfod, *Christian 3.s flåde*, Copenhagen, 1995, pp. 123-42.
27. J.E. Olesen, 'Dominium Maris Baltici. Kampen om Østersøen 1625-1643', *Militært Tidsskrift*, 1984, p. 214.
28. Bill, Poulsen, Rieck and Ventegodt, *Dansk Søfarts Historie*, vol. 1, pp. 193-4.
29. J. Lavery, *Germany's Northern Challenge. The Holy Roman Empire and the Scandinavian Struggle for the Baltic, 1563-1570*, Boston/Leiden, 2002, pp. 21, 89.
30. Ibid., p. 89.
31. Ibid., p. 90.
32. J. Glete, *Navies and Nations*, p. 138.

CHAPTER 9

The Dutch Republic—A Water-Borne Power?

Naval Power and the Maritime Sector in the Netherlands (c. 1590-1795)

KAREL DAVIDS

INTRODUCTION

The Dutch Republic was an alliance between seven more or less sovereign provinces,[1] sharing a number of central agencies concerned chiefly with the conduct of war and foreign relations. This Republic was one of the great maritime powers of the early modern period. How was that possible? The Swedish maritime historian Jan Glete has taken Dutch historians to task for emphasizing the supposed shortcomings in the organization and operation of the navy of the United Provinces which had their origins in the federal, decentralized nature of the republican constitution. The focus, Glete has argued, should instead be on the efficiency with which resources for the deployment of naval power were mobilized as well as the effectiveness with which this power was actually used in relation to its major opponents.[2] The nature of these resources, however, is left unspecified in Glete's account, except that they are said to have been raised through custom duties and, temporarily, through taxes. Nor does it adequately transpire from Glete's overview, why and to what degree the 'fiscal–military state' in the Dutch Republic actually succeeded in mobilizing resources for the deployment of naval power.

The resources for the naval power of the Dutch Republic are the central theme of this paper. The argument here focuses on the relation between the Dutch Navy and the maritime sector at large. The central question raised is: To what extent was Dutch maritime power based on the sea? Or, in other words, to what extent did the naval power of the Dutch Republic rest on its maritime sector, or the sector of overseas trade and shipping respectively, and to what extent did it rely on other resources? In order to answer this central question, two key aspects of naval power, i.e. money and manpower, will be examined. Where did the financial and human resources of the Dutch Navy come from? After demonstrating that the burden of the maintenance of Dutch naval power was in course of time partly shifted to sources outside overseas trade and shipping, the paper analyses why this shift went further in some periods than in others, which alternative solutions for sustaining the burden were tried and why those solutions were adopted or discarded. The latter question also involves a discussion of the role of the East India Company (Verenigde Oostindische Compagnie, or VOC) in the naval power of the Dutch Republic.

II

MONEY

The administration of naval affairs in the Dutch Republic was entrusted to five separate Admiralties located in Amsterdam, Rotterdam (called the *Maze*), Zeeland, Friesland and the northern part of Holland (called the *Noorderkwartier*). The functions of these agencies of the central state were to provide protection to ships, ports and coastal areas, to recruit and pay crew of warships, to adjudicate on the seizure of prizes and to collect and administer custom duties.

The expenses for the execution of these tasks were paid from various sources,[3] which—historically and analytically—can be divided into primary and secondary sources of income. Primary sources of income were revenues earmarked for the Admiralties. These included the standard custom duties on commodities, called *convooien en licenten*, which were collected by officials of the Admiralties stationed at the land and sea borders of the Republic; a temporary surcharge was introduced in 1652 (which continued till 1725) known as the *derde verhoging*; a series of taxes on shipping and trade called the last- en veilgelden; contributions from the East-India Company compensating for its exemption from custom duties as well as last- en veilgelden; and a portion of the revenues from the sale of prizes. All these sources of income had a common feature—they were largely generated by the maritime sector; even the bulk of custom duties was raised in the seaports, not along the land borders of the Republic.

Secondary sources of income were revenues that were assigned to the Admiralties on an ad hoc basis. These included subsidies granted by the provinces of the Republic to defray expenses on equipment or construction of new ships; public loans contracted by the Admiralties with the approval of the highest authority of the Republic,—the States General; and a fund formed from the revenues of an extraordinary veilgeld on overseas shipping introduced in 1697, called the *verhoogde last- en veilgelden*. Except for the latter, these sources of income were not primarily generated by the maritime sector.

What was the relative importance of these sources of income for the maintenance of the Dutch Navy? Data presented in Table 9.1 reveal the picture for the period up to the end of the First Anglo-Dutch War (1652-4). This was the period of the so-called 'Old Navy', when the nucleus of permanent, specialized warships maintained by the Admiralties was still relatively small compared to the 'outer shell' of ships temporarily leased from private shipowners or trading companies. The first war with England marked the beginning of the transition towards the 'New Navy', which was almost entirely composed of full-time, specially built men-of-war.[4]

Although the total income of the Admiralties for later periods is not exactly known, several estimates are available highlighting the

TABLE 9.1: SOURCES OF INCOME OF ADMIRALTIES, 1629-54

	Zeeland 1629-49 (in per cent)	All Admiralties 1652-4 (excluding prize money) (in per cent)
Convooien en licenten	68	26
Prize money	11	
Last- en veilgelden		23
Contributions from VOC	4	3
Subsidies from provinces	6	33
Other (public loans, etc.)	11	14
Total abs. (guilders)	16,112,000 = 100	20,947,000 = 100
Average per year (guilders)	767,238	6,982,333

Sources: Enthoven, 'Slag bij Duins', p. 72. Id., 'Mercurius en Mars bijeen', p. 59.

relation between various sources of income over different periods of time. These relate especially to the most important Admiralty, the Admiralty of Amsterdam. Between 1682 and 1701, the combined income of the Admiralties (excluding Zeeland) deriving from subsidies granted by the provinces was twice as high as from the convooien en licenten: on average 4 million guilders a year as compared to 2 million.[5] With regard to the relation between prize money and the convooien en licenten, it has been calculated for the Admiralty of Amsterdam that during the First Anglo-Dutch War income from the former was slightly more than half of the latter, but was as least as high during the Second and Third Anglo-Dutch Wars (1664-7, 1672-4). During the Nine Years' War and the War of Spanish Succession, however, the amount did not exceed between 7 and 10 per cent.[6]

For the Admiralty of Amsterdam during the 1714-51 period, income has been broken down and a distinction made between primary and secondary sources in Table 9.2. The distinction between the periods before and after 1726 highlights the success of comprehensively restructuring the tariff rates, the collection of the *convooien en licenten* as well as the *last- en veilgelden*. The reforms were introduced by the States General in 1725.

TABLE 9.2: SOURCES OF INCOME OF THE ADMIRALTY OF AMSTERDAM, 1714-51

Source of Income (in per cent)	Period		
	1714-25	1726-51	1714-51
Convooien en licenten	47-55	55-63	
Ordinary last- en veilgelden	12-16	3-4	
Contributions from VOC	8-9	11-12	
Other	4-8	4-8	
Total primary sources			78.7
Extraordinary veilgelden			8.7
Subsidies from provinces			6.3
Public loans			6.2
Total secondary sources			21.3
Total abs. (guilders)			69,035,262 = 100 per cent
Average per year (guilders)			1,865,817

Source: Bruijn, *Admiraliteit van Amsterdam*, pp. 73-7.

Extant evidence on the income of the Admiralties strongly suggests that when the naval power of the Dutch Republic was at its height between the First Anglo-Dutch War and the end of the War of the Spanish Succession (1652-1714) it was supported to a greater extent from sources outside the maritime sector than before or after this period. This was particularly in the form of loans or subsidies paid by the provinces. The burden of financing the Dutch naval power shifted more significantly in the first half of the seventeenth century and again in the post-1714 period. During its clashes with England, Sweden and France, the Dutch Republic would have found itself unable to muster such sea power if the navy's finances had depended entirely on its primary sources of income deriving from overseas shipping and trade.[7]

In reality, the picture was more complex. On the one hand, the burden shifted far more than even these figures suggest, although its consequences cannot as yet be expressed in quantitative terms. In the late seventeenth and early eighteenth century, the range of the *convooi- en licentgelden* and also the *last- en veilgelden* were temporarily and sometimees permanently expanded beyond the sphere of overseas shipping and trade. The increase in the *convooi-en licentgelden* rates approved in 1652 (*derde verhoging*) also applied to overland and riverine trade.[8] Since 1652 the (ordinary) veilgeld was levied on rivers and overland trade as well. Although this duty was abolished in 1725 as part of the general reform of the tariff system, the *lastgeld* was simultaneously extended to all riverine shipping.[9]

On the other hand, shifting the burden was in reality not always as successfully accomplished as it appeared on paper. Subsidies promised by the provinces did not always materialize in practice; by 1755, the provinces had to pay arrears of nearly 9 million guilders to the Admiralties.[10] The partial default of the provinces in turn contributed to a substantial increase in debt held by the Admiralties themselves. At the end of the War of the Spanish Succession, the combined debt of the three Admiralties in Holland stood at nearly 9.4 million guilders. By 1790, the total debt of the five Admiralties amounted to no less than 16 million guilders.[11] A large part of their debt consisted of claims on the Admiralty Boards by suppliers and naval officers who often had to wait for years before their bills were settled. For example, of the debt of nearly 6.5 million guilders owed by the Amsterdam Admiralty at the end of the War of Spanish Succession, 2 million were owed to suppliers and 4 million to the Board's own naval officers.[12] The financial cost of sustaining Dutch maritime power was thus partly shifted to the superior officers of the Admiralties themselves.

III

MANPOWER

Manpower is another key aspect of maritime power. As in the case of financial resources, the question is: to what extent was the manpower of the Dutch Navy recruited from the (non-naval) maritime sector of the Dutch Republic? To what extent were the crews of the Dutch fleet drawn from the 'pool' of native seafarers in other branches of the Dutch shipping industry?

The (estimated) evolution of total employment in the Dutch maritime sector during the seventeenth and eighteenth centuries is shown in Table 9.3.

All the estimates given in Table 9.3 pertain to 'normal' times in the history of Dutch shipping, i.e. periods when the overall level of employment, or the ratio between different branches, did not abruptly change as a result of large-scale war or the expansion of the navy and privateering that accompanied it. Such changes occurred during the three Anglo-Dutch Wars of the seventeenth century, the wars with France during the reign of Louis XIV and the Fourth Anglo-Dutch War between 1780 and 1784. Employment levels in the navy during the first three Anglo-Dutch Wars as well as the Nine Years' War, for example, peaked at over 20,000 men and in the War of the Spanish Succession were between 14,000 and 17,000 men; the number of seamen sailing on Zeeland privateers during the latter war varied between 4,500 and 7,000. During the Fourth Anglo-Dutch War, the total number of seafarers employed on the Dutch fleet in the spring of 1783 was no less than 19,000.[13]

The extra demand from the navy and privateering in times of large-scale war was only partly balanced by a temporary reduction in activities in other branches of shipping, such as whaling or sea

TABLE 9.3: EMPLOYMENT IN THE DUTCH MARITIME SECTOR IN THE SEVENTEENTH AND EIGHTEENTH CENTURIES

Branch of Shipping	1610	1630-40	1680	1725	1770
Navy	3,000	8,000	3,500	3,500	2,000
Merchant marine	21,500	25,500	22,500	22,000	21,000
East India Company	2,000	4,000	8,500	11,000	11,500
Whaling		1,500	9,000	9,000	6,000
Sea fisheries	6,500	7,000	6,500	4,000	4,000
Grand total	33,000	46,000	50,000	49,500	44,500

Source: Davids, 'Maritime Labour', p. 42.

fisheries. The total demand in the Dutch maritime sector in these conditions far exceeded the ordinary limits of about 44,000-50,000 men. For its supply of manpower, the navy did not solely rely either in 'normal' or in 'exceptional' circumstances on the capacity of the Dutch maritime sector alone. A substantial proportion of seamen on Dutch warships were always recruited from outside the Dutch Republic, and even from outside the maritime sector. After an initial decline in the first decades of the seventeenth century, this proportion steadily grew from the later seventeenth through the eighteenth century, as samples from payrolls of Dutch men-of-war reveal (Table 9.4).

The presence of foreigners on board was in itself not a peculiar characteristic of warships. As a whole, the maritime sector of the Dutch Republic always relied on the employment of foreign seamen.

TABLE 9.4: GEOGRAPHICAL ORIGINS OF PETTY OFFICERS AND COMMON SEAMEN IN THE DUTCH NAVY IN THE SEVENTEENTH AND EIGHTEENTH CENTURIES

Geographical origin	Admiralty, year(s) of sample (in per cent)								
	Zeeland 1600	Zeeland 1669	Zeeland 1685-6	Zeeland 1694	Zeeland 1709	Amsterdam 1720-33	Zeeland 1745-6	Zeeland 1769-72	Noorderkwartier 1772-3
Zeeland	34	60	60	17	37	17	6		
Holland	10	8	5	36	14	38	14	29	24
Rest of Dutch Republic	7	7	2	10	4	12**	10	7	9
Total Dutchmen	51	75	67	63	55	50	41	42	33
Southern Netherlands	14	4	6	10	2				
British Isles	14.5	2	4	3	4		5		
Germany	8.5	2		7	12	19	17	31	35
Scandinavia/Baltic	8	7		10	14	24	17	16	23
Rest	4	10	23*	7	13	7	20	11	9
Total foreigners	49	25	33	37	5	50	59	58	67
Total (abs.)	422	118	454	558	150	1,243	2,128	268	373

Sources: Bruijn, *Dutch Navy*, pp. 133, 200. Id., *Varend verleden*, pp. 72, 169, 243.

Notes: *Distribution over Germany and Scandinavia/Baltic unknown.
**Distribution over Zeeland and other provinces unknown.

However, what was special about the navy was first, an increase in the proportion of foreigners from the later seventeenth through the eighteenth century to a level that was not matched by any other branch of shipping (not even by the VOC), and second, a growth in the numbers of inexperienced sailors, i.e. sailors who had never been to sea prior to their recruitment by the navy. The Admiralties increasingly employed men who had no previous experience in the maritime sector. Complaints about the 'incompetence' of newly-hired hands became louder and more frequent after the 1730s. At the outbreak of the Fourth Anglo-Dutch War in 1780, the armed readiness of the Dutch fleet was seriously hampered by the lack of sufficient numbers of skilled seamen.[14]

The diminished inflow of Dutch seamen from other branches of the maritime sector into the navy was partly due to the structural developments that were beyond the control of the navy and in part to specific policy decisions. Due to economic and demographic changes in the coastal provinces, the 'pool' of seafarers in the Netherlands as a whole dwindled in the course of the eighteenth century.[15] After stagnating from about 1680 onwards, the cost of living in Holland began to rise again after 1740.[16] In these circumstances, the Admiralties were less successful in recruiting seasoned seafarers from the Netherlands as such, because the navy's wages for petty officers and common seamen remained relatively low especially when compared to other branches of shipping. After an increase of nearly 50 per cent in the course of the 1620s and 1630s, the wages in the navy stagnated till the beginning of the nineteenth century. Wages in the merchant marine, by contrast, were less rigid and moved to higher levels. While an able seaman on a naval vessel between *c.* 1640 and 1800 could not earn more than 10 to 11 guilders a month, his colleague on a merchantman could earn a monthly wage of up to 15 guilders by the eighteenth century.[17] Thus, seamen employed in the navy suffered more from a decline in real wages than seafarers in the merchant marine. Faced with the almost perennial shortage of funds, the naval authorities were therefore unwilling to introduce a structural increase in wages. A temporary bonus during time of war was all they were prepared to offer.

Yet, the Admiralties did not swing to the other extreme either, i.e. resorting to forced labour to fill the complement of warships. Pressure or conscription was never used. Port cities and coastal areas of the Dutch Republic were not roamed by press gangs and merchantmen, whalers or fishing boats were not held up by naval vessels in search of able-bodied mariners. The States General or the Admiralties in wartime only went as far as to oblige other branches of shipping to deliver 20 per cent of their complements to the navy (or an equivalent in money) or arbitrarily prolonged term of service.[18] Like the refusal to raise wages, this hesitation to resort to outright force was also not the ineluctable outcome of a structural economic development, but rather the result of particular policy decisions.

IV

POLITICAL CONDITIONS

This overview of the changes in the financial and human resources of the Dutch Navy leads to the following question: How was it possible that the burden of maintaining Dutch naval power between 1652 and 1713 was shifted largely to sources outside overseas trade and shipping compared to the period after the War of the Spanish Succession? The best way to explain this shift is to refer to the dominant personalities in Dutch politics at that time, for instance, the Grand Pensionaries of Holland, Johan de Witt (1653-72) and Anthonie Heinsius (1689-1720), and Stadtholder Willem III (1672-1702), who in their formal roles as 'high officials' of the provincial estates were extremely adept in making the political system 'work' for the sake of building and maintaining a strong navy.[19] Yet, it would be fallacious to claim that the office of the Grand Pensionary was devoid of any skilful incumbent once Heinsius had disappeared from the scene. It would be even more difficult to defend the proposition that the stadtholders of the eighteenth century were never in a position to repeat the political feats of Willem III. In fact, after restoring the stadtholderate in all provinces of the Republic in 1747, stadtholders obtained more leverage over the political system, not just through the power of their office, but also by conferring patronage. It will be hypothesized here that the system after 1713 could have been used to produce the same results for the navy as in the period 1653-1713, if other political circumstances had remained constant.

The crucial point is, of course, that other political circumstances did not remain unchanged. The arrangements made in the later seventeenth and early eighteenth centuries for shifting the burden of maintaining naval power to sources outside overseas trade and shipping, meant in practice that an enhanced part of the costs was borne by the province of Holland as well as by traders, carriers and shipowners using the roads and rivers for entering or leaving the Republic. Other provinces of the Union, together with other branches of the economy, contributed less than their due proportionate share in the costs, or shied away from contributing anything toward the upkeep of the fleet. At a deeper level, the relative success in shifting the burden to sources outside overseas trade and shipping can be ascribed primarily to the willingness of Holland to pay a disproportionate share of the expense. The province of Holland undertook not only to pay nearly 60 per cent of all subsidies earmarked by the States General for the five Admiralties of the Republic (and some 90 per cent of all subsidies for the three Admiralties in Holland itself),[20] but was also far more meticulous in honouring its commitments than any other province of the Union. During the 1701-12 period, for example, Holland remitted more than 6 million guilders toward the subsidy of 11 million guilders promised to the Admiralty of the Maze. By contrast, the other provinces contributed no more than one-seventh (or 245,000 guilders) toward the total sum of 1.7 million guilders they had agreed to contribute.[21] Of the 2,175,000 guilders promised by Utrecht, Gelderland and Overijssel to the Admiralty of Zeeland during the Nine Years War, 1.6 million remained unpaid by 1694.[22] In the early eighteenth century, the provinces of Zeeland and Friesland were not only tardy in funding the Admiralties under own respective jurisdiction, but also borrowed money from those very organizations they had pledged to subsidize![23]

The crucial change in this political equation occurred in Holland. Although not always keen on consenting to the decisions of the States General to subsidize the navy, Holland certainly did more than any other province of the Republic to keep the Admiralties afloat financially, and this, too, over a sustained period of time. Between 1714 and 1741, Holland was the only province to provide financial assistance to the Admiralties.[24] However, the ability of Holland to sustain the navy diminished as its own debt soared during the Nine Years' War and the War of the Spanish Succession from around 160 to 310 million guilders. Its willingness to bear a disproportionate share of the burden finally turned into growing resistance when the War of Austrian Succession led to an increase in its public debt from approximately 300 million to over 360 million guilders. The need to set its own finances in order became paramount.[25] When the stadtholder and the inland provinces began to press for an expansion of the army after *c.* 1770, Holland, led by Amsterdam, refused outright to agree to any decision that did not provide for a proportionate expansion of the fleet and at the same time did not contain rock solid guarantees that the other provinces would in future fully honour their commitments to the financing of the navy.[26]

The disastrous performance of the fleet during the Fourth Anglo-Dutch War (1780-4) finally let to an initial restructuring of the navy's financial base. A reform committee calculated in 1787 that of the navy's estimated expenses totalling 3.6 million guilders, 1.2 million guilders could not be met from the primary sources of income of the Admiralties and should, therefore, be borne by the Union.[27] In 1792, the budget of the Union was enlarged permanently with an entry for expenses on the yearly equipment and construction of new warships. All provinces were hereafter firmly committed to contribute toward the maintenance of the fleet. Holland managed to obtain a commitment from the other provinces that they settle in full their outstanding debts with the Admiralties. The budgetary sum that was earmarked for the navy was almost as high as the amount estimated by the committee in 1787—1 million guilders.[28]

V

ALTERNATIVE ARRANGEMENTS: THE NAVY AND THE EAST INDIA COMPANY

Given that the primary sources of income of the Admiralties often proved woefully inadequate to fund the Dutch naval force, the question arises as to how the financial burden of sustaining Dutch maritime power could have been serviced by any other means. Theoretically, there were several alternative solutions even within the existing system of financing. Income from the *convooien en licenten* or from the *last- en veilgelden* could be raised by changing tariff rates and/or introducing more effective systems of collection that reduced operating costs as well as the possibility of fraud. Another solution was to delegate part of the tasks of the Admiralties to other organizations. A third alternative was to enhance the contribution of the East India Company.

Each of these three alternatives was tried. The tariff rates of the *convooien en licenten* and the *last- en veilgelden* were reversed several times in the seventeenth century, both upwards and downwards, but eventually reduced by a 1725 ordinance of the States General that remained in force until 1816. The structure of tariffs and the method of collection were also simplified. The underlying purpose of this ordinance was to assure the Admiralties of sufficient, regular income by boosting the volume of trade and shipping as well as reducing the possibility of fraud.[29] Two experiments were conducted that farmed out the collection of *convooien en licenten* at least in part, between 1625 and 1638 and again between 1687 and 1690. The objective was to raise the overall revenue from this source of income.[30] Between 1631 and 1656, the Admiralities' duty of providing protection at sea was partly assumed by 'directorates' comprising merchants and supervised by urban governments. These equipped their own warships and financed operations from separate, locally collected, sources of income known as the *directiegelden*.[31] During the War of Spanish Succession, the revenue generated by a special increase of the *last- en veilgelden* was used entirely to promote privateering rather than strengthen the navy; it was not until after the war that the supplementary funds from the higher *last- en veilgelden* were used to equip additional warships for the protection of merchantmen.[32] With regard to the VOC, monetary contributions from 1673 onwards wholly replaced contributions in kind (i.e. ships or cannon). The annual sum to be paid by the VOC as compensation for its exemption from all custom duties was fixed at 300,000 guilders by the States General in 1683, half of which was due to the Admiralty of Amsterdam, a quarter to the Admiralty of Zeeland and one-eighth to each to the Admiralties of the Noorderkwartier and the Maze. The sum was raised to 364,000 guilders in 1690 but remained unchanged thereafter.[33]

These alternative solutions either produced little effect or—in so far as they could have been effective—were obstructed or rejected. The reduction of tariff rates and the simplification of their structure and method of collection only led to a higher income from the convooien en licenten for a few years and resulted in a substantial loss of income from the *last- en veilgelden*: 50,000 to 75,000 guilders a year, instead of 200,000 to 300,000 collected before the mid-1720s.[34] Tax evasion was far from eradicated. Scholarly estimates for the late eighteenth century put the evasion of *convooien en licenten* at slightly more than 30 per cent, with percentages varying from around 30 in the region of the Maze, 40 in the territory under the Admiralty of Amsterdam and nearly 80 in the area under the Admiralty of Zeeland.[35] Farming out the collection of such duties might have led to a substantial rise in total receipts, as the experiments in the 1630s and 1680s had clearly shown. The estimated increase in the 1630s was between 20 and 25 per cent.[36] The reason why these solutions ultimately failed to provide an alternative means of financing Dutch naval power (even if they could be proven effective) lay principally in the resistance from mercantile interests, and foremost in the resistance of commercial lobbies in Amsterdam and Zeeland. Merchants opposed or evaded any new arrangement which they thought compromised the leading position of the Dutch Republic in European trade by raising the burden on commerce.[37] The Admiralties themselves proved to be bastions of resistance on occasion. They were set against the devolution of certain tasks to the urban directorates, a trend that started around 1631 and lasted till the mid-1650s.[38]

The most viable means of financing the naval power was the third option: enhancing the contribution of the East India Company. If the States General had agreed with the VOC in the 1680s to receive a fixed percentage of the revenues generated by the sales of its Asian produce in the Netherlands, say 10 per cent, instead of collecting a fixed sum of money, the income of the Admiralties would have vastly increased. Between 1680 and 1730 the average annual revenues of the sales of the VOC rose from 10,340,000 to 18,560,000 guilders. This would have translated into an increase of payments to the Admiralties from 1,034,000 to 1,856,000 guilders per year.[39] Incidentally, that was almost five times the sum they actually received from the VOC and chose to the average income of the Amsterdam Admiralty (see Table 9.2).

It could be argued that such contributions would have overtaxed the VOC, because the Company already bore part of the expenses for the Admiralties by funding its own escort fleets to merchant shipping east of the Cape of Good Hope for most of the seventeenth and eighteenth centuries. Dutch warships were not dispatched to Asian waters, because the VOC itself acted as a naval power. In the eighteenth century the Company evidently did not invest much in its own fleet that could have acted as an effective force against its European or Asian foes. A telling example of its growing naval impotence was the unsuccessful expedition of 1739 against privateers of Angrey along the Indian coast between Bombay and Goa. This was launched in retaliation for the seizure of two small Company vessels in the previous year.[40] After the 1780s, the VOC was no longer able to uphold its position in Asia on its own. A naval squadron was sent from Holland in 1783 to relieve the VOC forces in the Straits of Malacca, and warships thereafter sailed to Asian waters on a regular basis, escorting East Indiamen along the way.[41] Considering that the dividends paid by the Company between 1680 and 1740 seldom dipped below 20 per cent, and during the 1710s even reached 40 per cent,[42] it is not unreasonable to suppose that the VOC could have contributed much more to the upkeep of the Dutch Navy than it actually did. The reason why this solution was never chosen lay in the political structure of the Dutch Republic itself:

councillors of the Admiralty, urban magistrates and representatives of the States General were often also shareholders and sometimes even served as directors of the East India Company. Shifting a larger part of the burden to the VOC thus was an option not taken.

VI

EPILOGUE

The maritime sector of the Dutch Republic was not surprisingly always an important pillar of Dutch naval power, but it was not able to bear the entire burden of maintaining maritime power on its own. As far as human resources are concerned, the capacity of the Dutch maritime sector to sustain the power of the navy actually decreased steadily after the late seventeenth century. The proportion of foreigners among the crew of Dutch warships rose to a level that was not matched by any other branch of shipping, and the number of untrained sailors markedly increased. With regard to finance, the burden of maintaining the Dutch naval power in the seventeenth and eighteenth centuries shifted to a varying degree to sources outside overseas trade and shipping. While the share of these outside sources diminished after the War of Spanish Succession, the Admiralties' primary sources of income remained insufficient to maintain an efficient or effective navy. One should take into consideration the huge debts of the Admiralties, the inability of the navy to offer competitive wages to seamen and the hapless performance of the fleet in the Fourth Anglo-Dutch War. Alternative solutions for sustaining the burden of maritime power within the existing framework of financing, which would have entailed a more efficient diversion of resources from the maritime sector to the navy, were conceived, as has been shown, and alternative arrangements of finance were sometimes implemented. However, opposition from mercantile circles and the political system of the Republic thwarted the realization of these options. The resources of the maritime sector could have been utilised more effectively for maintaining naval power, if it had not been for the resistance from mercantile interests and the typical features of the Dutch federal system.

NOTES

1. Namely the maritime provinces Holland, Zeeland and Friesland and the inland provinces Utrecht, Gelderland, Overijssel and Groningen.
2. J. Glete, *War and the State in Early Modern Europe: Spain, the Dutch Republic and Sweden as Fiscal-Military States, 1500-1660*, London/New York, 2002, pp. 162-71.
3. H.E. Becht, *Statistische gegevens betreffende den handelsomzet van de Republiek der Verenigde Nederlanden gedurende de 17e eeuw (1579-1715)*, Den Haag, 1908, passim. J. Hovy, *Het voorstel van 1751 tot instelling van een beperkt vrijhavenstelsel in de Republiek*, Groningen, 1966, pp. 88 ff. W.G. Heeres, 'Annual Values of Amsterdam's Overseas Imports and Exports, 1697 to 1798', in *From Dunkirk to Danzig: Shipping and Trade in the North Sea and the Baltic, 1350-1850*, eds. W.G. Heeres et al., Hilversum, 1988, pp. 263-80.
4. On this distinction and shift see J.R. Bruijn, *The Dutch Navy of the Seventeenth and Eighteenth Centuries*, Columbia, 1993, pp. 67-82.
5. J.R. Bruijn, *Varend verleden. De Nederlandse oorlogsvloot in de 17de en 18de eeuw*, Amsterdam, 1998, p. 134. J.C. de Jonge, *Geschiedenis van het Nederlandsche zeewezen*, vol. 3, Haarlem, 1860, p. 735. Becht, *Statistische gegevens*, Appendix I.
6. F. Snapper, *Oorlogsinvloeden op de overzeese handel van Holland, 1551-1719*, Amsterdam, 1959, pp. 301-3.
7. Enthoven's observation in V. Enthoven, 'Mars en Mercurius bijeen. De smalle marges van het Nederlandse maritieme veiligheidsbeleid rond 1650', in *In het kiel zog. maritiem-historische studies aangeboden aan Jap R. Bruijn*, eds. L. Akveld et al., Amsterdam, 2003, p. 60, is thus also applicable to the period between 1652 and 1713.
8. Becht, *Statistische gegevens*, pp. 151 ff.
9. Ibid., p. 175. Heeres, 'Annual Values', p. 267.
10. Hovy, *Het Voorstel*, p. 644.
11. J.R. Bruijn, *De Admiraliteit van Amsterdam in rustige jaren 1713-1751. Regenten en financiën, schepen en zeevarenden*, Amsterdam, 1970, pp. 80 ff. E.H.M. Dormans, *Het tekort. Staatsschuld in de tijd der Republiek*, Amsterdam, 1991, p. 163.
12. Bruijn, *Admiraliteit van Amsterdam*, pp. 80 ff.
13. K. Davids, 'Maritime Labour in the Netherlands, 1570-1870', *Research in Maritime History*, vol.13, 1997, pp. 42 ff. G.J.A. Raven, '"Aanhoudend

sukkelen om bootsvolk". Een keerpunt in het personeelsbeleid van de marine, 1775-1795', *Tijdschrift voor Zeegeschiedenis*, vol. 1, 1981, p. 135.

14. Bruijn, *Admiraliteit van Amsterdam*, pp. 157-62; Raven, '"Aanhoudend sukkelen"', pp. 135-8.
15. A summary of the discussion in Davids, 'Maritime Labour', p. 70, and P. Boon, *Bouwers van de zee. Zevarenden van het Westfriese platteland, c.1680-1720*, Leiden, 1996, chaps. I, III and V.
16. J. de Vries and A. van der Woude, *The First Modern Economy: Success, Failure and Perseverance of the Dutch Economy, 1500-1815*, Cambridge, 1997, pp. 627-30.
17. Davids, 'Maritime Labour', pp. 67 ff.
18. Examples in J.Th.H. Verhees-Van Meer, *De Zeeuwse kaapvaart tijdens de Spaanse Successieoorlog 1702-1713*, Leiden, 1986, p. 49. Raven, "Aanhoudend sukkelen", p. 138.
19. De Jonge, *Geschiedenis zeewezen*, vol. III, p. 21. J.K. Oudendijk, *Johan de Witt en de zeemacht*, Amsterdam, 1944, pp. 47 ff. J.E. Elias, *De vlootbouw in Nederland in de eerste helft der 17e eeuw 1596-1655*, Amsterdam, 1933, pp. 131-44. J.S. Bartstra, *Vlootherstel en legeraugmentatie 1770-1780*, Assen, 1952, pp. 14-19. On the operation of the political system in the Dutch Republic in general, see J.L. Price, *Holland and the Dutch Republic in the Seventeenth Century. The Politics of Particularism*, Oxford, 1994, esp. pp. 122-48.
20. Bruijn, *Varend verleden*, p. 134.
21. Bartstra, *Vlootherstel*, pp. 20 ff.
22. Bruijn, *Varend verleden*, p. 134.
23. Hovy, *Het Voorstel*, p. 125.
24. Bartstra, *Vlootherstel*, p. 20. Hovy, *Het Voorstel*, p. 124. Bruijn, *Admiraliteit van Amsterdam*, p. 76.
25. Dormans, *Het Tekort*, esp. pp. 78 ff., 99-111.
26. Bartstra, *Vlootherstel*, pp. 38f. and chaps. 2-5.
27. N. Habermehl, *Joan Cornelis van der Hoop (1742-1825). Marinebestuurder voor stadhouder Willem V en koning Willem I*, Amsterdam, 2000, p. 134.
28. Bruijn, *Varend verleden*, p. 214.
29. Becht, *Statistische gegevens*, chaps. 2 and 3. Hovy, *Het Voorstel*, pp. 119-25, 140-3. J.L.F. Engelhard, *Het generaal-plakkaat van 31 juli 1725 op de convooien en licenten en het lastgeld op de schepen*, Amsterdam, 1970, chaps. 3-5.
30. Becht, *Statistische gegevens*, pp. 143-8. J. de Jong, 'De verpachting van

het kwart van de Convooien en Licenten, 1625-1639', *Tijdschrift voor Zeegeschiedenis*, vol. 15, 1996, pp. 147-62.

31. Becht, *Statistische gegevens*, pp. 149 et seq. Engelhard, *Het generaal-plakkaat*, p. 224. Enthoven, 'Mars en Mercurius bijeen', pp. 48 ff.
32. Verhees-Van Meer, *Zeeuwse kaapvaart*, p. 77. Bruijn, *Admiraliteit van Amsterdam*, p. 76.
33. A. Staarman, 'De VOC en de Staten-Generaal in de Engelse Oorlogen. Een ongemakkelijk bondgenootschap', *Tijdschrift voor Zeegeschiedenis*, vol. 15, 1996, pp. 3-24, Becht, *Statistische gegevens*, p. 181. Bruijn, *Admiraliteit van Amsterdam*, p. 74. Hovy, *Het voorstel*, p. 142.
34. Hovy, *Het Voorstel*, pp. 143 et seq. Bruijn, *Admiraliteit van Amsterdam*, pp. 74 ff.
35. J. de Vries, *De economische achteruitgang der Republiek in de achttiende eeuw*, 2nd edn., Leiden, 1968, p. 22.
36. De Jong, 'De Verpachting', p. 159.
37. Becht, *Statistische gegevens*, chaps. 2 and 3. M. 't Hart, *The Making of a Bourgeois State. War, Politics and Finance during the Dutch Revolt*, Manchester, 1993, pp. 110 ff. De Jong, 'De Verpachting', esp. pp. 155 ff. Engelhard, *Het generaal-plakkaat*, chaps. 3 and 8. Hovy, *Het Voorstel*, passim. J.F. Meijer, 'Voorstellen tot de herziening van de heffing van convooien en licenten in de jaren 1714-1720', in *Doel en middel. Aspecten van financieel overheidsbeleid in de Nederlanden van de zestiende eeuw tot heden*, eds. W. Fritschy, J.K.T. Postma and J. Roelevink, Amsterdam, 1995, pp. 97-113.
38. Engelhard, *Het generaal-plakkaat*, pp. 223 ff.
39. J.P. de Korte, *De jaarlijkse financiële verantwoording in de Verenigde Oostindische Compagnie*, Leiden, 1984, Appendix 1. F.S. Gaastra, *De geschiedenis van de VOC*, Zutphen, 2002, p. 147.
40. H.C.M. van de Wetering, 'De VOC en de kapers van Angria. Een expeditie naar de westkust van India in 1739', *Tijdschrift voor Zeegeschiedenis*, vol. 10, 1991, pp. 117-30.
41. J.R. Bruijn, F.S. Gaastra and I. Schöffer, *Dutch-Asiatic Shipping in the 17th and 18th Centuries*, vol. I, The Hague, 1987, pp. 246-9. Gaastra, *De geschiedenis van de VOC*, pp. 59 ff.
42. De Korte, *De jaarlijkse financiële verantwoording*, Appendix I.

CHAPTER 10

Circumventing State Power—Scottish Mercantile Networks and the English Navigation Laws, 1660-1707

ALLAN I. MACINNES

From its insular location, its limited indigenous resources and its subordinate political standing as one of the three kingdoms ruled by the Stuart dynasty, Scotland was dependent on overseas trade, commercial networks and an entrepreneurial willingness to set aside international regulations for its very survival as a distinctive European nation in the later seventeenth century. Scotland was neither a major European power nor a significant imperial presence in the Americas or in the East Indies. Yet Scottish overseas connections and mercantile activities between the Restoration of the Stuart monarchy in 1660 and political incorporation with England in 1707 offer a particularly apposite case study and, indeed, a corrective to the narrow focus on empire that results from a preoccupation with conflicts for colonial hegemony, such as the territorial ambitions of England in competition with Spain (and Portugal), France and the Netherlands or even Denmark and Sweden. The distinctive activities of the Scots and the Irish, no less than the Flemings, the Norwegians, the Finns, the Poles and the Jews, like that of adventurers from the Italian city states or colonists from German principalities, were not exclusively tied to the service of one imperial power. In the case of the Scots, their association with the English in the Americas contributed to the British character of the Stuarts' overseas dominions, but did not preclude their association with the Swedes and the Dutch on the Delaware, with the Dutch in Brazil, New Amsterdam, Surinam and Tobago, and with the Danes in St. Thomas.[1]

A case can certainly be made for the simultaneous intensification of state authority within the British Isles and the extension of that authority into the Stuarts' American dominions during the later seventeenth century.[2] However, the creation of a common elite identity based on shared notions of authority and civility within the three kingdoms is a far more vulnerable proposition. Again, the Scots provide an apposite corrective to an Anglocentric reading of British history. By the 1690s, the clannish cohesion of their landed and commercial elite, their diligence in securing positions of influence and their collusive disregard for the Navigation Laws were perceived by English merchants, colonial officials, diplomats and ruling ministries as highly threatening. Not only did the Scots challenge the English elites with the Darien Scheme to create an international entrepôt for the Pacific as well as the Atlantic on the Panama Isthmus, but also through their expansion into Ireland and the Delaware basin. If the Scots made a success of Darien, there seemed a real prospect that their domestic market would expand to include Ireland and that their entrepreneurial endeavours along the Delaware would lead to the secession of the three counties to form a Scottish middle colony on the American mainland.[3] Only political incorporation, through the Treaty of Union in 1707, put an end to Scottish flouting of English state power.

II

The Restoration of Charles II in 1660 led to constitutional settlements in all three kingdoms, as in the overseas dominions of the Britannic monarchy, which revived the Stuarts' 'ius imperium' by land and sea. This exclusive sovereignty, which had been asserted since the establishment of the dynasty by James I in 1603, had all but been subsumed by civil war, regicide and republicanism during the 1640s and 1650s. Accordingly, the extent to which the Restoration marked a return to Britannic monarchy as an organically inclusive construct for the three constituent kingdoms of the British Isles remains questionable. In particular, the continuing political dominance of England, which was confirmed rather than checked by the Restoration, threatened to make Scotland a permanent political satellite like Ireland. With the Privy Council restored as the king's executive agency of government in England, with the city of London intimately involved in the permanent Commissions of Trade and Plantations,[4] and with the restored Erastian episcopacy reinforcing the purity of the Anglican Church, the Restoration bolstered the appropriation of Britain for England.[5] Adding force to the debate on the Stuart dynasty's ius imperium was the changing intellectual context. In contrast to the situation that prevailed in the aftermath of the regal union between Scotland and England in 1603, this debate was conducted primarily within the context of political economy rather than jurisprudence or confessional allegiance.[6]

Formally restored to independence in 1660, Scotland nonetheless continued to operate as a junior political partner in its regal union with England. The Scottish Council at Whitehall, a devolved committee of the English Privy Council, initially marked Scotland's provincial standing while serving as a channel for the Court to press for the constitutional settlement in Scotland to follow English practice. Although James Maitland, Second Earl (later First Duke) of Lauderdale was not the main political influence within Scotland at the outset of the Restoration, he soon turned the mendacity, venality and chicanery rampant throughout the regime dominated by the Scottish nobility to his personal advantage. His ascendancy, which was marked by the termination of the Scottish Council, led to his personal exercise of provincial government from 1667. Over the next thirteen years, Scotland served as a political laboratory. English fears that Lauderdale was using Scotland as a model for absolutism on the cheap were not groundless. Simultaneously, he exploited an exaggerated climate of religious dissent in the Lowlands and social disorder in the Highlands to build up not only standing forces, but also a militia sustained by cess and empowered to quell unrest anywhere within the king's dominions at home and abroad.[7]

In reality, restored Stuart rule over the three kingdoms represented a compromise between Britannic and Gothic perspectives. The

Britannic, as represented by the monarchy, was grounded in an imperial vision, which ensured that Britain was always something more than the kingdom of England; the prerogative powers of the monarchy allowed them to suspend or dispense with laws inimical to other constituent interests within the British Isles. The Gothic was rooted in an English parliament with sole powers to vote for supply and enact statutes that reinforced English common law. Accordingly, the Gothic proponents of the supremacy of parliamentary statute and the common law placed contractual emphasis on rights, liberties and privileges which were applicable to all freeborn Englishmen, but were exclusively English at the expense of differing Scottish legal traditions or Irish customs. Alternative Scottish and Irish perspectives, respectively for a federative Britain and for equal dominions, were now subordinate if not subliminal.[8] The inclusive Britannic perspective of the monarchy was highlighted by the Dutch academic, Rutgerius Hermannides, in his *Britannia Magna* of 1661, which chronicled English hegemony over Scotland and Ireland. The exclusive Gothic perspective was articulated forcibly by the Swedish jurist, Samuel von Pufendorf, who viewed England as a composite monarchy with Scottish and Irish dependencies. Charles II carried on the mantle of Oliver Cromwell and his republican regime of the 1650s in maintaining English greatness through dominion over the seas and the promotion of commerce.[9]

Although the Restoration clearly marked a return to regal union, the resurgence of European mercantilism reawakened the debate on state formation in Britain. As Duke of York, the future James II had played a key public role in upholding a Britannic perspective for imperial monarchy which sought to be inclusive of Scottish, Irish and Welsh as well as English interests. Notwithstanding the association of the Gothic perspective with civil war and popular insurrections during the Restoration era,[10] the imposition of the Navigation Laws by the English Parliament in 1660, 1663, 1667 and 1671 and the rise of London to global significance had facilitated a Gothic mercantilism as well as the English appropriation of the Britannic Empire by cartographers like Richard Bloome (alias Nathaniel Crouch).[11] After the first imposition of the English

Navigation Laws, Charles II had used his prerogative powers to grant individual dispensations to Scottish entrepreneurs wishing to sustain sugar works in Glasgow and Edinburgh through trade to the Americas, which was also broadened to encompass trading ventures to Africa and Asia. However, James was instrumental in using these same powers to suspend laws restricting Scottish no less than Irish participation in English overseas ventures. The issuing of letters of marque to Scottish privateers, the pressing of Scots into service in the royal navy, and the conscription of Scottish seamen to serve in the Second (1666-7) and Third (1672-4) Dutch Wars against their main commercial partner further encouraged a laxity in applying trading prohibitions.[12] Having been awarded New York as a proprietary colony on its wresting from the Dutch in 1664, James had been an assiduous and tolerant promoter of a durable Scottish and Dutch commercial network from 1673 that was based in Albany, named after his Scottish ducal title. He subsequently opened up opportunities for participation from all three kingdoms in the Hudson's Bay Company during the 1680s.[13]

The Duke of York also attempted to moderate the Gothic mercantilism that sought to secure the fishing resources around the British Isles solely for English benefit. The Company of the Royal Fishery of Great Britain and Ireland established in 1661, which drew upon the expertise of agents involved in the common fishing of Charles I that was wholly miscast in the 1630s, was a Thames led initiative regulated by the English common law. Money realized by lottery as well as public subscription having proved more corrupting than remunerative, the Company was remodelled in 1664.[14] Its continued functioning was compromised by the existence of a separate Scottish initiative operating through provincial associations from 1661 that were refashioned in 1670 as the Royal Company for Fishery in Scotland. This venture, which stuttered on till 1690, remained distinct from and detrimental to the viability of the complementary Company of the Royal Fishery of England established under the duke's leadership in 1677. Regardless of any resolution on respective territorial waters claimed for Scotland and England, neither company could operate independently of

Dutch fishing expertise in the deep sea waters around the British Isles.[15]

Whereas fishing was part of the debate on national improvement through commerce in England, it was integral to the debate on national survival through entrepreneurship in Scotland. Bilateral discussions on commerce and constitutional affairs had tended to posit either closer political union or access to the claimed English colonies in the Americas and the Indies. As in Ireland, overtures for union with England also featured as issues of political economy. Sir William Petty promoted Anglo-Irish union in order to facilitate social engineering, if not ethnic and cultural assimilation, through the transplantation of peoples. Although Petty recognized that Scotland had separate fiscal powers, he viewed English leadership, and the prodigious use of public duties to increase wealth from trade and shipping, as the key to accumulating wealth in all three kingdoms.[16] However, the principal governing agency in Scotland, the Privy Council based in Edinburgh, preferred Scottish initiatives. In 1661, in retaliation to the English Navigation Acts, the Council had instigated a debate, backed up by resolutions from the commercial interest in town and country and reinforced by legislation to encourage trade through the establishment of companies for manufacture, shipping as well as fishing. The Scots had certainly benefited from the prohibition of the import of Irish cattle to England in 1667, which they had consolidated with their own simultaneous ban on Irish imports. Thus, the droving of cattle and sheep from Scotland under licence had a clear run in English markets. Nevertheless, as the Privy Council's committee of inquiry into trade made clear in 1681, when calling for another round of protection, the Scots lacked the political muscle to ensure that the other mercantilist measures became effective.

Proposals for commercial confederation that issued from Scotland in 1664 and 1668 had run up against English fears about the competitive edge enjoyed by the Scottish carrying trade,. the close Scottish trading links with the Dutch and, above all, the perceived Scottish threat to vested coal and salt interests in the north-east of England. Support for a commercial union was effectively a power play by Lauderdale to establish his supremacy at Court as adviser on Scottish affairs. However, his advocacy of political incorporation in 1668 and his subsequent wrecking of negotiations between the commissioners of the English and Scottish parliaments two years later was an even more cynical ruse to cover up secret negotiations between Charles II and Louis XIV of France. Revived proposals for commercial confederation from England in 1674 never got off the drawing board as the Scots opted for colonial expansion which remained a chimerical if not an entirely fruitless pursuit over the next two decades. When James established his court in Edinburgh following his retreat from the Exclusion Crisis in England, he reinvigorated these Scottish endeavours and added the targeted pursuit of colonies as the commercial alternative to a union. In 1681, the Committee for Trade reported to the Privy Council that the only effective way for the country to cope with mercantilism and growing dependence on English markets was either to seek closer union or develop overseas colonies. James duly authorized Scottish ventures in South Carolina in 1682 and East New Jersey from 1685.[17]

Of the two colonies, South Carolina was the more transient. This venture, which was ostensibly promoted by Presbyterian nonconformists, actually resulted from extensive commercial networking on the Scottish western seaboard. The Scots planters along the Ashley river were based at Stuart's Town, named in honour rather than in defiance of their royal patron. They insisted on separate administration according to Scottish law rather than incorporation with the English colonial government. This uneasy arrangement, which sought confederation but was accorded a federal accommodation, was brought to a conclusion by Spanish reprisals that did not end the Scottish venture, but certainly terminated separate constitutional experimentation. While the New Jersey colony had drawn off some planters from South Carolina, this served to enhance and deepen the colonial expertise among a commercial network that drew support from the Highlands as from the north-east of Scotland. Its principal patrons being well connected at the Court, the plantation around Perth Amboy effectively enjoyed a confederal relationship with the associated English proprietary colony; a relationship that failed to be sustained beyond the Revolution, however.[18]

Nevertheless, there was little political will either at the Court (even after James II succeeded Charles II), in the English Privy Council, in the Commissions of Trade and Plantations, or in the English Parliament to sustain an inclusive Britannic agenda within the Stuarts' dominions. When William of Orange superseded James II in all three kingdoms between 1688 and 1691, he assumed the mantle of Pufendorf, projecting himself internationally by his English nomenclature as William III. For the purposes of making peace and war, and conducting trade and commerce, the interests of England were paramount. Scotland, like Ireland, was an ephemeral consideration.[19]

III

The 'Glorious Revolution' that brought William of Orange to power in England can be viewed as a triumph of Gothic constitutionalism and mercantilism: the Anglican ascendancy in the Church was confirmed, limited monarchy was consolidated and the Navigation Laws were reasserted comprehensively and exclusively. Albeit distinctive in each of the three kingdoms, the Revolution settlements effectively privileged baronial politics in alliance with military engagements that were predominantly Francophobe, and with commercial opportunism on a global scale. The proclaimed Gothic achievement of constitutional monarchy in place of Stuart autocracy glossed over the continuation of the fiscal–military state instigated in the Stuarts' dominions outwith England in the Restoration era. Ostensibly under parliamentary control once the Revolution, imperialism was moderated rather than contained by votes of supply and was fructified by the creation of the National Debt in 1693 that was financed through the Bank of England from the following year. The Revolution was not so much glorious as bloody in the other two kingdoms. In Ireland, the forcible replacement of James II by William (and Mary) established an Anglican ascendancy for the English interest that rigorously excluded Irish Catholics and Ulster-Scottish Presbyterians from public life. In Scotland, the Revolution was uncompromisingly Whiggish. Notwithstanding the re-establishment of Presbyterianism in the Kirk, the resurgence of radical constitutional activity was the most remarkable feature. The unicameral Scottish estates attempted to secure permanent checks on the executive power wielded on behalf of the British Court. In turn, politicians favourable to the Court used the prospect of Anglo–Scottish union as a diversionary ploy to fundamental constitutional reform.[20]

The defining feature of William's reign in Scotland, as in England and Ireland, was not the pursuit of political union, but the processes as well as the policies associated with political economy, which also served as the key pointer towards modernity at the turn of the eighteenth century. Caution must be exercised in accepting a Whig interpretation of modernity through the triumphalist linking of Protestantism, property and progress with the 'Glorious Revolution'; a linkage that overplays the causal relationship between political revolution and commercial revolution and severely underplays the engagement in commercial enterprise of Jacobites (who, as supporters of the exiled James II, did not accept the Revolution) and Tories (who acquiesced in the Revolution).[21] For the Jacobites and Tories also had an alternative approach, which valued land over trade, mercantilist regulation and monopolistic companies over free enterprise. But Jacobites and Tories as well as Whigs were engaged in co-partneries to exploit manufactures, fisheries and colonies. A further complication was the ongoing national rivalries between Scotland and England, which actually cut across political allegiances among Whigs, Jacobites and Tories. Scottish commercial endeavours under William were looked upon no more favourably by English Jacobites and Tories than by the Whigs.[22] Although William failed to equitably check these rivalries, the enduring legacy of his reign in Scotland was the opening up of political discourse on state formation, which had not only British but also transoceanic ramifications. By the end of his reign the continuance of regal union was no longer viable.

Of critical significance for the discourse on state formation was the transformation during the Revolution of the Britannic Empire based on the Stuarts' royal prerogative into an English empire subject to constitutional oversight by the English Parliament. At the same time, Scots were markedly disadvantaged in both the British Isles and the colonies by reinforced Navigation Laws, which instigated a tariff battle with England from 1693 and treated Scots as aliens in the American colonies after 1696. Notwithstanding the undoubted structural weaknesses in the Scottish economy, its relative lack of depth and diversity and its vulnerability to mercantilist policies applied by the leading European states, trade and commerce was neither stagnant nor on an irreversible downward spiral.[23]

Considerable caution must be exercised before accepting official reports, customs records, fiscal returns and unfulfilled commitments to military and civil expenditure as accurate indicators of the Scottish economy. Scottish mercantile communities in Iberia, France, the Netherlands, northern Germany, Scandinavia and the Baltic sustained levels of inward and outward investment that have yet to be accurately measured. At the same time, the expansion of Scottish commercial networks into Boston, New York and Philadelphia, on the Delaware and Potomac rivers, and on the Leeward Islands complemented rather than superseded longstanding networks that also operated aggressively throughout Scandinavia and the Baltic, from Bergen via Gothenburg, Danzig and Stockholm and Königsberg on to Narva (later St. Petersburg). The Atlantic connection certainly contributed to the reinvigoration of Scottish networks in Bordeaux and their installation in Lisbon and Cadiz well in advance of 1707.[24] Core networks, that linked not only the Scottish cities of Edinburgh, Glasgow, Aberdeen and Dundee, but also lesser ports such as Ayr, Greenock and Dumbarton in the west, Bo'ness, Kirkcaldy and Montrose in the east, Inverness and even the Shetland Isles in the north to London, Hamburg, Amsterdam and Rotterdam, served both these transatlantic and continental communities. Within the British Isles, émigré communities of Scots not only in London, but also in Norwich, Newcastle, Belfast, Dublin and the Isle of Man colluded in privateering, disguised ownership of shipping, smuggling, tax evasion and other illicit commercial practices that facilitated trade between Scotland and the American colonies. This trade involved the direct import of tobacco, sugar, cotton, indigo and ginger, and, above all, the transfer of tramping practices with which the Scots were particularly associated in the Baltic to the Caribbean and subsequently to the Indian Ocean and the China Seas in the eighteenth century. This practice ensured that illicit trading, customs evasion and smuggling continued well beyond the Treaty of Union's concession of free trade with the colonies to Scottish mercantile networks.[25]

The Scottish alternative to mercantilist regulation in the later seventeenth century was the transoceanic pursuit of capitalism as characterized by economic self-interest, the relentless pursuit of profit and the resourceful investment in goods, services and people. Capitalism, whether viewed as organic or contractual constructed, was also adept at circumventing the power of the state no less than the municipality or the corporation.[26] In the Scottish context, circumvention went hand in glove with commercial innovation. Thus, Glasgow merchants used both consignment and store systems first to penetrate the staple Atlantic trade in tobacco and then to secure dominance in it. Their participation in this trade since the 1630s seemed compromised by the restrictive English Navigation Acts. Under the consignment system the planter bore the risk of marketing, whereas the risk was borne by the merchant under the store system, which tied advances of credit on tobacco sales in Europe to the purchase of merchandise from the colonial store. This latter system, which was particularly suited to the expansion of small plantations along the Chesapeake Bay and into the hinterlands of Maryland, Virginia and the Carolinas, had higher risks but greater profits. Whitehaven, hitherto third after Bristol and Liverpool in the Atlantic trade, was so eclipsed by the Glasgow merchant's use of the store system in tandem with smuggling through the Isle of Man, that the Cumbrian town actually petitioned for repeal of the Treaty of Union in 1710. Scottish entrepreneurs duly extended the store system perfected by the Glasgow tobacco lords into the Caribbean in order to enhance profits from sugar and rum.[27]

At the same time as Scottish entrepreneurship was proving remuneratively illicit, the public debate on political economy, galvanized by the Gothic nature of the Revolution Settlement in

England, was accompanied by polemical rebuttals that Scotland was in any way subordinate to England. This debate belied the notion that Scottish commercial aspirations were enshrouded in gloom or that trade and manufactures were in terminal decline. Growth was achievable through flexible credit arrangements facilitated by commercial and land banks and by the revival of Scottish colonial aspirations with overtures for a plantation in the West Indies resurfacing by 1693. This proposal was to be carried out in a conscious spirit of emulation of England, but the anonymous Scottish adventurers were also adamant that it was 'in the interest of England that Scotland have plantations in the West Indies' which would together serve as a bulwark against other European competition.[28]

IV

Cooperation with Scotland was not a pressing concern of the political economy in England, where the servicing of the military–fiscal state under William III was accorded priority. In December 1697 and January 1698, the Council of Trade and Plantations completed a review of English trade from 1670 until the Peace of Rijswijk with the French. Focusing on commercial exchange, the balance of payments and the competitive impact of mercantilist regulation, the Council noted that the expansion of English trade in the Restoration era had measurably declined since the Revolution. Global threats to English trade were more pressing than transatlantic opportunities for colonial expansion. English trade was in general decline in Scandinavia, France, Russia and the East Indies, where the pepper trade had been effectively ceded to the Dutch. While continuous war with France certainly diverted national resources by land and sea, war had helped reverse the decline in English trade with Holland and Flanders. English trade was only vibrant in Hamburg and in Iberia, the Mediterranean and Africa. Serious misgivings were expressed about woollen manufacturing, fishing and the carrying trade, particularly that from the plantations. The uncooperative presence of Scottish commercial networks loomed large. Not only was wool necessary for English manufacturing being exported out of England, Ireland and Scotland, but also Scottish carriers were dominating this trade from the three kingdoms. There was no evidence that the Scots were any further inclined to revive a British fisheries project, and in the colonies, the Scots were taking particular advantage of the lack of designated ports in the plantations for the loading and unloading of overseas vessels. The activities of Scottish entrepreneurs in the rivers and creeks, 'far removed from the places where the Collectors and other Officers of the Customs are directed to keep their offices', were regarded as no less competitive than the Dutch and no less damaging than that of pirates in the Americas.[29]

As an opponent of Irish claims for parliamentary independence of England, John Cary, a Bristol merchant and commercial commentator, expressed concern in 1695 that Scotland should not be encouraged to develop companies for textiles, fishing and colonies. As the Scottish domestic market was limited, these putative companies could only be successful if Scotland attained dominance in Irish markets at English expense. Accordingly, Ireland should be reduced to an English colony and every effort made to contest Scottish commercial expansion by ensuring that it was not attractive to English investment. Cary stated in public what English diplomatic and colonial officials had expressed in private. Indeed, the Council of Trade and Plantations had become particularly apprehensive about the purported dominance of Scottish commercial networks in Ireland since the Revolution. Not only did Scottish merchants in the trading towns and the Scottish gentry in plantation districts actively collude, but they 'are generally Frugall, Industrious, very nationall, and very helpful to each other agst any Third [party]'.[30]

William III was caught in the horns of a British commercial dilemma. Government ministers and officials, merchants and commercial commentators were determined to ensure that English—not British—interests prevailed in the colonies as on the continent. William's Scottish government, however, was by no means averse to the promotion of schemes for economic growth. Building upon an Act of 1693 for the encouragement of foreign trade through the creation of commercial companies as co-partneries based on joint stock investments—that had its origins in past legislation to promote manufactures and fishing in 1661, to which colonies were added in 1681—the Scottish estates licensed two flagship endeavours in 1695. The Bank of Scotland and the Company of Scotland trading to Africa and the Indies were effectively national co-partneries. When subscription lists were opened in 1696, both the Bank and the Company of Scotland attracted respectively individual and corporate pledges for £ 60,000 and £ 400,000 and sums in hard currency totalling to £ 6,000 and £ 34,000. As Scotland was also in the grip of an intensive, five-year famine, these levels of investment could be taken as indicators of a blind optimism that would destabilize a fragile domestic economy. Yet, these subscriptions were not unrealistic in terms of inward investment that reflected the close integration of Scottish mercantile communities at home and abroad. A key group in the promotion of both ventures were the London Scots, the same group which had taken the lead in developing textiles, notably the manufacturing of coarse cloth and linen in and around Edinburgh using purloined English pattern books.[31]

Under the far from benign entrepreneurial influence of one of these London merchants, William Paterson, polemicist, colonial adventurer and founder of the Bank of England, the Company of Scotland was persuaded to concentrate its endeavours on an American settlement that would serve as an entrepôt capable of attracting trade from the East and West Indies through its location on the Panama Isthmus at Darien. Recent Scottish colonial experience was not so much lacking as mixed, notably with regard to governance as well as settlement. In addition to the federal model that flourished briefly in South Carolina and the confederal accommodation that was applied initially in East New Jersey, there were effectively three other models for Scottish colonial engagement prior to the Revolution. First, there were the distinctive Scottish networks in the Caribbean, New England and the Middle Colonies that were sustained by British enterprise and supported by indentured service. However, the Scottish networks were also subject to sustained criticism from the English colonial administration for their clannishness and their connived breaching of the Navigation Laws to benefit their fellow countrymen. Second, there were disparate Scottish networks associated with Dutch colonies that had limited prospects for development, as mercantilist competition was constricting the close commercial association the Scots had long enjoyed with the Dutch. Third, there was the lingering desire that Scotland should pursue a separate colony that would still be under the protection of the Stuart dynasty but no more dependent on England than on Spain. Darien seemed to fulfil this desire. The Scottish directors, investors and colonists can certainly be accused of over-optimism, incompetence and even profiteering. That they were obliged to proceed unilaterally, however, transformed Darien from a visionary enterprise into a fiasco.[32]

Notwithstanding his sanctioning of both the Bank of Scotland and the Company of Scotland in 1695, William of Orange could not endorse the Darien venture without the support of the English Parliament, which preferred to tighten its Navigation Acts to the detriment of Scottish commerce in 1696. Although the proposed colony did fit the legislative requirement that commercial activity was to be conducted in any part of the world not then at war with William, the Company of Scotland was conceived as a rival to the English East India Company. Its established block of members in the English Parliament was more than capable of impeding William's need for financial supply. As the legality of English residents investing in the Company of Scotland was ambivalent, the East India Company, with royal approval, successfully pushed through the Houses of Lords and Commons a series of hostile measures in December 1695. The threat of impeachment as interlopers for any investor resident in England aborted subscriptions to the Company of Scotland in London. Although frustrated, England based investors formed a new company trading to the East Indies in 1698 challenging the monopoly of the old East India Company. William turned this situation to his financial advantage by securing a loan of £ 2 million from the latter to further his war effort. Scottish antipathies were not abated by the old East India Company continuing to earn a drawback on customs from all goods exported to Scotland. At the same time, William's desire to appease Spain that claimed sovereignty over the Panama Isthmus and the expendable nature of Scottish interests as he sought to broker a military alliance against Louis XIV, conspired to reduce Darien from a confederation of Scottish, English, Dutch and north German commercial interests to a separatist endeavour. William clearly accorded higher priority to the balance of power in Europe over the balance of trade in Scotland.[33]

In denying funding, expertise and assistance to the Company of Scotland, William was undoubtedly responding to the real determination within governmental as well as mercantile circles in England that the Darien enterprise should not succeed. The Council for Trade and Plantations, together with the Commissioners of the Customs in London were determined that the colonial governors rigorously implement the Navigation Laws. Scots resident in the colonies were to be stripped of public office. Not only were they treated as aliens, but they were also the only residential group denied naturalization. Indeed, there was a concern in government circles that if Darien became a success, the Scots would lay claim to a settlement in the counties of Newcastle, Kent or Sussex on the southern shore of the Delaware bay. The Swedes and later the Dutch had originally settled these counties, which sat uneasily between the colonies of Philadelphia and Maryland. A persistent Scottish presence since the 1630s was now deemed particularly disruptive. Their indigenous mercantile community was not only past master at evading the Navigation Laws but also considered capable of establishing an independent staple for European manufactures. Such a free port would be considerably more menacing to English interests in North America than that operated by the Dutch on the island of Curaçao. William Blathwayt, William's resident agent at The Hague from where Dutch assistance was discouraged, undertook the task of coordinating between diplomatic and colonial officials. More blatantly, the resident in Hamburg, Sir Paul Rycaut, openly admonished the city's senate that William would perceive the licensing of subscriptions to the Company of Scotland as a hostile act.[34]

Moreover, although English diplomats and colonial officials sowed doubts at home and abroad about the legality of the Scottish enterprise, their concern for the sovereign rights of Spain over the

Panama Isthmus were somewhat tempered by the lack of current Spanish settlement in the area and by its suitability for an English entrepôt. Private ventures there by English entrepreneurs had come to grief prior to the Scots embarking for Darien. Making the area notably attractive for entrepreneurial exploitation was the fact that the overland route lay in Panama for the silver mined in Peru prior to its shipping to Spain from Portobello and Cartagena. Indeed, English concerns for Spanish interests were far from altruistic. A naval squadron, under the command of Admiral John Benbow, operated off these Caribbean ports when the Scots mounted their ill-fated endeavours to settle Darien, which met with disaster in 1700, after successive expeditionary fleets that sailed in 1698 and 1699 failed to establish a permanent colony. Funded eventually as a national enterprise, as a commercial compact between God and the Scottish people, surveying, provisioning and leadership were deficient notwithstanding additional assistance provided by Scottish mercantile communities in Boston and New York.[35] The defeat of Spanish forces at Tubuganti on 15 February 1700 by a combined force of Scots and Indians under the command of Colonel Alexander Campbell of Fonab, offered no more than a brief respite. English polemicists declared open season in ridiculing the audacity of the Scottish enterprise. Duly glossed over was William's instruction to the governors of Jamaica and the other Caribbean colonies to deny assistance to the Scots, admittedly issued when Darien was reportedly thriving in December 1699. Spanish tenacity on the issue of the Panama Isthmus was wholly underestimated. The fiasco was in no small measure due to misplaced British—not just Scottish—disrespect for Spain as 'the sick man of Europe'.[36]

V

The political fallout of Darien was the mobilization of public opinion within Scotland by polemic, petition and pulpit against the Court. Mass mobilization, on a scale unprecedented since the revolutionary convulsions of the mid-seventeenth century, supplemented by public rioting and the inflammatory bribing of members of the Scottish estates, imperilled the continuation of regal union. In the course of the Darien venture, Scottish polemicists moved from demonstrating that the Company of Scotland was a calculated investment, to bolstering the country's commercial confidence in the face of English hostility and to a strident defence of a Caledonian right of presence in the Caribbean.[37] The public clamour for reparations from England and Spain led to parliamentary addresses to William supplicating him to take such measures 'as may vindicate the rights and privileges' of the Company of Scotland. Beyond extending the duration of the Company's trading privileges and a promise to consider any reasonable plan for compensating for Scottish losses, William was not prepared to take any specific remedial action. He also deferred plans for a placatory visit to Scotland in 1700, the sole occasion when he considered visiting his northern kingdom. However, he did recommend that the Scots should concentrate on the improvement of their manufactures and native produce as both assured the foundation of foreign trade and the most suitable means of rectifying widespread Scottish destitution.[38]

This suggestion did serve to re-channel the ongoing debate on political economy. Measures for national recovery became integral to the political discourse on state formation in Britain. The commercial impact of Darien was a critical but not a crippling loss of venture capital, less than £ 200,000 from the £ 434,000 pledged or paid in cash. The Company of Scotland continued to operate and licence ships to Africa and the East Indies. Collateral damage to the Bank of Scotland was contained by an accommodation with Edinburgh merchant houses that had hitherto acted as competitors. Scottish commercial networks of merchants and planters continued to operate, albeit even more clandestinely, in the Americas.[39] Nonetheless, the failure of the Scots to break out of the mercantilist prism increased their reliance on access to English domestic and colonial markets. The models for colonial development, in turn, became models for state formation. The Scots preferred a federative arrangement; the English were intent on incorporation. Undoubtedly, the Darien fiasco contributed to the national sense of defeatism that facilitated the English drive for parliamentary incorporation, but the Scots remained opportune negotiators.[40]

The revived prospect of an incorporating union was initially proposed in the House of Lords as a means of placating the Scots at the outset of 1700. English misgivings about the negative Scottish impact on woollen manufacturing, fishing and the carrying trade from the plantations were not abated by the Darien fiasco. An implacably hostile House of Commons rejected the union. At this juncture, William faced more formidable opposition from within Scotland. A confederated opposition that became known as the country interest had emerged intent on using Darien as a means of breaking the dominance of the Court and the English ministries over Scottish affairs.[41] Another distinctive Scottish grievance surfaced when, twelve months after the rejection of the union with England, the Parliament passed an Act of settlement in 1701, which unilaterally prescribed the succession of the House of Hanover following the death of the designated heir, William's sister-in-law, Princess Anne of Denmark. On the death of Anne's father, James II, that same year, Louis XIV had immediately proclaimed the exiled king's son as James III. The immediate threat from William's continuous neglect of Scottish affairs was a British debacle. There was a distinct possibility that at his own death in 1702 his last continental preoccupation, the War of Spanish Succession, would turn into the War of British Succession. At the same time, the succession issue strengthened the negotiating position of the Scots driven by the issue of political economy to seek closer association with England.[42]

Ongoing commercial contacts with the Americas and the continuing evasion of mercantilist regulations bolstered Scottish confidence to oppose political incorporation and to pursue a federative outcome with guaranteed access to the colonies. The Scottish estates did not lack confidence either to question the Act of Settlement or to play the Jacobite card and leave the issue of succession unresolved. Anglo–Scot antipathy was compounded by a legislative war. Scottish retaliation was two-pronged. The act anent peace and war provided for an independent Scottish foreign policy on Anne's death. The act of security threatened to dissolve the regal union unless the sovereignty of Scotland, the power of its parliament and the freedom of its religion and commerce were secured from English interference by Anne's successor. At the same time, those within the Scottish administration who were treating covertly for union with the English ministry were told peremptorily to desist.[43] Instead of the placatory gesture counselled by Queen Anne, the English were not persuaded to share 'the imperium Britannicum that they had usurped'. However, Scottish retaliation was trumped by the alien Act of 1705 and by the mobilization of troops on the borders and across the North Channel in Ireland. Along with the threat of subjecting the Scots to the same punitive tariffs as foreigners was an invitation to treat for incorporating union.[44]

In this legislative stand off, the English ministry had several distinct advantages. It was clearly intent on an incorporating union; it was prepared to use the resources of the Treasury to facilitate Scottish politics of influence; and it could rely on the support of key Scottish politicians whose thirst for power was enhanced by their lucrative playing of the English marriage market.[45] Incorporation also offered a viable way out of the mercantilist prism reaffirmed by the alien act, a theme taken up by Scottish merchants resident in London, especially those with interests in colonial plantations. The abolisher of protective tariffs through free trade, though exposed Scottish manufacturing and extractive industries to risk from English competition, opened up unfettered access to the English colonies. On the Scottish side, John Spreull from Glasgow, the city which was the main beneficiary of the illicit transatlantic trade, led a vigorous rebuttal of Scottish vulnerability to the alien act on a global scale; a rebuttal which was reinforced by an attack from within the Scottish merchant community on the Anglo–Scot trading houses in London. The dubious prospect of free trade was not 'a sufficient Equivalency for our Sovereignty, Independency and Laws'. A communication of trade through commercial confederation would allow the Scots to harmonize rather than subordinate their economic regulation to English interests.[46]

While there was a broad consensus against an incorporating union among the Scottish Estates as it entered what proved to be its last session in 1706-7, there was no agreed alternative with variations ranging from a federal executive to confederal legislatures. In this situation, the inveterate polemicist and none too secret agent, Daniel

Defoe, was despatched by the English ministry to Scotland to propagate the mutual benefits from partnership through the union. Defoe claimed it was imperative that Scotland be part of a British incorporation; he extolled the advantages for Scottish commerce of free access to English and imperial markets; and he countered religious scruples and other national prejudices standing in the way of the treaty being ratified.[47] However, the Scots were not necessarily committed to a British constitutional settlement any more than they were convinced that parliamentary incorporation was the best guarantee of economic prosperity.[48]

An alternative European confederation, notably a coalition with the Dutch, held real attraction for the Scots. Not only were the United Provinces Scotland's foremost trading partner until the 1690s, but the Scots had also served for as long and more extensively in the Dutch colonial service as they had in the English. The Dutch were deemed to operate a more cost-efficient colonialism based on commerce rather than plantations. The Scots could further benefit from Dutch expertise in developing deep sea fishing as an alternative national venture to colonialism. At the same time, the constitutional structure of the United Provinces was deemed more supportive of distinctive Scottish interests, particularly Presbyterianism. Notwithstanding the persuasiveness of these polemical arguments, there was no corroborative evidence that the Dutch were prepared to confederate with the Scots other than hints from Prussian diplomats that money was being sent from the United Provinces, through Scottish networks, to bolster the resolve of politicians to resist political incorporation.[49] Defoe's implacable opponent, James Hodge, a London Scot, shipped north for his polemical abilities by the Country party, forcibly made the point that breakaway areas from incorporating unions, notably Sweden from Denmark in the sixteenth century and Portugal from Spain in the seventeenth, had advanced their wealth as nations rather than being consigned to poverty as provinces. The discriminatory and prejudicial treatment of Protestant dissenters, American colonists and, above all, the Irish in the wake of the Revolution reinforced religious, commercial and political doubts about incorporation at the dictate of the English ministry.[50]

VI

Scottish engagement in empire, an ongoing rather than an occasional process between 1660 and 1707, ensured that the making of union involved issues of principle on both sides. At the same time, commercial networking that linked traditional markets in northern Europe with the Americas and the Indies restored the importance of political economy in effecting the United Kingdom of Great Britain.[51] The accomplishment of a parliamentary union signposted a collective crisis of political will among the Scots to pursue a separate commercial agenda, not an entrepreneurial lack of ambition. The British nature of the empire was reasserted through Scottish networks within an English governmental framework. State power was now to be consolidated rather than circumvented. However, the Gothic realities of state formation in Britain were expressed appositely on 9 May 1707, eight days after the Anglo–Scottish Treaty of Union became operative, when Governor Thomas Handasyd of Jamaica was notified by the Council of Trade and Plantations, 'that Scotchmen are thereby to be looked upon for the future as Englishmen to all intents and purposes whatsoever'.[52]

NOTES

1. 'Direktionens Korrespondance - Supplikationskopibøger' (1690-1712), A 4/465-7, Vestindisk-Guineisk Kompagni, 1671-1755, Dansk Rigsarkivet, Copenhagen (RA). J. Clifford, *The Conduct of the Dutch Relating to the Breach of Treaties with England*, London, 1760. *Narratives of the Netherlands, 1609-1664*, ed. J.F. Jamieson, New York, 1909, pp. 66-96, 257-63, 307-8.
2. M.J. Braddick, *State Formation in Early Modern England, c. 1550-1700*, Cambridge, 2000, pp. 340-419.
3. 'Papers relating to Trade, etc.', Sloane MS 2902, ff. 137-8, 218, British Library (hereafter BL). Bridgewater & Ellesmere MSS, EL 9776-7, 9802-3, 9880, Huntington Library (hereafter HL), San Marino, California.

4. 'Hastings Irish Papers', box 22/HA 15352, HL. R. Hutton, *The Restoration: A Political and Religious History of England and Wales, 1658-1667*, Oxford, 1985, pp. 125-84. G. Holmes, *The Making of a Great Power: Late Stuart and Early Georgian Britain, 1660-1722*, Harlow, 1993, pp. 27-43.
5. William Prynne, The first tome of an exact chronological vindication and historical demonstration of our British, Roman, Saxon, Danish, Norman, English kings supreme ecclesiastical jurisdiction, in, over all spiritual, or religious affairs, causes, persons, as well as temporal within their realms of England, Scotland, Ireland, and other dominions, London, 1665. J. Syith, *The Making of the United Kingdom, 1660-1800*, Harlow, 2001, pp. 77-87. N.H. Keeble, *The Restoration: England in the 1660s*, Oxford, 2002, pp. 109-31.
6. S. Pincus, 'Neither Machiavellian Moment nor Possessive Individualism. Commercial Society and the Defenders of the English Commonwealth', *American Historical Review*, vol. 103, 1998, pp. 705-36.
7. 'Hastings Irish Papers', box 11/HA 14779, 14958, 15993, HL. J.M. Buckroyd, 'Bridging the Gap. Scotland 1659-1660', *Scottish Historical Review* (hereafter *SHR*), vol. 66, 1987, pp. 1-25. A.I. Macinnes, 'Repression and Conciliation: The Highland Dimension, 1660-1688', *SHR*, vol. 65, 1986, pp. 167-95. Like the Irish parliaments and constitutional assemblies in Caribbean colonies, the Scottish estates in 1661 awarded Charles a substantive annuity (£ 40,000 sterling) for life raised mainly through excise. Such awards obviated the need for regular parliaments to vote supply.
8. A.I. Macinnes, *The British Revolution, 1629-1660*, Basingstoke, 2004, pp. 8-39.
9. R. Hermannides, *Britannia Magna*, Amsterdam, 1661. S. [von] Puffendorf, *An Introduction to the History of the Principal Kingdoms and States of Europe*, London, 1699.
10. J. Davies, *The Civil Warres of Great Britain and Ireland Containing an Exact History of Their Occasion, Originall, Progress, and Happy End*, London, 1661. J. Howell, *Divers historical discourses of the late popular insurrections in Great Britain and Ireland tending all, to the asserting of the truth, in vindication of their Majesties*, London, 1661. J. Heath, *A Chronicle of the Late Intestine War in the Three Kingdoms of England, Scotland and Ireland*, 1676.
11. *The English Empire in America: Or a Prospect of His Majesties Dominions in the West-Indies*, London, 1685 (RB). J. Evelyn, *Navigation and Commerce, their original and progress containing a succinct account of traffick in general: its benefits and improvements, discoveries, wars and conflicts at sea, from the original of*

navigation to this day, with special regard to the English nation, 1674. G. Collins, *Great Britain's Coasting-Pilot, Being a New and Exact Survey of the Sea-Coast of England*, London, 1693.

12. 'Maitland & Lauderdale Papers', 1532-1688, Add. MSS 35,125 fol. 74 (BL). Calendars of State Papers (hereafter CSP), *Colonial: America and the West Indies*, eds. W.M. Sainsbury, J.W. Fortescue and C. Headlam, London, 1880-1916 (1660-8), nos. 543, 849 (1669-74), nos. 42-3, 50-1, 163. Registers of the Privy Council of Scotland (hereafter RPCS), third series, vols. 1-16 (1661-91), eds. P.H. Brown, H. Paton and E.W.M. Balfour-Melville, Edinburgh, 1908-70, vol. 1 (1661-4), pp. 600-1, 606-7, 641-3, vol. 2 (1665-69), pp. 512-13, vol. 3 (1669-72), pp. 463, 499-505, vol. 4 (1673-76), p. 42.
13. 'Maitland & Lauderdale Papers' 1532-1688, Add. MSS 35,125, fol. 74 (BL). 'Letters and Papers of Thomas Bannatyne', RH15/14/41, National Archives of Scotland (hereafter NAS). N.C. Landsman, 'The Middle Colonies. New Opportunities for Settlement, 1660-1700', in *The Origins of Empire*, pp. 351-74. A.I. Macinnes, M.D. Harper and L.G. Fryer, eds., *Scotland and the Americas, c.1650-c.1939: A Documentary Source Book*, Edinburgh, 2002, pp. 135-6. Moreland and Bannister, *Antique Maps*, pp. 158-60. Thus, James named the eastern shore of Hudson's Bay as North and South Wales and its western shore as New Britain.
14. J. Smith, *The Trade & Fishing of Great-Britain Displayed With a Description of the Islands of Orkney and Shetland*, London, 1662. [R. Codrington], *His Majesties Propriety, and dominion on the British Seas asserted: together with a true account of the Neatherlanders insupportable insolencies, and injuries, they have committed; and the inestimable benefits they have gained in their fishing on the English Seas*, London 1665 and 1672. R. Coke, *England's improvements in two parts: in the former is discoursed how the kingdom of England may be improved; in the latter is discoursed how the navigation of England may be increased and the sovereignty of the British Seas more secured to the crown of England*, London, 1675.
15. 'Sir George Maxwell of Nether Pollock, Information for the Herring Fishing and Others Relating unto', Wodrow MSS, quarto ix, ff. 109-18, National Library of Scotland (hereafter NLS). 'Bruce of Sunburgh Papers', D8/31, Shetland Archives. W.R. Scott, *The Constitutions and Finance of English, Scottish and Irish Joint-Stock Companies to 1720*, 3 vols., Cambridge, 1911-12, vol. 2, pp. 361-82. T.W. Fulton, *The Sovereignty of*

the Sea: An Historical Account of the Claims for Dominion of the British Seas, Edinburgh, 1911, pp. 441-9, 461, 465, 494, 515-16.

16. J. Kelly, 'The Origins of the Act of Union. An Examination of Unionist Opinion in Britain and Ireland, 1650-1800', *Irish Historical Studies*, vol. 25, 1987, pp. 236-63. Sir William Petty, *Britannia Languens, or a Discourse of Trade*, London, 1680. Ibid., *Political Arithmetick*, London, 1690. Ibid., *The Political Anatomy of Ireland*, 1691.
17. *Aberdeen Council Letters*, 1552-1681, ed. L.B. Taylor, 6 vols., Oxford, 1942-61, vol. 4, pp. 152-7. RPCS, third series, vol. 1, pp. 89, 97-8, 114, 127, 158-9, 173, 182, 271, 315-16; vol. 7, pp. 651-73.
18. G.P. Insh, *Scottish Colonial Schemes, 1620-1686*, Glasgow, 1922, pp. 67-94. N. Landsman, *Scotland and Its First American Colony, 1683-1760*, Princeton 1985. L.G. Fryer, 'Robert Barclay of Urie and East New Jersey', *Northern Scotland*, vol. 15, 1995, pp. 1-17. T.M. Devine, *Scotland's Empire, 1600-1815*, London, 2003, pp. 36-40.
19. 'Breve, til Vels med Bilag fra Medlemmer af det engelske Kongehus til Medlemmer af det danske', 1613-1726, England, AI, 3-4 and 'Politiske Forhold', 1679-1701: State Papers Denmark-Greg's Diplomatic Papers, England, AII, 33-7, TKUA, DR. Sir John Clerk of Penicuik, *History of the Union of Scotland and England*, ed. D. Duncan, Edinburgh, 1993, pp. 81-3.
20. M.J. Braddick, *The Nerves of State. Taxation and the Financing of the English State, 1558-1714*, Manchester, 1996, pp. 27-45. T. Harris, 'Incompatible Revolutions. The Established Church and the Revolutions of 1688-9 in Ireland, England and Scotland', in *The Stuart Kingdoms in the Seventeenth Century: Awkward Neighbours*, ed. A.I. Macinnes and J. Ohlmeyer, Dublin, 2002, pp. 204-25. J.R. Young, 'The Scottish Parliament and the Covenanting Heritage of Constitutional Reform', in ibid., pp. 204-50. William of Orange had actively encouraged advocacy of an incorporating union by an overwhelmingly Whiggish Convention of Estates in the spring of 1689. Such Scottish lobbying, though ostensibly an ideological mark of Whig solidarity in Britain, was primarily driven by the military threat from Jacobitism, which did not abate until 1691. Lobbying for union, moreover, served as a device for the Convention to turn itself into a parliament that had the exclusive powers to commission bilateral negotiations. Lobbying duly ceased when the Convention became a parliament in July 1689. *An Account of the Proceedings of the Estates in Scotland, 1689-1690*, ed. E.W.H. Balfour-Melville, 2 vols., Edinburgh, 1954, vol. 1, pp. 42, 50-109. R. Ferguson,

The Late Proceedings and Votes of the Parliament of Scotland Contained in an Address Delivered to the King, Signed by the Plurality of the Members Thereof, Stated and Vindicated, Glasgow, 1689. P.W.J. Riley, *King William and the Scottish Politicians*, Edinburgh, 1979, pp. 7-8, 27-33, 48-54, 160-2.

21. R. Saville, 'Scottish Modernisation Prior to the Industrial Revolution, 1688-1763', in *Eighteenth Century Scotland. New Perspectives*, ed. T.M. Devine and J.R. Young, East Linton, 1999, pp. 6-23.

22. S. Pincus, 'From Holy Cause to Economic Interest. The Study of Population and the Invention of the State', in *A Nation Transformed. England after the Restoration*, ed. A. Houston and S. Pincus, Cambridge, 2001, pp. 277-98.

23. T.C. Smout, *Scottish Trade on the Eve of Union, 1660-1707*, London, 1963, pp. 205, 244-51. C.A. Whatley, *Scottish Society, 1707-1830*, Manchester, 2000, pp. 31-9. Although Scotland undoubtedly suffered from trade deficits and falling exports in the concluding decades of the seventeenth century, with the outbreak of the War of the Spanish Succession, Scotland's maritime trade revived while the English and Dutch trading losses actually increased. E.J. Graham, 'In Defence of the Scottish Maritime Interest, 1681-1713', *SHR*, vol. 71, 1992, pp. 88-109.

24. 'Politiske Forhold, 1679-1701: 'State Papers Denmark (1694-1701)', England AII, 34, TKUA, DR. CSP, Colonial (1681-85), nos. 580, 885. *Minutes of the Provincial Council of Pennsylvania, 1683-1775*, ed. S. Hazard, 10 vols. (1851-52), vol. 1 (1683-1700), pp. 90-1, 527, 550-1. *Proceedings of the Council of Maryland*, vol. 8 (1687/8-1693), pp. 335-7, 358-9; vol. 20 (1693-97), pp. 236-7, 546-7; vol. 23 (1696/7-1698), pp. 11-12, 402, 551; vol. 25 (1698-1731), pp. 73, 80, 96, 98-9. *Proceedings of the Provincial Council*, vol. 69 (1679-1680/1), pp. 238-41, 300-9, http.//www.mdarchives.state.md.usa/ Archives of Maryland online. W.R. Brock, *Scotus Americanus: A Survey of the Sources for Links between Scotland and America in the Eighteenth Century*, Edinburgh, 1982, pp. 11-12.

25. 'Den af Isack Holmes Fuldmægtig, Seneca Torsen, holdne Journal paa alle engelske og skotske Skippere saavel fra Vestersøen som fra Østersøen, der har passeret Øresund', 1681-4, Diverse breve, documenter og akter, C.63-III, DK, DR. 'Scott of Ancrum', MSS GD 259/4/29 and 'Andrew Russell Papers', GD 1/885/2/23 and 'Journal of William Fraser, London merchant', CS 96/524 and 'Letter and Account Book of John Watson, Edinburgh Merchant', CS 96/3309, NAS. 'Glasgow Burgh Court Register of Deeds', B 10/15/1811/2135/2155,

Glasgow City Archives. Macinnes, Harper and Fryer, eds., *Scotland and the Americas*, pp. 73-4. Instead of making direct journeys to and from the Baltic, Scottish ships were often inclined to travel or tramp around the Baltic picking up and depositing cargoes at different ports before returning to Scotland sometimes one, two or more years after their departure. This tramping routine was transferred to the Americas by the later seventeenth century.

26. D. Harris-Sax, *The Widening Gate: Bristol and the Atlantic Economy, 1450-1700*, Berkeley, 1991, pp. 14-15, 251-77.
27. *Calendar of Treasury Papers* (1557-1728), 6 vols., ed. J. Reddington, London, 1868-89 (1708-1814), pp. 117, 170, 229, 241, 252-3, 261. T.M. Devine, *The Tobacco Lords*, Edinburgh, 1975, pp. 55-71. A.I. Macinnes, 'Scottish Gaeldom from Clanship to Commercial Landlordism', in *Scottish Power Centres from the Middle Ages to the Twentieth Century*, ed. S. Foster, A.I. Macinnes and R. MacInnes, Glasgow, 1998, pp. 162-90.
28. 'Convention of Royal Burghs', Moses Collection, SL 30/215, Edinburgh City Archives. Sir Thomas Craig, *Scotland's Soveraignty Asserted*, tr. G. Ridpath, London, 1695. H. Chamberlen, *Papers Relating to a Bank of Credit Upon Land Security*, Edinburgh, 1693. R. Murray, *A Proposal for a National Bank Consisting of Land, or Any Other Valuable Securities or Depositions, with a Grand Cash for Returns of Money*, London, 1695. [Ph. Verax], *A letter from a member of the parliament of Scotland to his friend at London concerning their late act for establishing a company of that kingdom trading to Africa and the Indies*, London, 1695.
29. 'Papers Relating to Trade, etc.', Sloane MS 2902, ff. 115-16, 171-80, 244, BL Ch. Davenant, *Discourses on the Publick Revenues, and on the Trade of England*, London, 1698. There was a tenuous balance of payments of £ 74,000 in the value of goods exported over those imported and a turnover in English customs of £ 6,174,000.
30. J. Cary, *A Discourse Concerning the Trade of Ireland and Scotland as They Stand in Competition with the Trade of England*, Bristol, 1695 and London, 1696. 'Papers relating to Trade, etc.', Sloane MS 2902, ff. 137-8, 218, BL. The Council was particularly concerned to establish the reliability of reports that the Scots controlled two-thirds of Irish trade as 30,000 were reported to have migrated to Ireland to take advantage of the reconstruction necessary after the Jacobite rising and another 20,000 were said to have come over following the outbreak of the famine in 1695.
31. Acts of the Parliament of Scotland (hereafter AP), 12 vols., ed.

T. Thomson and C. Innes, Edinburgh, 1814-72, vol. 9, c. 49-53, pp. 313-19, c. 10, pp. 377-81, c. 34, pp. 420-1, c. 41, p. 429, c. 43, pp. 430-1, c. 73, p. 463, c. 83, pp. 490-1, c. 88, pp. 494-7. 'Hamilton Papers', GD 406/1/6784, NAS. W.D. Jones, 'The Bold Adventurers: A Quantitative Analysis of the Darien Subscription Lists (1696)', *Scottish Economic & Social History*, vol. 21, 2001, pp. 22-42.

32. A.I. Macinnes, 'Union for Ireland failed (1703), Union for Scotland accomplished (1706-7)', in *Acts of Union: The Causes, Contexts, and Consequences of the Act of Union of 1801*, ed. D. Keogh and K. Whelan, Dublin, 2001, pp. 67-94. Devine, *Scotland's Empire*, pp. 40-8.-'Hamilton Papers', GD 406/1/4393, /9078, NAS.
33. Loudoun Scottish Collection, box 3/LO 7171, box 48/L0 10102 and Blathwayt Papers, BL 10. Scott, *The Constitutions and Finance of English, Scottish and Irish Joint-Stock Companies*, vol. 2, pp. 207-27. Anon., *Some considerations upon the late act of the Parliament of Scotland, for constituting an Indian company in a letter to a friend*, London, 1695. Anon., *Some considerations concerning the prejudice which the Scotch act establishing a company to trade to the East and West-Indies (with large priviledges, and on easie terms) may bring to the English sugar plantations, and the manufactury of refining sugar in England, and some means to prevent the same from Scotland and other nations*, London, 1696. Anon., *In the act for raising two million, and for settling the trade to the East-Indies are the following clauses*, Edinburgh, 1698.
34. Bridgewater & Ellesmere MSS, EL 9776-7, 9802-3, 9880, HL. *Proceedings & Acts of the General Assembly*, vol. 19 (1693-7), pp. 545, 582. *Proceedings of the Council of Maryland*, vol. 20 (1693-7), pp. 345-55, 569, http.//www.mdarchives.state.md.usa/ Archives of Maryland online. William's hostility, however, does not fully explain why the Scots, with their long-standing commercial associations in the East and West Indies, did not press the Dutch to assist them to ensure that Darien succeeded as a colonial venture. For the mercantile houses of Amsterdam, supplemented by those of Hamburg, effectively ran the Danish West Indian and Guinea Company, which used St. Thomas in the Virgin Islands less as a base for slave trading as an entrepôt for the exchange of Brazilian timber for Norwegian stockfish. The Danish Company offered a model of sorts for a colonial partnership, the African Company of Brandenburg also had its Caribbean base on St. Thomas. S. Murdoch, 'The Good, the Bad and the Anonymous. A Preliminary Survey of the Scots in the Dutch East Indies, 1612-1707', *Northern Scotland*, vol. 22, 2002, pp. 63-76. Direktionens Korrespondance

- Supplikationskopibøger (1690-1712), A 4/465-7, Vestindisk-Guineisk Kompagni, 1671-1755, DR. That William was aware of these alternative paths to colonialism can be no more than mooted. However, Blathwayt was fully informed from his diplomatic sources that there were long-standing tensions between the Danish and Brandenburg Companies, with the latter attempting to secure its own independent entrepôt elsewhere in the Virgin Islands (on Tortola or St. Croix). Dutch reluctance to support a working accommodation with the Scots can be attributed partly to their diversity of commercial and provincial interests. Clear concerns were also expressed from Surinam and Curaçao that the Scots should be viewed more as rivals than partners; concerns that were not abated by Scottish exploratory trading ventures in the Caribbean from their first attempts at settling Darien. Politiske Forhold, 1679-1701: Greg's Diplomatic Papers (1694-99), England, AII, 36, TKUA, DR. Anon,. *The Conduct of the Dutch Relating to the Breach of Treaties with England*, London, 1760, pp. 88-9. Douglas of Strathendry MSS, GD 446/39/15-6, NAS.

35. Bridgewater and Ellesmere MSS, EL 9740 and Blathwayt Papers, BL 6-9, HL. Leven & Melville MSS, GD 26/13/101/105 and Hamilton Papers, GD 406/1/4382-3/4392/4404/4462-4/4485/4541/4572/4749/6484/6553/6983/9078/9086/9115, NAS.
36. Huntington Manuscripts: West Indies, HM 32282-3, HL. E. Ward, *A Journey to Scotland Giving a Character of That Country, the People and Their Manners*, London, 1699. Anon., *Caledonia; or, the Pedlar turn'd Merchant: A Tragi-Comedy, as it was acted by His Majesty's Subjects of Scotland in the King of Spain's Provinces of Darien*, London, 1700. C. Storrs, 'Disaster at Darien (1698-1700)? The Persistence of Spanish Imperial Power on the Eve of the Demise of the Spanish Habsburgs', *European History Quarterly*, vol. 29, 1999, pp. 5-38.
37. Cf. Anon., *A letter from a gentleman in the country to his friend in Edinburgh wherein it is clearly proved that the Scottish African and Indian Company is exactly calculated for the interest of Scotland*, Edinburgh, 1696. [J. Holland], *A short discourse on the present temper of the nation with respect to the Indian and African Company, and of the Bank of Scotland also, of Mr Paterson's pretended fund of credit*, Edinburgh, 1696. Anon., *A proper project for Scotland to startle fools, and frighten knaves, but to make wise-men happy*, Edinburgh, 1699. [Philo-Caledon], *A defence of the Scots settlement at Darien. With an answer to the Spanish memorial against it. And arguments to prove that it is in the interest of England to join with the Scots and protect it*, Edinburgh, 1699.

[Philo-Britan], *The defence of the Scots settlement at Darien, answer'd paragraph by paragraph*, London 1699. Leven & Melville MSS, GD 26/13/95/111 and Breadalbane Collection, GD 112/39/182/21 and Hamilton Papers, GD 406/1/4362, NAS.

38. *Company of Scotland Trading to Africa and the Indies, Scotland's right to Caledonia (formerly called Darien) and the legality of the settlement asserted in three several memorials presented to His Majesty in May 1699*, Edinburgh, 1700. *APS*, X, pp. 126, 132, 134, 194, 201, 211, 242-8, 251, 254, 257, 282, 339, Appendix pp. 19, 36-41, 43, 73-86. William R., *His Majesties Most Gracious Letter to the Parliament of Scotland*, Edinburgh, 1700. Hamilton Papers, GD 406/1/4559/4594/4637/4778/6595 and Campbell of Barcaldine MSS, GD 170/641 & NAS, Leven & Melville MSS, GD 26/13/119, NAS.
39. G.P. Insh, *The Company of Scotland Trading to Africa and the Indies*, London, 1932, pp. 245-77. Leven and Melville MSS, GD 26/13/118 and Hamilton Papers, GD 406/1/4688/4697/4711/5640, NAS.
40. D. Armitage, *The Ideological Origins of the British Empire*, Cambridge, 2000, pp. 146-69. Anon., *An Essay against the transportation and selling of men to the plantations of foreigners with special regard to the manufactories, and other domestick improvements of the kingdom of Scotland*, Edinburgh, 1699. Sir William Seton of Pitmedden, *The Interest of Scotland in Three Essays*, London, 1700.
41. Papers Relating to Trade, etc., Sloane MS 2902, ff. 2-10, BL. Hamilton Papers, GD 406/1/4440/4510/4581/4583/4666/6986/7278/7281/7283/7285/7288/7291/10341, NAS. This incipient political party, which was led nominally by William Douglas-Hamilton, fourth Duke of Hamilton, consisted of three groupings—disappointed placemen and colonial adventurers headed by Hamilton and his considerably more principled kinsman, John Hamilton, Lord Belhaven; constitutional reformers galvanized by Andrew Fletcher of Saltoun's intent to secure fundamental limitations on aristocratic as well as monarchic power; and reinvigorated Jacobites who had attracted the likes of George Lockhart of Carnwath, an energetic organizer committed to maximizing national grievances to effect the restoration of the exiled house of Stuart.
42. Saltoun Papers, MS 17498, fol. 73, NLS. Loudoun Scottish Collection, box 18/LO 8600, box 20/LO 9532, box 39/LO 92832, HL. Hamilton Papers, GD 406/1/4552/4651/4670-1/4688/4790/4820/4907/4976/5018-19/6506/7419 and Douglas of Strathendry MSS, GD 446/40/2, NAS. 'A Journal of Proceedings upon the Union between the Two

Kingdoms of England and Scotland', 1702-03, SP 54/2/1, Public Record Office (hereafter PRO). D. Szechi, 'Constructing a Jacobite. The Social and Intellectual Origins of George Lockhart of Carnwath', *Historical Journal*, vol. 40, 1997, pp. 977-96. W.A. Speck, *The Birth of Britain: A New Nation, 1700-1710*, Oxford, 1994, pp. 44-5.

43. [G. Ridpath], *Proceedings of the Parliament of Scotland Begun at Edinburgh, 6th May 1703. With an Account of All the Material Debates Which Occur'd During that Session*, Edinburgh, 1704. The pro-English ministry, Court Party, in a feeble attempt to regain the political initiative, sponsored the wine act, which maintained French links despite the current English trade embargo. Tensions with England were generally aggravated by a largely fabricated Jacobite plot, which was supposed to implicate Scottish politicians across the party spectrum. This 'Scotch Plot' was investigated judicially by the House of Lords without reference to the Scottish Estates (Loudoun Scottish Collection, box 20/L0 9532, /L0 9536-7, HL; ICA, bundle 17/3).

44. Clerk of Penicuik, *History of the Union of Scotland and England*, pp. 81-5. D. Daiches, *Scotland and the Union*, London, 1977, pp. 68-125. P.W.J. Riley, 'The Union of 1707 as an Episode in English Politics', *English Historical Review*, vol. 84, 1979, pp. 498-527.

45. W. Ferguson, *Scotland's Relations with England: A Survey to 1707*, Edinburgh, 1977, pp. 232-69. P.W.J. Riley, *The Union of England and Scotland*, Manchester, 1978, pp. 254-338.

46. Smout, *Scottish Trade on the Eve of Union, 1660-1707*, pp. 261-75. [G. Ridpath], *The Case of Scots-men Residing in England and in the English Plantations*, Edinburgh, 1703. J. Spreull, *An Account Current betwixt Scotland & England Balanced Together with an Essay of a Scheme of the Product of Scotland, and a few Remarks on Each*, Edinburgh, 1705. *A Letter Concerning Trade from Several Scots Gentlemen that are Merchants in England, to their Countrymen that are Merchants in Scotland*, London, 1706. *Answer to a Letter concerning Trade Sent from Several Scots Gentlemen, that are Merchants in England to Their Countrymen that are Merchants in Scotland*, Edinburgh, 1706. D. Black, *An Essay upon Industry and Trade showing the Necessity of the One, the Conveniency and Usefulness of the Other and the Advantages of Both*, Edinburgh, 1706.

47. J. Mackinnon, *The Union of England and Scotland: A Study in International History*, London, 1896, pp. 240-72. K.P. Penovich, 'From Revolution Principles' to Union. Daniel Defoe's Intervention in the Scottish Debate', in *A Union for Empire: Political Thought and the Union of 1707*,

ed. J. Robertson, Cambridge, 1995, pp. 228-42. On the political level, Defoe was to retain a watching brief that the Court Party did not accept any material alterations or amendments to the Treaty that would breach the financial reparations agreed as the Equivalents. Any such breach would open the door to the Treaty being questioned or impeded in the English Parliament.

48. Loudoun Scottish Collection, box 43/LO 10045, HL. [D. Defoe], *The Advantages of Scotland by an Incorporating Union with England, Compar'd with these of a Coalition with the Dutch or League with the French*, 1706. Scottish concerns to be informed of Dutch and French standpoints on the Treaty of Union had led the Privy Council to authorize the translation and publication of the Haarlem Courant and the Paris Gazette from the outset of 1706.

49. Parliamentary Memorandums, A 817/2, pp. 53-4, Dumfries House, Ayrshire. P. Abercromby, *The Advantages of the Act of Security Compared with These of the Intended Union Founded on the Revolution Principles Publish'd by Mr Daniel De Foe*, 1706. Anon., *An Essay on Removing Rational Prejudices Against a Union with England, 1706* in three parts. Prussia—State Papers, 1706-8, SP 90/4, ff. 171-5, 313-14, 327-33, 337-40, PRO.

50. [J. Hodge], *The Rights and Interests of the Two British Monarchies with a Special Respect to an United or Separate States. Treatise III*, London, 1706. There was a general recognition Defoe shared with his sympathizers and detractors among Scottish polemicists, that the Treaty did not entail the absolute surrender of Scottish sovereignty. Should ensuing British parliaments breach fundamental safeguards for the Presbyterian establishment, education, Scots law and local government, Scotland would be reduced from partnership to the satellite status of the Irish which would, in turn, imperil the continuance of Union (F. Grant), *The Patriot Resolved*, 1707. L. Dickey, 'Power, Commerce and Natural Law in Daniel Defoe's Political Writings' in *A Union for Empire*, pp. 63-96.

51. T.C. Smout, 'The Anglo-Scottish Union of 1707, vol. 1: The Economic Background', *Economic History Review* (Second Series), vol. 16, 1963-4, pp. 455-67. A.M. Carstairs, 'Some Economic Aspects of the Union of Parliaments', *Scottish Journal of Political Economy*, vol. 2, 1955, pp. 64-72.

52. CSP, *Colonial*, 1707, p. 431.

PART IV

EUROPE: HYDRAULIC STATES

CHAPTER 11

Water Control—A Network of Knowledge and Know-how.

Europe, America and Asia (Fifteenth to Nineteenth Century)

SALVATORE CIRIACONO

At the end of the Middle Ages and right through the sixteenth century, water control and scientific knowledge underwent fundamental transformations. This was due to geographical exploration and the relative decline of the Islamic tradition that had played an important role in the transmission of knowledge from Asia to Europe. At the same time, the economic standing of the Mediterranean was in decline—with the Italian economy, in particular, falling behind those of the Atlantic and northern European countries. More importantly, during these centuries, different scientific and technological traditions interacted more closely than generally realized or accepted. In the Mediterranean, Venice serves as a classic example, which constituted first a water city, second, a world economy (during the fifteenth and sixteenth centuries), and third, was able to draw on the traditions of the Islamic countries of the eastern Mediterranean, Spain and western Europe, and thus played a key role in the transfer of water technology.

The sixteenth century also saw the transfer of some legislation and technological knowledge pertaining to water regulation from Spain to Lombardy—and, thus, indirectly to Venice. Spain, in turn, had inherited such knowledge from the Islamic world. The process of transmission is not entirely clear or even well researched. Indeed, recent scholarship from the Iberian Peninsula challenges the view that Spain failed to acknowledge the influence of Islamic countries. Just one episode explains this assumption: Gabriel Alfonso de Herrera's influential treatise, *Obra de agricoltura*, published in 1513, attaches more importance to classical and Italian hydraulics than to the assimilation of the Islamic tradition in Spain.[1] Indeed, the analysis in Herrera's treatise raises another question. What was the role of Roman and the classical traditions in Mediterranean countries? What role did they play in the agronomical literature produced in other parts of Europe? It is certain that during the sixteenth century new editions of Frontinus, Pliny the Elder, Vitruvius and Columella—as well classics such as Euclid and Hero of Alexandria—proliferated in many European countries. Italy, and Venice in particular, assumed a crucial role in this context. According to Corinne Beutler, more agricultural books were published in Venice than in any other European city. It is worth noting that eminent writers like the Frenchmen Bernard Palissy or Olivier de Serres, were also influenced by the hydraulics and agronomy of classical antiquity.

Nevertheless, as important ancient hydrology may have been, modern hydraulics solved fundamental theoretical questions only during the Scientific Revolution of the seventeenth century, such as by the calculation of the speed of water, investigated in a thoroughly scientific manner in Benedetto Castelli's seminal work *Della misura delle'acque correnti* (1628).[2] Till then, the quantity of water flowing through a section of a canal (for irrigation purposes or as a source of energy) was calculated by taking into account only the area of the section passed through by the water itself, time and speed were not taken into consideration—a situation that permitted all sorts of abuse (for example, the consumption of far more water than permitted by authorities). As observed, technology in Roman times considered the quantity of water (Q) equal to the area (i.e. $Q = A$), and during the Renaissance, scientific hydraulics did not extend much beyond these theoretical parameters. The ancient tradition was vital in any context during the sixteenth century: in Italian treatises, French science and agronomy, British know-how, Church science, the Spanish Empire, as well as in the colonization of the Americas.

Another essential question is the extent to which oriental knowledge was transmitted to Europe, either through the mediation of the Islamic world or as a result of direct Euro–Asian contacts (the vast and complex issue of possible reciprocal influence of Chinese and European know-how remains inconclusive even today). To some degree, one may extend the seminal observations in Karl August Wittfogel's 'Oriental Despotism' to Europe and America, and that is essentially what is attempted in this paper. In fact, whilst initially formulated with reference to China, the tenets of 'Oriental Despotism' have also been applied to the historiography of Latin America, where 'the aggressive warriors of Navarra and Castille [. . .] destroyed the hydraulic core of the high American civilizations with the self-same political and economic weapons they had used against the centres of Moorish irrigation—Cordoba, Seville, and Granada'. It is now clear that the centralist tenets of Wittfogel cannot be applied to other regions—and even some regions in China have revealed that local communities succeeded in managing water in a more rational way than the central authority. Contrary to what one may surmise, it was the Middle East that emerged as the cradle of democratic management of water resources. This can be seen from the nascent Mesopotamian civilization that also stands in sharp contrast to the rigid despotism which later developed there. In fact, one should underscore the dangers of applying excessively broad generalizations in this regard—generalizations such as 'Hydraulic Society' and 'Oriental Despotism'.

Over the past few decades, a lively debate has ensued between historians, anthropologists and economists on this very issue. Geographers first expressed serious doubts about a univocal relation between geographical environment and social development and questioned the claim that there is 'an environmental determinism which embraces any explanation of societal change'. However crucial irrigation may be, it does not itself determine particular forms of despotic government. Water control schemes should be analysed in relation to other variables which are not only politico-economic and geographical-environmental, but also socio-cultural. Not only was 'Hydraulic Despotism' not a necessary precondition for the establishment of a modern bureaucracy and full territorial control, in some cases it actually hindered such development by protecting established forms of privilege and social status. This does not mean that there are no cases of 'despotism' or other forms of authoritarian administration conducive to establishing central institutions which promote embankment and irrigation schemes. What will be argued here, is that despotism was not the only socio-political system capable of organizing such schemes. Dutch *Hoogheemraadschappen*, whose origins go back to the Middle Ages, are—along with the irrigation projects in the Valencia region of Spain—perhaps the most obvious examples of the need to supplant Wittfogel's 'central theory' with a model based on an analysis of 'subordinate local systems'. Additionally, area studies of Cambodia, Burma (Pagan) and ancient Ceylon also defy Wittfogel's axiom and, it should be added, he did not take these regions into consideration when formulating his theory. The approach is further limited in its focus to arid and semi-arid regions, neglecting humid and subtropical areas which scholars are now studying in greater detail. A number of sociological and anthropological studies have amply demonstrated the need to connect Eastern and Western countries and to look at the similarities (and differences) in their water policies. Indeed, when Wittfogel studied other areas such as India, Mexico and pre-Spanish Peru, in the course of which he sought to confirm 'Asiatic conditions', he concluded that the transplantation of Spanish agricultural techniques (large scale farms, increase in livestock breeding, neglect of much of hydraulic engineering left by the Arabs) to Latin America induced a corresponding decline in native New World engineering.[3]

Certainly, reality was not as simple in the Americas as in other parts of the world, and Wittfogel is accredited with highlighting a close link between technology and modes of production, as well as between a scientific culture and the prevalent social, political and international conditions. Sometimes it is very difficult, or even impossible, to detect these relationships. As Norman Smith clarified when writing about hydraulics, the Romans had acquired technical skills from other societies, but clear evidence of precisely how this functioned is not so easy to unravel. It is also necessary to ask why a certain cultural and social environment is more likely than another to embrace innovation, especially when it emanates from a scientific milieu that is distinct from the popular culture which, until that point in time, has solved its hydraulic problems successfully on its own. There is no subject like water management in which the relationship, and sometimes the conflict, between cultural practice and scientific knowledge has been so obvious. All these aspects certainly came into play when the Spaniards arrived in Central and South America.

Another agent that should be taken into account in this process of technological transfer is the Church which played a role as least as important as the hydraulics of classical antiquity. The Church which was an autonomous source of scientific research in its own right and remained so for centuries, kept the heritage alive and also developed new technologies. It should be borne in mind that Benedetto Castelli was a cleric and that, as an ecclesiastical order, the Jesuits were engaged in various research projects that importantly included hydraulics. It was logical that, with the arrival of missionaries in the Americas, Church science also evolved, and clerics served as transmitters of basic information between the two worlds. When they returned to Europe in the eighteenth century, the Jesuits introduced knowledge to the Old World that had been developed in the Americas during the early modern period. They played a very similar role upon their return from Asia.[4] Setting aside theoretical science, it is known that priests in Mexico took charge of the construction of irrigation works, which overlapped with, and fed into, the ancient irrigation systems of the Mayas and the Aztecs.

Of similar importance in this general discussion of our subject is the Flemish–Dutch technology that was adopted in Europe, Asia and the Americas. Until the end of the sixteenth century, Italian hydraulics assumed a pivotal role in this field. A great deal of engineering and military technology was connected with hydraulics, a fact which is confirmed by the countless Italian engineers who were active in England, the Low Countries and Germany. Technological transfer in this domain was firmly in the hands of the Italian Peninsula. For instance, Giuseppe Aconcio, a mathematician and military engineer, was in England during the reign of Elizabeth I and presented a general project to drain the Fens.[5] In many European countries, fountains and urban aqueducts were built by Italian architects, who were no less important than the Germans or the French.[6] There were considerably more Italian than Flemish or Dutch brevets dating from the sixteenth century that devised schemes to raise water for irrigation purposes, channel it to mills, or exploit it generally for hydraulic power. From the end of the 1500s the situation began to change and Flemish–Dutch hydraulics moved from the Low Countries to England, to northern Germany, along the Marschen, to some extent to Italy and to the Americas as well. Dutch towns were encircled by canals built to original designs, and intended partly as defence against the Spanish army.

Spain offers the best example of the interconnection of different scientific traditions, both Roman and Islamic. How smoothly the management of agriculture and the manipulation of irrigation passed from Moslems to Christians in Spain is of course well known.[7] The problem is that the Reconquista provoked a kind of nationalistic approach that tended to hide or relegate to oblivion the achievements of Islamic tradition. Sometimes, as in the case of Alfonso de Herrera, the classical tradition appeared to be more evident than the Islamic one, even though the latter clearly survived in rural society.

Apart from the Roman and Islamic transfer of technology, a third aspect need be taken in consideration when discussing the Iberian Peninsula: the direct influence of contemporary Italian technology during the sixteenth century. This aspect merits more extensive investigation. According to Nicolás García Tapia, the presence of Italian engineers was overestimated, and he has done research and provided precise data on Italian as well as German, Flemish–Dutch, French and English engineers working in sixteenth-century Spain. He claimed that the Spaniards were ultimately more numerous than the Italians and not as insignificant as conventional historiography has argued. According to the conclusions of Tapia and also of José A.

García-Diego,[8] the most important treatise on hydraulics published in Spain ('The Twenty-one Books of Devices and Machines') should not be attributed, as it has long been, to the Italians Giovanni Francesco Sitoni (of Scottish origin but born in Milan) or Juanelo Turriano (born in Cremona), but to the Aragonese Pedro Juan de Lastanosa. Even if that be true one cannot overlook the fundamental contribution made by these Italians. There were various reasons for their presence and significance in Spain: several Italian states were under Spanish rule; Flemish and German engineers experienced considerably more difficulties with the language than their Italian counterparts; many Spanish engineers were educated in Flanders and in Italy, despite the opposition expressed by Philip II to their study abroad. In the long run, Spain had the great advantage over Italy of being involved in the colonization of the Americas and was thus in a position to develop new tools. For example, navigational instruments used to measure distance found additional applications in hydraulics. Spain was very innovative in this regard, introducing instruments such as the *corobate*, *nivel de tranco* and *nivelador de grados*.

In Spain, Italy and elsewhere, hydraulics remained closely linked to geometry, mathematics, topography, cosmography, astronomy and geography, in other words, to a largely interdisciplinary knowledge that had measurement as its primary aim. It is not surprising that Spanish engineers were preoccupied to a large extent with hydraulics. In fact, this was the second most important field after the construction and public works sector. Nautical science, artillery, and fortification—fundamental to the Spanish Empire—lagged behind the development of new machines for water lifting (a fundamental chapter in European Renaissance hydraulics) as well as technology for dam building, irrigation and transportation canals.[9]

In the construction of water reservoirs Spanish engineering aimed at innovation. During the reign of Philip II the Tibi dike was constructed. Designed by Italian engineers Juanelo Turriano and Cristobal Antonelli, it ranked among the highest dikes in the world at the time, measuring 42 m.

Flemish know-how appeared very decisive in this kind of project, especially in the construction of the so-called gravity dike that retained water behind two stone walls; the other design was the bow-type. After 1560, a Flemish engineer, Pieter Jasen, known as 'el Holandés', constructed under the auspices of Juan Bautista de Toledo several such dikes in El Pardo, at Casa del Campo, El Escorial and Aránjuez. According to Norman Smith, the sixteenth and seventeenth centuries witnessed important developments in dam building in Spain. By the seventeenth century, technology had advanced sufficiently to enable the use of arch action alone. Spanish technology possibly drew on what was developed in England: Pedro de Zubiaurre, for example, copied a water pump invented by Peter Morris and used on the Thames. He sought to introduce it in the region around Valladolid where advanced technology in this domain was used throughout the sixteenth century.[10] Indeed, willingness to copy from other successful projects, or in inviting technicians and engineers from abroad, are all positive aspects. With regard to Spain, the most intriguing question concerns the successful completion of water management projects. This is particularly the case if attention is focused on the transfer of technology from one continent to the other. The creation of a network of canals is a highly controversial issue in Spanish history, as the country's competence in improving interior navigation and enhancing agricultural productivity through irrigation reflects its ability to remain a great power during the sixteenth century. The control of huge resources of silver enabled the Spanish Empire to employ many engineers from across Europe, but this did not lead to the construction of a dense water network in a country that required water more than any other on the continent. The sixteenth and seventeenth centuries witnessed a string of failures, even though the projects and the technicians employed to complete them were most certainly not lacking in skills. Between 1548 and 1550, that is during the reign of Maximilian of Austria, Spain saw a revival of interest in inland navigation. During this period, technicians of German origin teamed up with the Italians, and near the monastery of San Benito outside Valladolid, a sluice was designed that conformed to Leonardo da Vinci's model. This was meant to restrain a strong river current (aceñas). Also, at the behest of Maximilian, the canal of Castilla was conceived, but construction was not commenced until 1753.[11] Additional navigation canals were planned during the reign of Philip II. One canal leading off from the river Tago was successfully completed by Giovanbattista Antonelli, to whom is also attributed the broader plan '*para la navegación de todos los ríos de España*' (for the navigation on all the rivers of Spain). Few of these schemes, however, were completed in the course of the sixteenth century and fewer still during the reign of Philip III. According to García Tapia, during the latter period the only public watercourse built was intended for strictly religious and not agricultural or commercial purposes; it was constructed to enable the king to pass over an *aceñas* so that he could visit the monastery of 'Los martires'.[12]

It is understandable that this approach to water resource management was transferred to colonial possessions in Central and South America. The techniques that the Spanish inherited from the Moslems, Romans and from their own tradition were further developed in the New World. Still, one cannot accept Wittfogel's conclusions entirely. The theory of 'Water Despotism' does not fit into the complexity of the American situation where European technology and political organization were in contact with older advanced water civilizations. In the absence of any contact with Europeans, these civilizations were in fact capable of developing original technology that was fully adapted to their own setting. The mountain regions of southern Peru and northern Bolivia, for example, witnessed advancement in canal building, revealing high skills in engineering. Although some aspects of 'Andean Despotism' were noted within the context of the Chimú civilization, the latter showed itself capable of adapting technological expertise to a particular geographical and geological setting. The construction of an extensive network of canals, both intra-valley and inter-valley—executed at correct gradients, and in a few instances involving the creation of reservoirs of modest size—was an impressive achievement of civil engineering. This required repeated adaptation to changing circumstances over time. In the face of adverse natural conditions, the engineers were qualified to irrigate and cultivate hostile land with the assistance of advanced skills in surveying and channel design. The sophistication and originality of Chimú know-how in this field becomes clear when one takes into account the fact that these people did not have the mathematical skills that accompanied the development of hydraulic engineering in Europe during the Scientific Revolution.[13]

Irrigation practice was also observed in some regions of the south-western United States (California, Arizona, Texas and New Mexico). Even there—such as among the Indian Pueblos—some forms of 'Andean Despotism' were discernible with which Spanish technological transfer had to cope.[14] As in Mexico, the role of the Church proved fundamental. Missions were established from Los Angeles to San Antonio that were responsible for erecting numerous dams and digging irrigation canals: the Old Mission, El Molino dam on the San Diego river and the Espada dam on the San Antonio river still survive. In fact, Spanish technology relied more commonly on diversion dams than on reservoir dams, but these were not introduced before the eighteenth century. According to Norman Smith, the influence of engineers from Extremadura is evident from this type of construction. In the south-western states, several buttress dams were constructed which were observed among in the major dams of Mexico as well, enriched with baroque decorations and—far more important—featuring a hydraulic power device installed in the body of the dam itself. Many dry regions could be irrigated and new towns supplied with water, say by diverting water from the river Lerma toward Salamanca, a town founded in central Mexico in 1603.[15]

The legal definitions and property rights transferred from Spain to the Americas were derived from Roman and medieval law. Before colonial expansion, in fact, such rights varied considerably across the Iberian Peninsula. In some regions, such as Valencia and Castellón, ownership of water was firmly linked to the ownership of the land. In other cases (Alicante, Elche, Novelda, where water and land was once owned by the same person) water and land were properties that could be controlled or sold separately. The case of the Canary Islands was entirely different from the sixteenth century onwards.

Heightened demand for water, chiefly linked to the irrigation of sugar cane plantations, completely transformed water rights on the islands. This resulted in the evolution of a mixed model that eventually led to the commercialization of water as a commodity.[16] Despite a form of *dula* (rotation in the distribution of water), Thomas Glick noted a similar process in San Antonio in Texas, where many colonists settled from the Canary Islands. By the end of the eighteenth and the early nineteenth century, ownership of water became distinct from ownership of the land through which it flowed. Even if this was the case in San Antonio, various forms of communitarian distribution of water survived in other areas in the south-western United States, as is evidenced by the *acequias* of New Mexico. As José A. Rivera and T. Glick underlined, the *acequias* or earthen canals constructed across all parts of the south-western United States (Texas, New Mexico, Colorado, Arizona and California) survived perhaps 'as a transplanted Iberian civil and social institution' because these territories remained relatively isolated compared to other Hispanic provinces notably Texas or California.[17]

If the geographical and social origins of the acequias have a historical explanation, doubts persist about the origin of the American qanats or infiltration galleries, which have been much more extensively studied in the Middle East. These underground canals (which tap into an aquifer and carry by gravity water below the surface into the fields or to the village; wells and outlet pipes made it possible to draw off water at regular intervals) can be found in a number of countries throughout the Middle East—from Iran (where they were probably first developed) through Oman and Iraq to the Yemen. Could these have been possibly developed independently in pre-colonial America? Some authors are inclined to believe so, for so many different systems could be found in Peru, Chile and Mexico in the period immediately following the Conquest 'that it is unlikely that they could have been built after the Conquest, especially as these areas had been heavily depopulated'.[18] But for others,[19] such as in Mexico, the infiltration gallery was probably introduced by the monks of the Franciscan order. Similar doubts have been raised by the spread of the *entarquinamento* in colonial

Mexico. This technique is similar to the process of the Italian *colmata* (colmatage in French), whereby alluvial material from a river or torrent is deposited with the objective of eventually reclaiming a predecided area of land. Several terms refer to this process in Latin America (*gavias*, *nateros*, *jessour*, *cajas de agua*) but, more often than not, they suggest the adaptation of a European process, rather than an independent development in pre-colonial America. This conclusion does not imply that Alexander von Humboldt erred, when in 1803 he observed that the wheat harvested in the Mexican Bajío reminded him of the Egyptian fields fertilized by the flood waters of the Nile. Of course, the technique has nothing to do with the Italian *colmata*. Whether the Mexican *bimbalete* (a sort of balance pile connected to a recipient) dates from the pre- or post-colonial period is doubtful. The other terms used to refer to it (*shaduf*, *shadoof*, *shadouf*, *chaduf* or *chadouf*), as Glick correctly argued, make it difficult to discard any Islamic-Hispanic origins.[20]

When analysing the construction of the *desagüe* in Mexico City, one doubtlessly has to turn back to Roman technology and Dutch influence. These were built to prevent the serious flooding that threatened the town during the colonial period. If Spanish engineers could introduce 'the full repertoire of techniques already commonplace in the mother country' for irrigation purposes (such as canal systems, dams, desilting sluices, waterwheels, *norias* and *qanats*), they shared with the Aztecs a problem in tackling land reclamation and drainage.[21] In fact, something similar to the *desagüe* (long subterranean tunnel) had been developed by the Romans, even though 'the 3½-mile tunnel that Claudius built (CE 41-51) to drain Lake Fucino into the river Liris'[22] was nowhere near the length of the 8.02 mile *desagüe* dug at the beginning of 1608 from Lake Zumpango to the Gulf of Mexico. Enrico Martinez, who received his technical education in northern Europe, executed this project. Although he boasted of 'these spectacular achievements, which many had believed impossible', the completed tunnel was soon beset with problems: the underground canal passed through soil that was so soft that it crumbled easily, even if parts of the tunnel had been strengthened. Moreover, the canal had been dug too steep, with the result that, as the water increased in speed, it also increased pressure on the walls. This made it necessary to utilize Dutch know-how, the fame of which quickly spread from Europe to Mesoamerica. Adriaan Boot was called in to present an alternative project, though admittedly, this was not based on the most famous model of Dutch land reclamation: the construction of an open air semi-circular canal (the innovative Dutch *boezem* or *slotring* that flow around the polders in the Low Countries), a protective dike and windmills to pump the water. As is often the case when political authorities are pushed to choose between different solutions of unproven or uncertain merit, the implementation of this new technique proved highly problematic. An open canal (*tajo abierto*) designed to solve the flooding problems of Mexico City was only dug at the beginning of the eighteenth century.

Still, this case allows one to draw two conclusions. The first is that Dutch technology, even though very innovative, was difficult to implement. A dike such as the one proposed by Boot, would certainly have impeded the heavy traffic of boats that carried food supplies to ancient Tenochtitlan. The geographical position of the town and its elevation (7,800 ft. above sea level) was better suited to an Italian-style gravity drainage canal. However, at that time it was Dutch rather than Italian expertise which was widely regarded as the best available, even if it was true that Dutch engineering, whilst successful in its homeland and in some other areas of Europe, was not always able to solve the problems encountered in different topographical settings. What is more, in Mexico, as in other Latin American countries, various factors worked against radical measures to improve irrigation and drainage projects: society was conservative; the economy was less diversified than those in northern Europe; the merchant class was much less influential than its European counterparts; and the intellectual climate was not conducive to innovation. The case of the Mexican *desagüe* is significant but not an exception. The pre-colonial heritage did not really lead to a new approach towards ancient problems in Latin America. In effect, the results revealed the relative decline of—or, at best, a tardy improvement in—an ancient technology.[23]

No less essential is the technological transfer that took place among the numerous Asian regions. Here, the hydraulic technologies found throughout the Middle East and Asia were particularly significant for the Indian subcontinent. The British brought with them French and Italian hydraulic engineering (the theoretical hegemony of which was unchallenged until the middle of the nineteenth century) and made heavy investments in irrigation projects.[24] There is no doubt that the new network of canals dug during the period of British colonialism was an epic feat of civil engineering. However, it is also true that some of these canals pre-dated the arrival of the British (such as the Western Jumna canal, the Eastern Jumna Canal and the Bari Doab canal), and that traditional engineering techniques had achieved remarkable results. Unfortunately, due to their sparse use of masonry structures, these earlier canals were vulnerable to the effects of floods and silt deposits, and were of little use for irrigation purposes. They were used mostly to supply fountains and imperial palaces.[25] The Ganges canal—the first entirely British-built canal—was the product of different traditions and know-how: military engineering (which in 1859 gave rise to a separate discipline of civil engineering), Italian hydraulics and French hydrodynamics (involving Du Buat, Prony, D'Aubuisson and Bazin).

Last but not least, China and Japan were certainly less influenced by European know-how, confirming that as a whole Asia was a continent 'of irrigation agriculture', where water exercised 'a great economic and social influence over the entire agriculture system'.[26] When looking at China, however, one should not fall for an entrenched historical tradition that considers only the traditional canal systems fed by the great rivers, but tends to ignore the large reservoirs and lakes that were used for irrigation purposes. Akira Morita argued that the transition in China 'from the irrigation by means of canals used in northern China [...] to irrigation by barrages and reservoirs in southern China' took place immediately after the T'ang dynasty (CE 608-907). With the advent of the Song dynasty (960-1280), 'creek irrigation also developed in the Yangtze delta', whereas under the subsequent Ming and Qing dynasties (1368-1644 and 1644-1912 respectively) intensive agriculture developed largely based on the cultivation of rice.[27] In effect, there was a sizeable increase in the number of planned and implemented irrigation schemes in the central and eastern provinces. For example, in Hunan province the number of water control projects increased from 26 in the fourteenth century to 187 in the sixteenth century (it was the highest rate in all China).[28] Studying Hunan province,[29] Peter C. Perdue demonstrated how during the Qing period the situation relating to Dongting lake on the Yangtze river was symptomatic for all the economic, political and engineering problems created by irrigation. The first point to be raised is that the situation here belies Wittfogel's thesis of 'Oriental Despotism'. Far from passively suffering autocratic control, Hunan province came into direct conflict with the central government. This is not to say that its aspirations for independence guaranteed a favourable hydrogeological equilibrium: in fact, the difficulty in collecting the necessary maintenance funds—due to the resistance put up by both large landowners and rural communities—meant that there was a steady decline in the state of repair of irrigation canals and dikes. Indeed, when at the beginning of the nineteenth century, a series of floods enforced direct and decisive action by the state, the fiscal and institutional power of the central government had been so undermined that it was incapable of responding adequately.

Just as in the other regions examined, water management in Japan played a structural role in the formation of the modern state and the territorial integrity of the nation. Both were made possible 'by the development of irrigation agriculture'.[30] In Japan, however, the model of development differs from the rest of Asia. It was characterized by 'small-scale farming units', each comprising only a few (1-5) hectares, spread over uneven hilly terrain supplied by equally small-scale irrigation canals.[31] These did not have to cope with any of the disastrous flooding that occurred elsewhere in Asia (as well as in Europe and the Americas). Given that there was no need to engage in complex drainage schemes, energies and resources could be concentrated on irrigation alone, which meant that output per farm outstripped that of other Asian nations (and was probably even higher than in many areas of Europe as well). In fact, whilst European resources were directed toward livestock and farm implements, investment in Japan was focused on water control and irrigation facilities, as well as on the development of new types of rice and fertilizers.

From the sixteenth century onwards, the Daimyo and the Tokugawa Shogunate encouraged the development of a school of hydraulics in the very heart of the country (the Aichi Prefecture). The spread of irrigation and drainage know-how enabled an increase in productivity and facilitated the cultivation of new tracts of land.[32] The techniques employed—such as the channelling of torrent water from the opening of valleys to fields some distance away, or the use of reservoirs and dikes to collect and redistribute water—were not totally unknown in Europe. Nor were the techniques used in draining coastal lands particular to Japan; one recall, for example, the work of Flemish monasteries during the Middle Ages or the Dutch schemes dating from the Middle Ages through to the end of the sixteenth century. What does appear to have been original in the Japanese approach was the practice of covering agricultural land with previously fertilized soil and silt without waiting for the regenerating effect of copious irrigation waters on the new land, as was the case with the *colmatage* in Europe. This was developed on the Italian Peninsula from the fourteenth century onwards, and is very similar to the one described by Herodotus as having been developed in ancient Egypt in the Nile valley.[33]

This last consideration underscores the need for a comparative approach to such questions. This has been accomplished by Francesca Bray when she insists upon the deeper connections brought to light via a comparative study of areas in Asia and Europe which may be geographically far removed from one another.

NOTES

1. G.A. de Herrera, *Obra de agricoltura*, Alcala, 1513, rpt., Valencia, 1979.
2. B. Castelli, *Della misura dell'acque correnti*, Roma, 1628.
3. S. Ciriacono, 'Introduction', in *Land Drainage and Irrigation: Studies in the History of Civil Engineering*, vol. 3, Aldershot, 1998, pp. xv-xxi.

4. U. Baldini, *Saggi sulla cultura della Compagnia di Gesù (secoli XVI-XVIII)*, Padova, 2000.
5. C. Holmes, 'Drainage Projects in Elizabethan England: The European Dimension', in *Eau, et développement dans l'Europe moderne*, ed. S. Ciriacono, Paris 2004, pp. 93-4.
6. S. Ciriacono, 'Wasser', in *Lexikon des Mittelalters*, Munich, 1998, pp. 2064-72. A. Guillerme, *Les temps de l'eau: La cité, l'eau et les techniques*, Seyssel (Champ Vallon), 1983. U. Sowina, 'Les maîtres fontainiers dans les villes de Pologne du bas Moyen Age et au début de l'époque moderne—experts étrangers ou spécialistes polonais?', in *Questiones Medii Aevii Novae*, vol. 3 (Foreign experts), Warszawa, 1998, pp. 205-20.
7. N. Smith, *Man and Water*, London/New York, 1975, p. 22.
8. J.A. García-Diego, *Giovanni Francesco Sitoni, ingeniero renacentista a servicio de la Corona de España. Con su códice inédito trattato delle virtù et proprietà delle acque, en su idioma original y traducido al castellano*, Madrid, 1990.
9. N.G. Tapia, 'Ingenieria civil española en el Renacimiento', in *Cuatro conferencias sobre historia de la ingenieria de obras publicas en España*, Madrid, 1987, pp. 7-30.
10. Smith, *Man and Water*, pp. 23-4, 100-1.
11. G. Pérez Sarrión, 'Hydraulic Policy and Irrigation Works in Spain in the Second Half of the Eighteenth Century', *Journal of European Economic History*, vol. 24, no. 1, 1995, pp. 131-43.
12. Tapia, 'Ingenieria civil española en el Renacimiento', pp. 32-6.
13. C.R. Ortloff, 'Canal Builders of Pre-Inca Peru', *Cambridge Archaeological Journal*, vol. 5, no. 1, 1995, pp. 55-74.
14. Á. Palerm, *Obras hidráulicas prehispánicas en el sistema lacustre del Valle de México*, México, 1973.
15. Smith, *Man and Water*, pp. 25-6.
16. A. Macías Hernandéz, 'Les Iles Canaries, 1480-1525. Irrigation et première colonisation atlantique: Le domaine de l'eau', in *Eau et développement dans l'Europe moderne*, pp. 37-48.
17. T.F. Glick, *The Old World Background of the Irrigation System of San Antonio, Texas*, El Paso, 1972. J. Rivera and T.F. Glick, 'Spanish Origins of the Community Acequias of New Mexico', Unpublished paper presented at the XIII International Economic History Congress, Section 17: Technological Exchange, Modes of Production and Water Utilisation in Europe and Latin America from Ancient Times to the XXth Century, Buenos Aires, 26 July 2002.

18. J. Palerm Viquiera and T. Martínez Saldaña, eds., *Antología sobre Pequeño Riego: Organizaciones Autogestivas*, vol. 2, Plazay Valdés (Mexico), 2000.
19. G.C. Wilken, *Good Farmers. Traditional Agricultural Resource Management in Mexico and Central America*, Berkeley, 1987.
20. T.F. Glick, *Muslim Fortress to Christian Castle. Social and Cultural Change in Medieval Spain*, Manchester, 1995.
21. Smith, *Man and Water*, p. 26.
22. L. Schell Hoberman, 'Technology Change in a Traditional Society: The Case of the Desagüe in Colonial Mexico', *Technology and Culture*, vol. 21, no. 3, 1980, pp. 386-407.
23. Smith, *Man and Water*, pp. 25-6.
24. I. Stone, *Canal Irrigation in British India. Perspectives on Technological Change in a Peasant Economy*, Cambridge/New York, 1984, p. 1.
25. Ibid., p. 14.
26. A. Akira, 'The Development Theory of Irrigation Agriculture', Institute of Developing Economies, Special Paper no. 7, Tokyo, 1977, p. 1.
27. A. Morita, 'Water Control in Zherdong during the Late Ming', *East Asian History* (Australia), vol. 2, 1991, p. 31.
28. D.H. Perkins, *Agricultural Development in China, 1368-1968*, Chicago, 1969, pp. 334-7. See also A. Osborne, 'Economic and Ecological Interaction in the Lower Yangzi Region under the Qing', in *Sediments of Time. Environment and Society in Chinese History*, eds. M. Elvin and Liu Ts'ui-jung, Cambridge/New York, 1997, pp. 203-34. P.-É. Will, 'The Zheng-Bai Irrigation System of Shaanxi Province in the Late-Imperial Period', in ibid., pp. 284-343.
29. P.C. Perdue, 'Water Control in the Dongting Lake Region during the Ming and Qing Periods', *Journal of Asian Studies*, vol. 41, no. 4, 1982, pp. 747-65.
30. I. Hatate, 'Irrigation, Agriculture and the Landlord in Early Modern Japan', Institute of Developing Economies, Special Paper, no. 9, Tokyo, 1978, p. 30.
31. P. Francks, *Technology and Agricultural Development in Pre-war Japan*, New Haven/London, 1984, pp. 100-2.
32. W. Kelly, *Irrigation Management in Japan. A Critical Review of Japanese Social Science Research*, Ithaca, 1982, p. 2. Hatate, 'Irrigation, Agriculture and the Landlord', pp. 5-7.
33. L. Gambi, 'Acque ed ecologia', in *Agricoltura e tras-formazione dell'ambiente Agricoltura e trasformazione dell'ambiente, secoli XIII-XVIII*, ed. A. Guarducci, Firenze, 1984, p. 662.

CHAPTER 12

Particularism, Canals and Watercourses in the Old Reich (Germany, Sixteenth to Eighteenth Century)

ANDREAS KLINGER

Particularism appears to be among the widest known features of early modern Germany. The 'patchwork' of colours seen on historical maps is a familiar sight. It distinguishes the fragmented Holy Roman Empire from the western European monarchies, especially France, which are perceived as unitary states. In contrast to a centralized France, therefore, the Old Reich comprised a complex amalgam of some larger and numerous smaller, arguably 'sovereign', states, but this grossly oversimplifies its historic evolution. The Reich and its members, the imperial estates or *Reichsstände*, formed a very complicated political system that simply cannot be adequately reduced to the basic formula of central vs. particular power. The process of state formation in early modern Germany took place at the level of the constituent territories, but it must be remembered that until around 1800, this process was invariably linked to the institutions of the Reich. Until its formal demise in 1806, the Reich rendered important state functions for most of its constituent territories, such as defence and protection of territorial integrity, or—and this is crucial for subjects of the Reich—the supervision of adjudication. Both levels form a functional unity that in recent historical research has been understood in terms of—'complementary statehood'.[1]

A specific economic policy, though, was almost solely pursued by the princely states as well as the imperial cities. But it must be underscored at this juncture that the Reich established the framework for this, especially with regard to questions pertaining to trade and commerce.[2] During the first half of the sixteenth century, the Imperial Diet tried to limit the strong market position of the upper German commercial firms by enacting anti-monopolistic legislation. Later, efforts were undertaken to command the guild-controlled crafts. Certainly, the most important economic task of the Reich pertained to financial policy. Imperial institutions sought to standardize coinage throughout the Reich and withdraw base coins from circulation. The results, however, were always unsatisfactory and such efforts were generally short-lived. No measures of commercial or financial policy formulated by the Reich could be enforced against the will of the territorial governments. The imperial institutions functioned primarily as a forum that moderated and also brought together the diverging political conceptions and intentions in the hope of enacting regulations that clearly transcended regional boundaries. In line with the theme of state and water and focusing specifically on the process of state formation with its connection to inland navigation, it is important to pay attention to the constituent territorial states and not the Reich, because the former emerge as the protagonists in matters relating to infrastructural politics.

By the middle of the sixteenth century at the latest, the princely states began to formulate and command their own commercial and infrastructural policies with the aim of boosting their respective economic standing. These were aimed primarily at the agricultural sector, not least because the economy of early modern Germany remained steeped in feudal methods of production, especially in this sector.[3] The main objective of these policies was to systematically increase profits reaped from farming. Soon, efforts were made to cultivate forests and maintain waterways in order to maximize economic benefits derived from these natural resources.

Where possible, the princes nurtured the establishment of mining industries, or supported the expansion of existing operations. They also encouraged industrial production, as revealed by documentation pertaining to the founding of the first factories. After the Peace of Westphalia (1648), it was not just the pioneers, but nearly all the princes who also pursued an active commercial policy according to their means. The rulers fostered economic revival, not least because they were strongly interested in rebuilding and consolidating their state finances.[4] This was absolutely necessary for enhancing the power and authority of the government. During the seventeenth and eighteenth century, the commercial policy pursued by the rulers came to be known as 'mercantilism'.[5] With reference to the German territories the term 'cameralism' is also commonly employed, because concerns about the *camera*, that is the princely coffers, assumed the centre stage of economic theories. In contrast to the French mercantile system that is closely associated with Colbert, German cameralism was not understood in terms of mere commercial politics, but rather a comprehensive economy of the public sector. It combined the goal of sustaining export surpluses with domestic politics. According to the patriarchal self-perception of Germany's territorial princes at the time, political interest in generating expanded revenues was invariably coupled with the princely duty to promote the welfare and 'common felicity' of its subjects (J. H. G. v. Justi).

At an early stage, territorial economic policy came to focus on questions of infrastructure. In an attempt to understand economic life within a respective territory, not just in terms of supplies of food and goods, but also in terms of enhancing profits for the state, rulers began to direct their attention beyond their (often very limited) borders. The question was: how could the existing inter-regional trade be stimulated for the benefit of one's own territorial economy and princely exchequer? Inland navigation offered the most obvious answer.

Like in other parts of Europe,[6] inland navigation was the preferred means of mercantile transportation in the Old Reich.[7] Goods could be transported swiftly and also in greater quantities by water than by the poorly developed roads. The latter may have been adequate to sustain local and, to a limited extent, regional trade in agricultural produce. But efforts to expand markets often demanded a link to water-borne traffic. Similar observations hold true for non-agricultural products as well. One should bear in mind that many of the new canals served more than just as a means of transportation. The rural population extensively used them for irrigation and drainage.[8]

In the Reich, the canalization of rivers or the building of canals served to improve infrastructure and stimulate trade. Perhaps the best known example is the Fossa Carolina or *Karlsgraben*. This canal was planned and partly constructed during the reign of Charlemagne at the close of the ninth century, and its purpose was to connect the Main river with the Danube.[9] Unfortunately, the project was never completed. Navigable canals and improved rivers, however, did exist in the late Middle Ages. One noteworthy example can be found in the north of Germany where the Hanseatic town of Lübeck was joined to the Elbe via the narrow Stecknitz river which had been rendered navigable with the assistance of watergates.[10] Canals were often constructed to transport supplies to larger settlements, for example, the canal near the Hanseatic town of Bremen at the end of the thirteenth century.[11]

It was only against the backdrop of state formation in the early modern period that these and similar projects were pursued more intensively and systematically, thus ensuring chances of their success. As will be discussed later, failures were not unavoidable. During the sixteenth century, there were plans and projects for the construction of canals in all parts of the Old Reich, but rarely did these state-subsidized activities bring about new forms of administration. An exception is the example of the *Floßcommission* (Water Traffic Committee) in the electorate of Saxony. In the first half of the sixteenth century, this small agency was created to regulate water-borne traffic.[12] But it was only with the introduction of mercantilist and cameralist policies that canals and canalization projects became commercial policy in a given territory. In the second half of the eighteenth century, an increasing number of princely states established special boards for the promotion of water navigation.[13]

The Duchy of Saxe-Gotha in the seventeenth century reflects the importance attached to watercourses and canals in smaller German states. It should be emphasized at this juncture that Saxe-Gotha is not a success story, but it serves to illustrate two points. The large-scale plans reveal the tremendous ambitions of small princely states. But the failure to bring many of these grand infrastructural plans to fruition exposes the Reich's centrifugal problems of particularism.

Saxe-Gotha was founded in 1640, because in that year, the Ernestine Dukes of Saxe-Weimar divided their lands. Duke Ernest the Pious was the first ruler of Gotha. He is remembered as the successful founder of a state as well as a ground-breaking reformer, especially in the areas of religion and education. At least this is what his epitaph claims. The widespread idealization of Gotha as a model state of the early modern period, however, ignores actual historical developments. Nevertheless, it is correct to claim that the seventeenth century Duchy of Gotha offers a unique opportunity to closely scrutinize state formation within the constituent states of the Reich in a comparatively focused geographic region as well as within a relatively limited time frame. This is because Ernest the Pious ambitiously sought to transform a territory that had been arbitrarily lumped together through inheritance into a 'well-ordered' princely state, and Gotha was successfully transformed within a relatively short period of time.[14]

Gotha lies in Thuringia, which was part of an area within central Germany that was steeped in particularist thinking. According to modern historiography, Thuringia was the paradigm of political 'fragmentation' in the Reich because it survived the far-reaching territorial changes that took place at the beginning of the nineteenth century. Such a view is clearly fallacious. In early modern Germany, Thuringia's situation was not at all unique. Several small states not unlike Gotha were found not only in central Germany, but were also scattered across the whole Reich. Also, with regard to infrastructure, Gotha does not necessarily stand out. The duchy had an agricultural economy and it had only a few sizeable towns. Economic life was based chiefly on the production of grain and wool. For a significant period, woad dominated trade in this region, but around 1600 this plant that yielded a blue dye could no longer compete with imported indigo. In the Franconian exclave to the south of Gotha, wine was grown and traded for export. The duke's efforts to promote glass works achieved only limited successes and were not sufficient to shift established trends and forces of industry on to another course. The country's main asset was its vast forest. Duke Ernest controlled large portions of the Thuringian forest, a low mountain range that separates Thuringia from Franconia.[15] Timber became a driving factor in the development of Saxe-Gotha's inland waterway and navigation projects.

The steps initially taken were fairly modest and were only intended to foster the regional timber trade.[16] Time and again the ducal government sought to boost its revenues from the sale of timber, mainly by improving conditions for rafting. For this purpose some smaller rivers were made navigable, at least for rafts. Canals were also constructed, including the one leading to the ducal seat in Gotha. Problems, however, lingered, not least because of the large number of mills located along the rivers was simply not economically viable. The government hesitated to take action against the mill owners because they were perceived as vital to the processing of grain, the backbone of Gotha's agricultural economy.

The duke's objective was to develop a passage to the seaports located in the north by utilizing a series of minor rivers flowing through his territory. These, in turn, were expected to feed into the main navigable waterways of the Weser and Elbe. The rivers Unstrut and Saale flowed into the Elbe, but at the time both were controlled in part by the Elector of Saxony and other princes connected to his family. The proposals from Gotha, however, did not elicit a favourable response from the princes associated with the ruling house of electoral Saxony, echoing fears that a successful completion of the project could divert trade away from the city of Leipzig. Other opportunities appeared far more promising. The Werra's headwaters lay in the territory of Gotha and after flowing westward feed into the Fulda river at Hannoversch Münden. The idea of using the Werra for water-borne commerce was, of course, not new. Since time immemorial, parts of the river had been used for transportation. In 1646, the Hessian town of Wanfried was reported to be a 'blissful place' because 'a lot of woad and grain were brought there from Thuringia and shipped down the Weser River'.[17] This involved only local trade with largely small boats and just along certain sections of the Werra. This trade brought Wanfried great advantages, mainly on account of its long established *Stapelrechte*. According to these privileges, no goods could be transported without using the town's stores, and ships were required to pay fees. Duke Ernest was ambitious and sought to meaningfully enhance Gotha's foreign trade by ferrying his own ships. A watercourse made navigable for larger craft in the Werra and Weser would allow for a direct connection to the port and city of Bremen. In 1648, a test was conducted by rafting some mast beams from the Thuringian Forest to Bremen. Proceeds from their sale in Amsterdam, however, failed to meet expectations because the wrong kind of logs had been shipped.[18] For the ducal counsellors, it now seemed possible to expand the flow of trade in a northerly direction.

Several attempts followed to channel trade from the Werra toward the Weser. In 1648, Duke Ernest invited two shipbuilders from the imperial city of Ulm who were experienced in building vessels for inland navigation. Records show that the crafts were built, but there is no available report of their commercial success. One can safely assume that this first attempt ended in failure.

The next attempt was far better planned. It also illustrates how closely the Gotha counsellors monitored market developments. In 1656, the government dispatched a person on a reconnaissance mission down the Weser. He was instructed to study the prevailing prices keeping in mind Gotha's main exports such as timber, grain and bricks. He was also specifically commissioned to collect information on the grain trade in Bremen and Amsterdam. The Gotha government evinced a keen interest in crop yields for Russia, England, France, Livonia, Holstein and Sweden, and exports were aligned accordingly. Evidently, the counsellors envisaged sustained improvement in Gotha's balance of trade by stepping up grain exports. After agricultural production had largely switched from woad to grain, the region was in a position to successfully emerge as a 'granary' and reap considerable export revenues. But for this plan to succeed, it was necessary to ensure reasonable conditions for shipping grain to the northern seaports. It is precisely in this respect that the government mercantilists encountered insurmountable difficulties.

First there were technical problems. The use of smaller vessels brought to light how shifting water levels, bridges, fish traps and mills posed serious obstacles to future success. For large-scale grain export to thrive, considerably bigger vessels needed to be deployed, and as a result, watergates and lifters would have to be built along the entire length of the river. Unfortunately, Ernest the Pious did not control the entire course of the Werra. Part of it ran through the territory of Hesse-Kassel and passed by the town of Wanfried. The Gotha government was dependent on co-operation, not least with its counterpart in Kassel. The authorities there were also interested in promoting a more active trading regime on the Werra, but for entirely different reasons. The financial counsellors in Kassel were mainly interested in generating revenue from customs. For a while the Gotha government reluctantly entrusted Hessian ships with the trade of its grain. This reduced the income of the Gotha merchants and, as a result, no stable export business could be established. Even Gotha's bold but very risky offer to make the entire length of the Werra navigable at its own expense, including the Hessian portion, was rejected by Kassel. The particularistic interests of the princely states of Saxe-Gotha and Hesse-Kassel were simply too far apart to achieve a compromise. While one prince sought to make a transit route as economical as possible and to serve the broadest possible market for the benefit of his territorial commerce, the other tried to use his advantageous location for precisely the same reasons. This insurmountable conflict of interest sealed the fate of all attempts at making the Werra navigable. After 1672, no renewed efforts were made, and throughout the eighteenth century, the Thuringian princes did not devise plans to that end. Only Hesse-Kassel improved its own segment of the Werra.

Gotha reaped profits when some wood was rafted down the Werra and Weser in 1667-8. This was in the aftermath of the Great London Fire of 1666 when Gotha hoped to profit from the urgent need for timber in the English capital. But the expectations of a stable wood export to England were quickly shattered because the

Gotha merchants were not in a position to compete effectively with the far better organized Scandinavian timber dealers.

In sharp contrast to the plans for river navigation along the Werra, Gotha's canal projects were far more ambitious. Despite the aforementioned problems, the Werra was again chosen as the starting point of a new project. The duke aimed at reaching the Main river and planned to this end the construction of a canal that would link the Werra and the Main. The goal was twofold. First, the planned canal wold connect the territory of Gotha via the Main with the Rhine. This idea received the needed support of the prince bishops of Bamberg and Würzburg. The Bishop of Würzburg strangely agreed to this scheme for reasons directly opposed to Duke Ernest's intentions. The former wanted to use the planned canal to plug into the Weser in the hope of avoiding the high custom duties levied along the Rhine. Second, the new canal was regarded as a means to improve the territorial infrastructure of Gotha. The canal was to extend to Königsberg, the regional capital of a sizeable Franconian exclave. If the canal was completed, this outlying region would become more closely connected to the commercial and political centre. But the existence of exclaves such as Königsberg posed a great hindrance to the process of state formation, and the canal could make up for the lack of a contiguous territory only to a limited extent. By the end of 1661, work on the canal had begun, but it soon became clear that it would never be completed because of insurmountable technical difficulties. Interestingly, there were a number of serious attempts to build such a canal well into the twentieth century.[19] In retrospect, Duke Ernest's project remained intangible mainly because of problems relating to technology and engineering. Other projects such as the Weser–Lippe canal were truly visionary[20] and belong to a world too large for the limited capabilities and means of a small territory like Gotha in the seventeenth century.

Plans for canals and inland navigation, however, clearly reveal that the rulers of the small German principalities did not content themselves with the limited space of their political domains, at least in the realm of economics. This is not limited strictly to the structural policy of water-borne commerce. In Gotha, for instance, the government often sought to link the small territory with larger economic regions. For this purpose, it attempted to strike agreements with neighbouring states regulating the wages of servants and day labourers in the hope of forestalling attrition through emigration.[21] Such standardizations reached their limit as soon as they affected public revenues. The Gotha government pursued an active fiscal policy with respect to important transit routes, and this would have aroused the ire and suspicion of its neighbours. Gotha placed identical constraints on overland routes as Hesse did on water-borne trade along the Werra river.

The case of Saxe-Gotha illustrates some of the basic, underlying problems associated with German particularism. Obstacles to making the Werra navigable were akin to those encountered in the case of the Main and Rhine. States that were territorially larger than Gotha faced similar problems. There are innumerable examples of feasible, affordable and—in terms of trade—reasonable canalization projects that failed, or were never completed because of territorial custom policies or entrenched medieval prerogatives. Economic interests were simply too great for anyone to abandon.

One of the most illustrative examples of how particularism affected inland navigation as well as the construction of canals in the Old Reich can be found in the territory of Hesse-Kassel. The residence of Kassel was situated on the Fulda river, a well-navigable watercourse. Since the Fulda feeds the Weser, the conditions were favourable for water-borne commerce in a northerly direction. But at the confluence of the two rivers is situated the town of Hannoversch Münden which at the time was part of the Duchy of Brunswick-Calenberg-Göttingen. Münden enjoyed privileges that could be traced to the thirteenth century. As a result the town had established a virtual monopoly of trade along the Weser and Fulda toward Kassel.[22] Because of this, the landgraves of Hesse-Kassel did not command over their own direct access to the Weser. They sought this as they wanted to trade directly and independently with Bremen. Fortunately, the Hessian territory touched the Weser north of the town of Münden. In 1699, Landgrave Carl founded his own port town there under the name of Karlshafen. But this does not appear to have helped him much. The Hessian merchants could reach the Weser without passing through Münden, but to do so they had to transport goods overland between Karlshafen and Kassel, an expensive undertaking at the time. For this reason, the landgrave considered building a new canal, known as the Carls-canal, which was intended to connect the new river port to the city of princely residence. This project was financially a bottomless pit and only a third of the canal was eventually completed. Kassel's prestigious independence from the ships of Münden's merchants was simply too costly. A connection between the port of Karlshafen and the capital Kassel was finally completed in the nineteenth century. In 1850, the first Hessian railway was introduced there. Commemorating the ambitious canal project, it was called Carls-Bahn (Carl's Railway).[23]

There are many more examples. At the beginning of the eighteenth century, the imperial city of Esslingen, which lay in the heart of the Duchy of Württemberg, thwarted plans of the ducal government to render the upper reaches of the Neckar navigable. This river, which was an important traffic artery of the duchy, runs through the city of Esslingen, but the town's council rejected all plans to improve navigation. Esslingen even withstood the political pressure of a far larger territory and only neighbour. The magistrates pursued twin goals. First, as a matter of principle, the proud city did not want to submit to the will of the ducal government. Second, promoting water-borne trade along the Neckar would have resulted in heavy losses for the city's treasury because the town earned good money from tolls levied on roads and bridges.[24] Downstream, the imperial city of Heilbronn also opposed the plans of Württemberg for much the same reasons.[25]

In the eighteenth century, merchants from Münster who depended on trade with the United Provinces decided to build a canal between Münster and the Dutch city of Zwolle on the Ijssel river. The prince bishops of Münster enthusiastically supported this plan because they believed that it would not only enhance the wealth of their residency, but also of the entire region. The so-called Max Clemens Canal was built in two phases and the parts completed were extensively used.

The canal, however, never reached Holland because the Prince of Bentheim did not allow it to pass through his territory.[26]

As long as a princely state did not have the option of coaxing its neighbours into accepting plans, backed by credible threats or naked political force, cross-border projects were doomed. The trade and custom privileges of the imperial estates and the territorial towns were sacrosanct. The slightest infringement led to the intervention of the supreme courts of the Reich. During its conflict with Württemberg, the town of Esslingen appealed to the Emperor for assistance. As the protector of the imperial cities, the Emperor could do little more than preserve the *status quo*. Toward the close of the sixteenth century, the powerful, but not independent city of Brunswick stymied a canalization project launched by its own sovereign, the Duke of Brunswick-Lüneburg, and it achieved this with the help of the Imperial Cameral Court (*Reichskammergericht*). The reasons cited were hardly surprising. The city feared that the planned canal would adversely affect its commerce.[27]

In the eighteenth century, connecting the Prussian Rhine territories Mark and Cleves via the Ruhr river was possible because Prussia ruled the confluence of this river with the Rhine. King Frederick II threatened to cut-off all those who held territories along the Ruhr from having access to the Rhine if they opposed his proposal.[28]

If projects failed, it would be fallacious to blame the princes and magistrates. They were convinced that the policies which they pursued were good as well as beneficial. They tried to extract as much financial gain as possible in order to fill the coffers of their treasury, and many wanted to shield their subjects from economic competition. They cannot be held responsible for the particularism that created and sustained countless internal barriers. As members of the political elite, they only reaped profits from custom duties, shipping and warehousing privileges. In some cases, substantial customs revenues ensured the political survival of rulers.[29] The elites wanted to safeguard the hard, tangible income generated by the *status quo*, and they profoundly distrusted the largely elusive benefits of co-financed ventures, including canalization projects that spanned two or more territories. Why should the Saxon Elector jeopardize the trade profits of his fair town Leipzig by allowing other princes to bypass this city with their own trading ships? Why should the town of Münden voluntarily surrender a major portion of its revenue and allow contracts to be taken away from its shippers? New canals often meant changing old and established trade routes. When roads lost their importance, carters and innkeepers together with toll collectors who earned their livelihood from the traffic along these roads had to face heavy losses. No patriarchal ruler could tolerate this, and a mercantilist prince would only agree if the new infrastructure clearly promised higher yields. But this was highly uncertain.

Attentive contemporaries, however, recognized the inherent contradictions of the system. Time and again, one state withheld approval for another neighbour's projects because its own interests were at stake. In 1672, a political publicist, Johann Eberhart Wassenberg, presented an exposé to the Imperial Diet in Regensburg. To compete with the economically successful and politically menacing power of France, Wassenberg suggested the successful exploitation of Germany's naturally abundant watercourses. To achieve this end, two conditions had to be met: new canals had to be built with the objective of connecting large rivers that lead to the North and Baltic Seas, as well as the Black Sea (Danube). Second, territorial tariff barriers needed to be dismantled.[30] In the end, these proposals championed a centralized imperial economic policy based on the water-borne transport system. Wassenberg complained that Germany failed to utilize one of its 'goldmines', the watercourses, and appeared to block them deliberately. His appeal fell on deaf ears, though it should be stated that at the outset there were other political and economic treatises clamouring for the establishment of a nationwide canal system that interlocked navigable rivers.[31] The political system of the Old Reich lacked a strong central authority that could push through such projects. When Wassenberg approached the Imperial Diet, he spoke to the same governments that jealously guarded their prerogatives.

This explains why the largest and economically successful navigation and canalization projects were completed within single territories. As long as waterways did not cross borders, such government projects could come to fruition. Brandenburg-Prussia is a well-known example in this regard. The central authority succeeded in interconnecting different parts of the territory by building canals such as the Frederick William Canal,[32] the Plau Canal[33] and the Finow Canal.[34] This not only led to economic improvement as well as better development of certain regions, but also politically integrated them into the monarchy.[35] At the centre of this interlocking web of canals was the capital of Berlin, and these new waterways were meant to stabilize and enhance its centralizing functions. Another success was the Schleswig-Holstein canal built on the Eider river, connecting the North and Baltic Seas. In 1784, the original plan for this project, which was traced back to the sixteenth century, was realized by the King of Denmark who also ruled as the Duke of Schleswig and Holstein.[36]

In retrospect one can discover the strong influence of particularism on the development of German waterways in the Old Reich. In 1803, the political map of Germany changed fundamentally, chiefly under the severe pressures of Napoleonic expansion. The ecclesiastical principalities were wiped off the map as well as most of the imperial cities and the tiny domains of the imperial knights. This territorial consolidation led to the emergence of princely states with comparatively compact territories. Three years later, the Holy Roman Empire was dissolved and the German princes became true sovereign rulers. After the final victory over Napoleon, they came together in 1815 to form the German Confederation. At the Congress of Vienna, which was responsible for the new German Confederation, the states negotiated for the right of river navigation. Soon, long held trading privileges were repealed. Everyone was allowed to use the rivers for trade, and only the duties remained until the founding of the German Customs Union (*Zollverein*) in 1834 which included most of the German states.

States that had increased in size in 1803 and had control over the whole course of a river quickly leveraged on their new position. Württemberg made the Neckar navigable. After 1815, the course of the Lippe was completely controlled by Prussia, and its government developed it in order to secure easier access to the Rhine.[37] About ten years earlier, the French occupation on the left bank of the Rhine had spurred authorities on the right bank take concerted action. France and the Reich had signed an agreement on free navigation on this river that remained in force even throughout subsequent times of war.[38]

While examining the various canals built during the nineteenth century, it is clear that many of them drew on plans already devised in the early modern period. During the first half of the 1800s, the Ludwig Canal connecting the Danube and Main was built by Bavaria. This was the realization of an earlier plan to reach the Danube from the Rhine via the Main river.[39] At that time the water navigation engineers were no doubt far more skilled than their predecessors, but people in the seventeenth and eighteenth centuries had the ability to conceive viable plans which could not be executed as the times were not favourable. The railway provided serious competition to water-borne transport. Inland navigation no longer reigned supreme as the only means of low cost transportation.

With regard to the building of canals and inland navigation, the particularism of early modern Germany cannot be held solely responsible for creating a modernization gap. In line with mercantilist economics, several territorial states sought to improve their infrastructure for the benefit of trade, though admittedly there was no 'canal mania' like in England or the United States toward the close of the eighteenth century.[40] The noble objective of reaching larger markets by developing waterways rarely led to success. With regard to inland navigation, and especially from a modern, market-focused economic and political perspective, there was no central decision-making body capable of enforcing a consistent transport infrastructure policy that treated the Reich as an integrated economic region.[41] Despite acknowledging the necessity and the possible benefits of cross-border trade, the individual governments were too selfish and politically myopic and they failed to see the larger picture. Political reasons, such as the numerous territorial custom barriers, explain the unsatisfactory use of the natural watercourses. With regard to canal building, one must bear in mind the tremendous, technical problems which often rendered such projects unviable or too costly to be considered a realistic enterprise. The full financial burden fell on the territorial states alone that also acted as the exclusive initiators of the canal projects.[42] In the end, particularism, which rendered trade across borders unavoidable, also hampered trade at the same time.

NOTES

1. G. Schmidt, *Geschichte des Alten Reiches. Staat und Nation in der Frühen Neuzeit*, Munich, 1999.
2. M. North, 'Von der atlantischen Handelsexpansion bis zu den Agrarreformen (1450-1815)', in *Deutsche Wirtschaftsgeschichte. Ein Jahrtausend im Überblick*, ed. M. North, Munich, 2000, pp. 170 ff. F. Blaich, *Die Wirtschaftspolitik des Reichstags im Heiligen Römischen Reich. Ein Beitrag zur Problemgeschichte wirtschaftlichen Gestaltens*, Stuttgart, 1970.
3. H. Wunder, 'Agriculture and Agrarian Society', in *Germany: A New Social and Economic History*, vol. 2, ed. S. Ogilvie, London, 1996, pp. 63-99. W. Abel, 'Landwirtschaft 1500-1648', in *Handbuch der deutschen Wirtschafts- und Sozialgeschichte*, vol. 1, eds. H. Aubin and W. Zorn, Stuttgart, 1971, pp. 386-413. W. Abel, 'Landwirtschaft 1648-1800', in ibid., pp. 495-530.
4. See, for example, V. Sellin, *Die Finanzpolitik Karl Ludwigs von der Pfalz: Staatswirtschaft im Wiederaufbau nach dem Dreißigjährigen Krieg*, Stuttgart, 1978.
5. North, 'Von der atlantischen Handelsexpansion', pp. 176 ff. F. Blaich, *Die Epoche des Merkantilismus*, Wiesbaden, 1973.
6. H. Kellenbenz, 'Landverkehr, Fluß- und Seeschiffahrt im europäischen Handel (Spätmittelalter bis Anfang des 19. Jahrhunderts)', in id., *Kleine Schriften*, vol. 1: *Europa, Raum wirtschaftlicher Begegnung*, Stuttgart, 1991, pp. 327-441.
7. F.-W. Henning, *Handbuch der Wirtschafts- und Sozialgeschichte Deutschlands*, vol. 1, Paderborn, 1991, pp. 872 ff. North, 'Von der atlantischen Handelsexpansion', pp. 166 ff. P. Kriedte, 'Trade', in *Germany: A New Social and Economic History*, vol. 2, pp. 103 ff.
8. M. North, *Kommunikation, Handel, Geld und Banken in der Frühen Neuzeit*, Munich, 2000, p. 57.
9. W. Bader, *Die Verbindung von Rhein und Donau. Zur Geschichte eines bemerkenswerten Wasserstraßenprojektes*, Munich/Düsseldorf, 1982,

pp. 5-29. Flüsse und Kanäle, *Die Geschichte der deutschen Wasserstra ßen*, ed. M. Eckoldt, Hamburg 1998, pp. 451-7.

10. Ibid., pp. 348 ff.
11. Ibid., p. 14.
12. Ibid., p. 17. T. Klein, 'Kursachsen', in *Deutsche Verwaltungsgeschichte*, vol. 1, eds. K.G.A. Jeserich, H. Pohl and G.-C. von Unruh, Stuttgart 1983, pp. 818 ff. K. Blaschke, 'Die Ausbreitung des Staates in Sachsen' [1954], in K. Blaschke, *Beiträge zur Verfassungs- und Verwaltungsgeschichte Sachsens: Ausgewählte Aufsätze*, ed. U. Schirmer, Leipzig, 2002, p. 50.
13. Flüsse und Kanäle, p. 17.
14. A. Klinger, *Der Gothaer Fürstenstaat. Herrschaft, Konfession und Dynastie unter Herzog Ernst dem Frommen*, Husum, 2002.
15. Ibid., pp. 42 ff.
16. The following passages are based on the older biography by A. Beck, *Ernst der Fromme, Herzog zu Sachsen-Gotha und Altenburg: Ein Beitrag zur Geschichte des siebenzehnten Jahrhunderts*, Weimar, 1865, pp. 711-46, and the recent description by U.J. Wandel, 'Herzog Ernsts Schifffahrts- und Kanalpläne', in *Ernst der Fromme (1601-1675): Staatsmann und Reformer*, ed. R. Jacobsen and H.-J. Ruge, Bucha bei Jena, 2002, pp. 227-48.
17. Flüsse und Kanäle, p. 153.
18. Kammer Immediate Nr. 1201, Thüringisches Staatsarchiv Gotha.
19. O. Hennicke, 'Chronik der Versuche, die Werra schiffbar zu machen', *Thüringer Heimat*, vol. 1, 1956, pp. 162-76.
20. Wandel, 'Herzog Ernsts Schifffahrts- und Kanalpläne', p. 246.
21. Klinger, *Gothaer Fürstenstaat*, pp. 202 ff.
22. J. von Stockhausen, *Hann. Münden und die Schiffahrt auf Werra, Fulda und Weser*, Göttingen, 2003. Flüsse und Kanäle, pp. 159 et seq.
23. K. Röttcher, J. Tondera and F. Tönsmann, 'Der Kanal des Landgrafen Karl: Planung und Bau einer Kanalverbindung von Karlshafen über Kassel bis nach Marburg', in *LandgrafKarl und die Gründung von Karlshafen 1699-1999*, ed. G. Fenner, Kassel, 1999, pp. 92-131. Flüsse und Kanäle, pp. 138 ff., 160.
24. I. Sonnenstuhl-Fekete, 'Der Neckarkanal. Esslinger Beiträge zur Kanalisierung des Flusses vom 18. bis in das frühe 20. Jahrhundert', *Esslinger Studien*, vol. 40, 2001, pp. 121-66.
25. W.-I. Seidelmann, *Der Neckar-Donau-Kanal: 200 Jahre Planung für eine Wasserstraße quer über die Alb*, St. Katharinen, 1988, p. 37.
26. Flüsse und Kanäle, pp. 358 ff.

27. Ibid., p. 357.
28. Ibid., p. 107.
29. For instance at the Rhine river. F. Irsigler, 'Grenzen und Wirtschaftsentwicklung in Mittelalter und früher Neuzeit. Eine Skizze', in *Natürliche und politische Grenzen als wirtschaftliche Herausforderung*, ed. J. Schneider, Stuttgart, 2003, p. 37.
30. [E. Wassenberg], *Frantzösische Gold-Grube/Denen Römischen-Reichs-Ständen eröffnet/und verschlossen von Everardo Wassenbergio*, 1672, pp. 28 ff.
31. L. Schnabel and W.E. Keller, *Vom Main zur Donau. 1200 Jahre Kanalbau in Bayern. Karlsgraben, Ludwig-Donau-Main-Kanal, Rhein-Main-Donau-Kanal*, Bamberg, 1984, p. 27. Bader, *Verbindung von Rhein und Donau*, pp. 30 ff.
32. Flüsse und Kanäle, pp. 446 ff.
33. Ibid., pp. 223 ff.
34. Ibid., pp. 439 ff.
35. W. Neugebauer, *Zentralprovinz im Absolutismus. Brandenburg im 17. und 18. Jahrhundert*, Berlin, 2001, pp. 142 ff. K.-H. Manegold, 'Technik, Handelspolitik und Gesamtstaat. Brandenburgische Kanalbauten im 17. Jahrhundert', *Technikgeschichte*, vol. 37, 1970, pp. 101-29.
36. North, *Kommunikation*, p. 10. G. Andresen, 'Kanalprojekte in Schleswig-Holstein vom 15.-18. Jahrhundert und der Bau des Eiderkanals', in *1000 Jahre Verkehrswege in Schleswig-Holstein. Dokumentation*, ed. Thomas Riis, Kiel, 1996, pp. 57-78.
37. Flüsse und Kanäle, p. 112.
38. Ibid., p. 48.
39. Ibid., pp. 458 et seq. Schnabel and Keller, *Vom Main zur Donau*. Bader, *Die Verbindung von Rhein und Donau*, pp. 34 ff.
40. H.-U. Wehler, *Deutsche Gesellschaftsgeschichte*, vol. 1, Frankfurt (Main), 1987, p. 120. Ch. Hadfield, *British Canals. An Illustrated History*, 7th edn., Newton Abbot, 1984, esp. pp. 107 ff.
41. H. Jaeger, *Geschichte der Wirtschaftsordnung in Deutschland*, Frankfurt (Main), 1988, p. 18. R. Walter, 'Merkantilpolitische Handelshemmnisse (im territorialen Vergleich) am Beispiel eines territorial relativ zersplitterten Gebietes', in *Die Auswirkungen von Zöllen und anderen Handelshemmnissen auf Wirtschaft und Gesellschaft vom Mittelalter bis zur Gegenwart*, ed. H. Pohl, Stuttgart, 1987, pp. 84-120. But early modern German particularism is not to be understood as the only obstacle to a market economy. The competition among territorial states could also support this

development, for instance, by eliminating market barriers. See for this aspect O. Volckart, *Wettbewerb und Wettbewerbsbeschränkung im vormodernen Deutschland 1000-1800*, Tübingen, 2002, esp. pp. 233 ff.

42. H. Hassinger, 'Politische Kräfte und Wirtschaft 1350-1800', in *Handbuch der deutschen Wirtschafts- und Sozialgeschichte*, vol. 1, p. 646. This is true especially for the post-1648 period, after the decline of the cities in the Thirty Years' War. Prior to this, they had occasionally built their own canals. Flüsse und Kanäle, p. 15.

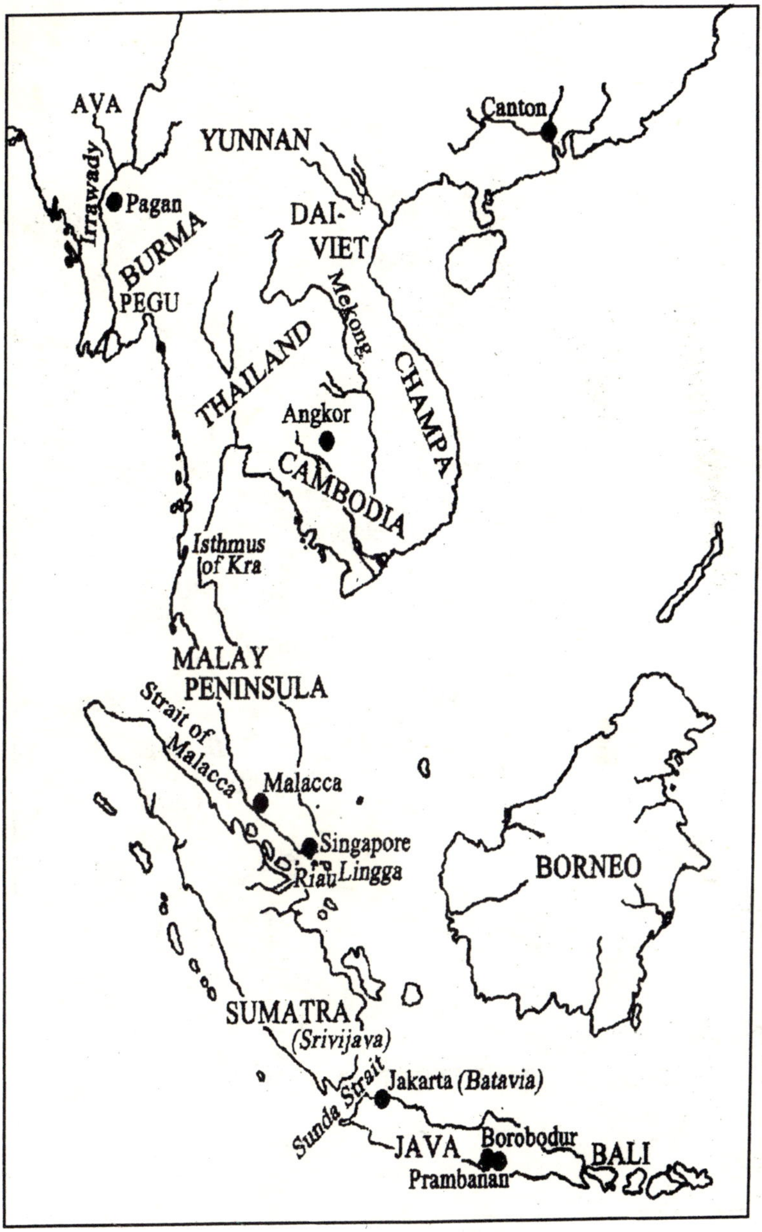

MAP 1: SOUTH-EAST ASIA

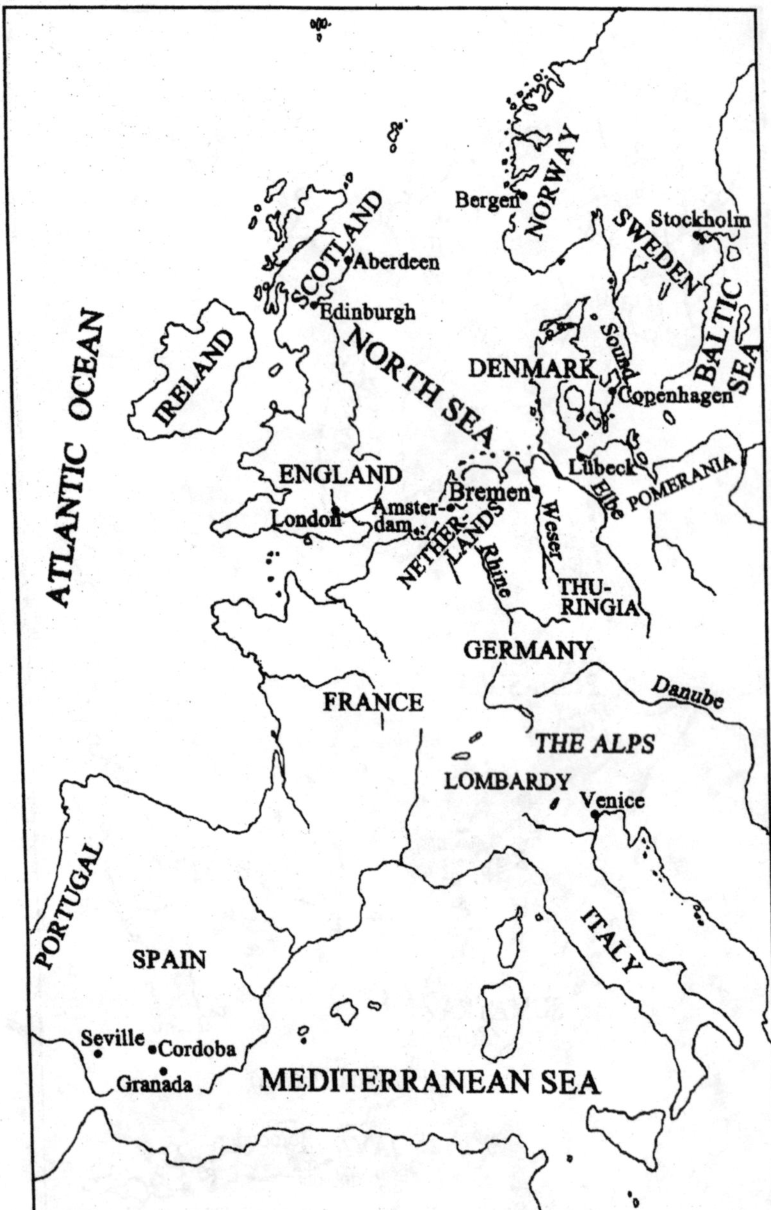

MAP 2: EUROPE (WESTERN PART)

Index